Norse Mythology, Vikings, Magic & Runes

Stories, Legends & Timeless Tales From Norse & Viking Folklore + A Guide To The Rituals, Spells & Meanings of Norse Magick & The Elder Futhark Runes.

History Brought Alive

Free Bonus from HBA: Ebook Bundle

Greetings!

First of all, thank you for reading our books. As fellow passionate readers of history and mythology we aim to create the very best books for our readers.

Now, we invite you to join our VIP list. As a welcome gift we offer the History & Mythology Ebook Bundle below for free. Plus you can be the first to receive new books and exclusives!

Remember it's 100% free to join.

Simply follow the link below to join.

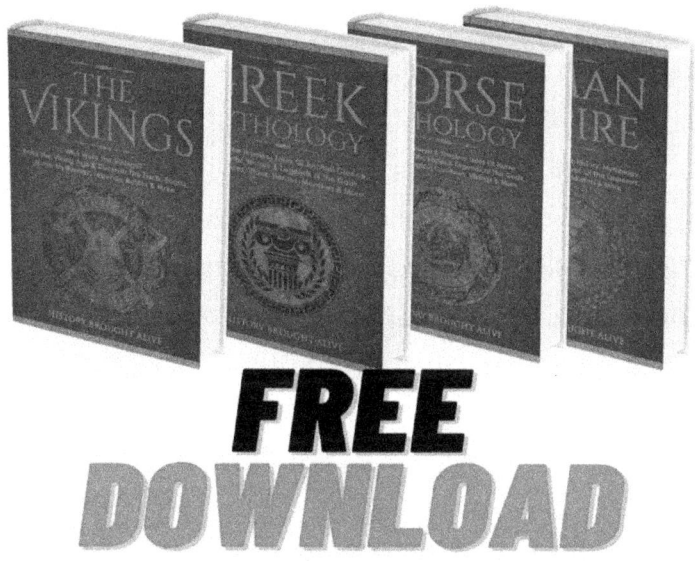

(https://www.subscribepage.com/hba)

Keep up to date with us on:

YouTube: History Brought Alive
Facebook: History Brought Alive
www.historybroughtalive.com

© **Copyright 2021 - All rights reserved.**

The content contained within this book may not be reproduced, duplicated or transmitted without direct written permission from the author or the publisher.
Under no circumstances will any blame or legal responsibility be held against the publisher, or author, for any damages, reparation, or monetary loss due to the information contained within this book, either directly or indirectly.

Legal Notice:

This book is copyright protected. It is only for personal use. You cannot amend, distribute, sell, use, quote or paraphrase any part, or the content within this book, without the consent of the author or publisher.

Disclaimer Notice:

Please note the information contained within this document is for educational and entertainment purposes only. All effort has been executed to present accurate, up to date, reliable, complete information. No warranties of any kind are declared or implied. Readers acknowledge that the author is not engaged in the rendering of legal, financial, medical or professional advice. The content within this book has been derived from various sources. Please consult a licensed professional before attempting any techniques outlined in this book.

By reading this document, the reader agrees that under no circumstances is the author responsible for any losses, direct or indirect, that are incurred as a result of the use of the information contained within this document, including, but not limited to, errors, omissions, or inaccuracies.

Norse Mythology

Captivating Stories & Timeless Tales of Norse Folklore. The Myths, Sagas & Legends of the Gods, Immortals, Magical Creatures, Vikings & More

History Brought Alive

Table of Contents

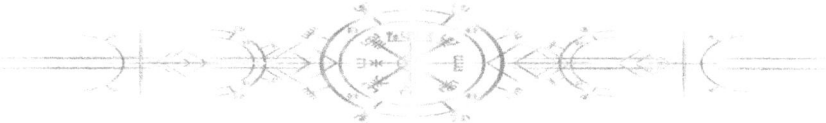

Introduction 12

Chapter 1: The Geography and Realms of Norse Mythology 17

    The Nine Realms 18

    Niflheim 20

    Muspelheim 21

    Asgard 22

    Midgard 24

    Jotunheim 26

    Vanaheim 27

    Alfheim 28

    Svartalfheim 29

    Helheim 30

Chapter 2: Norse Mythology Origins 32

    The Creation of the Universe, the Gods, and Man 33

Chapter 3: Norse Traditions, Worship, and Sacrifice 40

    Norse Mythology Religious practices and Rituals Practiced by Vikings 41

    Blot Sacrifice 43

    Human Sacrifice 44

    Yule Celebration 46

    Burial Traditions 50

Warding Off Draugr 54
Wedding Ceremonies 56
Infant Rituals and Naming Ceremonies 59
Chapter 4: The Gods of Norse Mythology 61

Odin 62
Frigg 65
Baldur 69
Thor 71
Heimdallr 74
Loki 77
Freya 80

Chapter 5: The Poems of the Poetic and Prose Edda 82

The Poem of Vafþrúðnismál (Vafthundnir's Sayings) 84
The Poem of Þrymskviða (Thrym's Poem) 86
The Poem of Hymiskviða (The Lay of Hymir) 88
The Poem of Skírnismál (Skirnir's Journey) 91

Chapter 6: The Myths of Norse Mythology 95

The Creation Myth of Thor's Hammer, Mjölnir 96
The Myth of Brunhilde 101
The Aesir vs Vanir War 103
The Binding of Fenrir 107
Asgard's Wall 109

Chapter 7: Ragnarok Explained 111

How it's All Meant to Unfold 112
The Final Battle 115
The Rebirth of the Cosmos 118
The Meaning of Ragnarok to the Vikings 119

What Ragnarok Meant in the Minds of the Vikings 121

How the Thought of Ragnarok Influenced the Vikings 122

Chapter 8: How Norse Mythology Influenced Modern Pop Culture 124

    Marvel's *Thor* 125

    How the Vikings and Norse Mythology Influenced J.R.R Tolkien and *The Lord of the Rings* 127

    Viking Metal 132

    God of War 134

    Hellblade: Senua's Sacrifice 137

    Ragnarok 137

    Game of Thrones 139

Conclusion 142

References 149

Introduction

Norse mythology is a truly fascinating ancient mythology filled with epic myths, battles, stories, folklore, gods, goddesses, customs, traditions, and beliefs. Norse mythology can be quite a daunting feat to sink your teeth into due to the immense size and lore associated with the mythology; however, that is where History Brought Alive comes in. We want to help you truly appreciate the marvels and wonders of Norse mythology by providing you with all you need to know in one single read. At History Brought Alive, we are history and mythology enthusiasts and are inherently fascinated with all the secrets these ancient beliefs, customs, traditions, and myths hold. Join us on a discovery to uncover the path of Norse paganism and learn from the ancient beliefs and customs from one of the most interesting civilizations the world has ever known—the Vikings.

Within these pages, we will not simply rehash the ancient myths, but rather provide context, background, and discussion regarding what life was like during the Viking Age, how life during that era influenced these myths, and how the myths influenced the Vikings. Upon reading, we will help you peel back the complex layers of history that surround these fascinating stories to take a peek at the accurate accounts of the myths, beliefs, customs, and traditions as they actually were.

We will uncover the geography of Norse mythology by understanding how the Vikings viewed the world. The nine realms of Norse mythology included Niflheim, Muspelheim, Asgard, Midgard, Jotunheim, Vanaheim, Svartalfheim, and Helheim. The realms played an integral role in providing explanations to the Vikings about how the world worked, how the gods operated, and how Earth coexisted in the cosmos. The nine realms were not only used to map out the cosmos, but were also used as a means to make sense of the phenomena the Vikings were experiencing.

The creation of the world in terms of Norse mythology will be unpacked, and we will take note of how the world was formed through fire and ice; the story of how the realms were created and the unusual origin of the gods, giants, and mortals; how the gods reigned supreme, and how the dynamic of the cosmos came to fruition. The creation myth is highly significant, as it provides the much-needed context of the history of the cosmos and the nine realms that coexist within it.

We will unpack what the customs, traditions, and worship looked like during the Viking age. How did the Vikings live their lives? How did they worship the gods? What did a day in the life of a Viking look like? Understanding how the Vikings worshipped the gods and what traditions they practiced provides us with a sneak peek back to the age of the Vikings to see how the myths influenced their daily lives.

Next, we will introduce the Norse gods in all their glory and signify what they stood for and their sphere of influence over Nordic culture. What they represented, who they were, and the myths surrounding their legacy will all be discussed. Understanding the gods and goddesses is vital, as they are the key characters that will be present in the myths of this fascinating mythology. Gods and goddesses such as Odin, Frigg, Baldur, Thor, Heimdallr, Loki, and more will be discussed and analyzed in detail throughout these pages. We need to understand the gods and their power to truly understand the essence of Norse mythology, as without the gods, there are no myths.

While it is important to uncover the myths, it is as important to highlight where the myths come from. The myths come from two crucial sources of evidence, which together is practically all we know about Norse mythology to date. The sources from which practically every story, myth, or folklore comes from are either thanks to the Poetic Edda or Prose Edda. We will uncover the epic poems of the Edda, as within these poems lies all the secrets and knowledge we know about the Norse gods.

Without the poems from the Eddas, we would largely be left in the dark regarding the ancient beliefs of the Vikings, and thus, it is critical to uncover the poems that lie within these ancient scripts. Over and above, the poems from Eddas' many other myths will be uncovered and discussed. The ancient stories of Norse mythology will slowly begin to unravel, and we will marvel at the fascinating adventures and tales the Nordic people had to tell. One myth, in particular, is truly frightening, and that is the myth of Ragnarok. This is the myth that ends all myths. It is the equivalent of the apocalypse, and signifies the destruction of all that we know and everything in the cosmos, including the Norse gods.

However, it is not just us that are fascinated with Norse mythology. Norse mythology has had a modern resurgence in the public consciousness through various depictions and portrayals of the Norse myths and gods through pop culture. Norse mythology's influence over Marvel's comic line Thor, the Lord of the Rings, Game of Thrones, God of War, and many more has truly relit the torch of ancient mythology. The legends, myths, and stories are all here just waiting to be read. Everything you need to know about the Vikings and the Norse pantheon is neatly wrapped up in one single read; all you need to do is uncover the secrets of Nordic history. Discover what life was like as a Viking and what governed their customs, traditions, and beliefs.

Chapter 1: The Geography and Realms of Norse Mythology

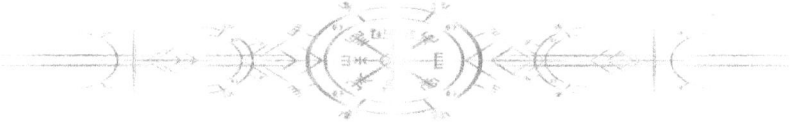

Norse mythology originated in the Scandinavian region located in Northern Europe. This region is categorized by the Scandanavian peninsula. There are five countries that make up this region, which include Norway, Denmark, Sweden, Finland, and Iceland. Scandinavia was home to the Vikings (a collective term for all people who lived in the Scandinavian region), or more correctly known as Norsemen.
Due to the Vikings living right on the cuff of the Scandinavian sea, they would often go on voyages to different lands and pillage there. They were infamous in England, as the Vikings would often set voyage there and raid nearby villages. Vikings were seen as heathens and pagans by the English. Due to the excessive and violent raids on England, the Vikings became public enemy number one to them, and the fact that they were pagans and heathens only enraged the English even more.

However, England was not the only target on the Vikings' radar; they would raid and voyage all over Europe, and during the period of 800AD and 1100AD, they left a crucial fingerprint on the history of Europe. However, although the Vikings were leaving a mark in Europe at the time, that was only one of nine realms that the Norsemen believed in. The Norsemen followed the teachings and traditions of Norse mythology as a guiding light for their actions.

The Nine Realms

Within Norse mythology, there are said to be nine realms within the universe. These made up the cosmos and were interconnected with one another. These included Niflheim, Muspelheim, Asgard, Midgard, Jotunheim, Vanaheim, Alfheim, Svartalfheim, and Helheim (Skjalden, 2011). Each realm has specific purposes and features that distinctly separate them from one another. Each one of these nine realms was home to various kinds of beings and mythical creatures. Jotumheim was home to the giants, Asgard was home to the gods, and Midgard was home to the humans. Norsemen believed that the nine different realms were held together by the world tree of Yggdrasil. Yggdrasil was the instrument that would ensure each realm was connected within a larger universe (Skjalden, 2011).

The first two realms include Niflheim and Muspelheim. These two are believed to have been created out of Ginnungagap. Ginnungagap consists of two words being merged together; the words in question were ginnunga and gap. Gap can be directly translated, as it is in English, but the word ginnunga is more difficult to translate. According to the Dutch scholar of Germanic linguistics and Germanic mythology, the word 'ginnunga' can be understood as something that is 'magically-charged' (Skjalden, 2020). Thus, Ginnungagap is known as the yawning void of absolute emptiness with a magically charged center that led to the creation of the first two realms. The cosmos had not been created yet, as all that had been created was Niflheim in the north and Muspelheim in the south.

However, the other seven realms were birthed out of Ymir's body (a hermaphroditic giant and one of the first-ever giants to ever exist in Norse mythology), which was initiated by Odin and his brothers during the creation of the cosmos (Skjalden, 2020). The fact that there are nine realms is no coincidence. The number nine holds great significance, much of which can be found in various poems, such as in the Eddas by Snorri Sturluson. Just to mention a few occurrences of the significance of the number can be found when Odin was hung on Yggdrasil for nine days and nights, Heimdallr birthed nine daughters, and Njord (the god of the wind and the sea) waited nine days for his wife Skadi (Skjalden, 2011).

Niflheim

Niflheim can be described as the realm of fog and mist. Niflheim, also known as *Niðavellir* in Old Norse, can be translated to 'mist home' or 'mist world.' Niflheim is located in the Northern region of Ginnungagap and is the first realm and was created at the same time as Muspelheim. Niflheim is the darkest and coldest realm of all the worlds. Hvergelmir is the oldest spring in all of Norse mythology, and is located in Niflheim. It is believed Hvergelmir is protected by an enormous and ferocious dragon known as Nidhug, or *Níðhöggr* in Old Norse (Skjalden, 2011).

According to Norse mythology experts, it is said that freezing cold rivers branch off of Hvergelmir and are believed to be the primary source of the eleven rivers (*Élivágar*) of Niflheim. These eleven rivers were the first rivers the universe had ever known as they were the only rivers in the only realm that existed at the time that had water. Hvergelmir is incredibly significant, as it was the primary source of all that is living, as well as the spring that all living beings will return to one day. It is said that the freezing water that flowed from Élivágar down the vast mountain ranges of Ginnungagap gradually solidified into a large dense layer of frost and ice, forming new land. Yggdrasil, the world tree, began to grow, stretched one of its three roots into the spring of Hvergelmir, and drew the necessary water needed to branch out (Skjalden, 2011).

Muspelheim

Muspelheim, or *Múspellsheimr* in Old Norse, can be described as the realm of fire. This realm was created at the same time as Niflheim; however, it is located in the South of Ginnungagap. Muspelheim is the polar opposite of Niflheim. Niflheim is the coldest realm while Muspelheim is the hottest. According to Norse mythology experts, Muspelheim is a scorching hot world that is filled with erupting volcanoes, lava rivers, flames, sparks, and heavy soot (Skjalden, 2011). It is believed that the sun, the moon, and the stars were created from the sparks of Muspelheim.

According to some traditions, it was believed that the warm air from Muspelheim resulted in the ice of Niflheim melting, thus creating the form of Ymir, the father of the evil giants and the first known being to inhabit the world. Ymir would be killed by Odin and other gods. His death would result in the creation of the other realms, as Odin and his brothers created the rest of the worlds with the corpse of Ymir. Ymir's death would also be the catalyst of Ragnarök and the end of the world by fire. Thus, Ymir was both responsible for the creation and destruction of the world (Britannica, 2019).

Muspelheim is home to the fire giants and the fire demons and is ruled by the great fire giant Surtr. Surtr is a sworn enemy of the Aesir (the inhabitants of Asgard such as Odin, Thor, Heimdallr, Loki) and has declared war on them for the death of his father Ymir. He would one day lead the sons of Muspelheim to destroy the world by fire during Ragnarök (Britannica, 2019). Ragnarök will be discussed in greater detail in a later chapter.

Asgard

Asgard, or *Ásgarðr* in Old Norse, is the third realm and is located in the middle of the world high up in the sky, which is unapproachable to mortal men. Asgard is the home of the gods, the goddesses, and the Aesir tribe. It is home to well-known gods such as Odin, Thor, Heimdallr, Loki, Frigg, Idun, Bragi, Tyr, and many more. The ruler of Asgard is Odin. He is known as the All-Father, and he is the chief ruler of the Aesir tribe. Odin's wife is Frigg, and she is the queen of all of Asgard (Skjalden, 2011). Many scholars believe that Asgard was a magnificent celestial city full of palaces made out of gold and silver, which was built entirely by the Aesir.

Asgard in itself is further divided into 12 smaller realms. The most significant of these realms include Valhalla and Fólkvangr. Inside these gates are inhabited by the gods alongside Viking warriors who died in battle. The fallen warriors are divided equally regarding where they spend the rest of eternity post mortem. Half of these warriors would end up in Valhalla, which is ruled by Odin, and the other half of the warriors would end up in Fólkvangr, which is ruled by the goddess Freya (Skjalden, 2011).

Asgard is protected by a giant wall that surrounds the entire realm. The wall was built during the battle against the Vanir (the other tribe of gods who were sworn enemies of the Aesir). If it were not for the wall, the Aesir and Asgard would be defenseless. This wall was impenetrable and was incredibly strong, which offered the Aesir complete protection against their enemies such as the evil giants, fire demons, the Vanir, and many more. There was only one entry within the wall that would lead into Asgard, and it was known as the Great Gate.

Within Asgard, there is a bridge that connects Asgard to all the other realms, including Midgard (the home of mortals). This bridge is known as Bifrost, but it has also been known to be called the rainbow bridge. Bifrost is described as a rainbow that consists of three plaited strands of fire. Bifrost was expertly guarded by the Norse god Heimdallr, who made sure that no trespassers or ambushes would fall upon Agard. Heimdallr had extraordinary powers and possessed remarkable sight that would help him spot enemies from a mile away. Whenever Bifrost was in danger, Heimdallr would blow his trumpet, the Gjallarhorn, and warn the gods of any danger ahead (Ancient Pages, 2016).

Midgard

Midgard, also known as *Miðgarðr* in Old Norse, is the fourth realm, and can be translated as "middle earth." Midgard is the realm that is home to human beings and animals. Midgard is located in the center of the world right below Asgard, which floats above Midgard. According to legend, Midgard was created from the body of Ymir. When Odin and his brothers killed Ymir, they are said to have rolled the evil giant's body into the central void of the universe, which began the formation and geographical creation of Midgard.

Ymir's flesh is said to be the land of Midgard. The oceans are the blood of Ymir; his bones became the mountains; his teeth became the cliffs; his hair became the trees, and Ymir's scattered brain became the clouds. It is said that four dwarves, known as Nordi, Surdi, Austri, and Vestri, who represent the four points of the compass, held up Ymir's skull, and thus, his skull became the dome of the heavens. The moon, the stars, and the sun, as we know them, were created from the scattered sparks that were caught within the skull of Ymir (Britannica, 2019a).

The first-ever humans in Norse mythology are believed to be Ask and Embla, who were sent down to Midgard after they were created from tree logs by Odin and his brothers (Skjalden, 2011). Midgard and Asgard are connected by Bifrost, which is guarded by Heimdallr. Scholars believed that Midgard was surrounded by an enormous ocean that was impassable by mere mortals.

It is believed that this impassable ocean was occupied by a ferocious sea serpent, known as the Midgard Serpent, which would devour any person who dared try to cross the ocean. The serpent was so large that it was believed it could encircle the realm of Midgard in its entirety with ease.

Jotunheim

Jotunheim, als0 known as *Jötunheimr*, is the fifth realm, and is home to the giants, or *jötnar*, as they are called in Old Norse. Jotunheim is only separated from Asgard due to the river Iving, which is believed to ever freeze over, thus acting as a barrier between the two realms. The giants are yet another sworn enemy of the Aesir and strive for the downfall of the gods. The geography of Jotunheim mainly consists of vast dense forests, rocky landscapes, and wilderness. Jotunheim is also said to be very cold and lies on the snowy region of the outermost shores of the ocean, thus is inhabited by many frost giants (Skjalden, 2011).

Due to this, the giants would eat fish from the rivers and oceans, as well as the animals from the forest, as it is believed that there was no fertile land in Jotunheim to grow crops or vegetables. The Aesir and the giants are said to have been constantly waged in the battle against one another; however, interestingly enough, it was said that their love affairs between the two races would sometimes occur and mixed-race offspring were conceived. It is said that even gods such as Thor, Loki, and even Odin himself, had lovers who were giants. Loki, the god of mischief, was actually born in Jotunheim, and was the adopted son of Odin. Loki was accepted with open arms by the Aesir and lived peacefully in Asgard for many years until he was punished and exiled and sent back to live in Jotunheim.

Utgard is the stronghold that protects Jotunheim, and can be described as the giants' version of Asgard's great wall. Utgard is said to be so tall that it is almost impossible to see the top of it. Utgard is a fortress that has been formed as a result of carved blocks of snow and sharp glistening icicles. Inside this fortress lives the much-feared giant ruler, king Utgard-Loki (Skjalden, 2011).

Vanaheim

Vanaheim, also known as *Vanaheimr* in Old Norse, is the sixth realm in Norse mythology and is home to the Vanir gods. The Vanir gods were associated with health, fertility, and wisdom. The Vanir gods are an old branch of gods who have had a conflict with the Aesir throughout their history. The Vanir gods and Aesir gods once lived in Asgard as one; however, conflict broke loose and the two branches of gods battled it out to fight for who got to live in Asgard. The bloody warfare eventually came to an end and the Aesir came out victorious. As a result, almost all of the Vanir gods were banished from Asgard; however, some Vanir gods still lived in Asgard after the war. At the end of the Aesir-Vanir war, three of the main gods of the Vanir clan stayed in Asgard as a token of peace. The Vanir gods in question were Njord, Freyr, and Freya (Skjalden, 2011).

Much of the geography of Vanaheim is a mystery. Many scholars have struggled to find any reputable sources or documentation about the realm of Vanaheim. It is known the Vanaheim is a place of magic and sorcery, as the Vanir gods were masters of the magic arts and were also believed to have been able to predict the future. However, nobody actually knows where the land of Vanaheim is located, nor are there any accounts of what it looks like.

Alfheim

Alfheim is the seventh realm in Norse mythology and is also known as *Álfheimr,* or *Ljósálfheimr* in Old Norse. It is located right next to Asgard in the heavens. Alfheim is home to the light elves, who are described as the most beautiful creatures known to man; they have even been described as being more beautiful than the sun itself. Not much is known about the home of the Alfheim, but considering its inhabitants being the light elves, it is considered by scholars to be a world of grace, light, and overwhelming beauty.

The light elves are widely considered to be guardian angels of Norse mythology. The Vanir god Freyr is the ruler of Alfheim. The light elves are considered gods in themselves; however, they are believed to be minor gods. They are gods of nature and fertility, and they help assist or even hinder humans with their knowledge of magical powers. The light elves often appear in art, such as paintings and music, and are believed to be the inspiration for many artists during the Viking Age (Norse Mythology for Smart People, 2018).

Svartalfheim

Svartalfheim is the eighth realm in Norse mythology, and is also known as *Niðavellir* or *Svartálfaheimr;* the word Svartalfheim can be translated to 'dark fields.' Thus, the realm was dark and consisted of many dense forests and caves that spread across the realm, almost like a whimsical, magical forest.

Svartalfheim is home to the dwarves. The dwarves of Svartalfheim are believed to have lived under rocks, in caves, or have found shelter underground. The dwarves were believed to be incredibly talented craftsmen and had gifted the gods of Asgard many powerful gifts such as the magical ring Draupnir and Odin's spear, Gungnir (Skjalden, 2011).

The king of the dwarves was Hreidmar, and was the ruler of the realm right up until he was killed by Fáfnir. Heirdmar had a lavish house built out of glittering gold and flashing gems and was guarded by none other than Fáfnir himself. Fáfnir grew ill-natured, killed Heirdmar, and stole all of Heirdmar's gold. He then ventured into the deep forests, where it is believed that Fáfnir turned into a serpent or a dragon (it varies in different sources) in order to guard his stolen treasure against thieves (Wikipedia, 2021).

Helheim

Helheim is the ninth and final realm, and is home to the dishonorable dead. Helheim can be understood as the Norse hell. In Norse mythology, Helheim is often simply referred to as Hel. This is where all the souls of the wicked and dishonest end up after death, such as thieves, murderers, cowards, and anybody who the gods and goddesses feel are not worthy or brave enough to enter Valhalla or Folkvangr.

Helheim is ruled by Hel, who is the daughter of Loki. Unlike hell, as we know it from a Christian perspective, where hell is described as scorching hot, Helheim is the complete contrast. It is believed to be freezing cold. Helheim is described as a dark, grim, and freezing realm where nobody will ever feel joy or happiness for the rest of eternity. Hel is believed to use all the dead in Helheim as her own personal army at her disposal to attack the gods and goddesses during Ragnarök and unleash her troop of the undead at the plains of Vigrid. When this happens, it is believed to be the end of the world. (Skjalden, 2011).

Chapter 2: Norse Mythology Origins

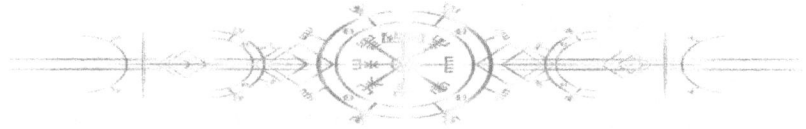

Every culture, religion, and region has its own interpretation of how the universe came into fruition and how the gods were created. Norse mythology is no different. Norse mythology has its own interpretation of the creation of the universe, and is used to explain the workings of the universe. It was used to explain aspects of life that mankind was unable to explain at the time, and the unknown phenomenon that the Vikings experienced in their everyday lives was often attributed to deities, monsters, and fate.

Throughout history, one of the biggest questions on everybody's minds has always been how the world and mankind was created. Before the breakthrough of scientific discoveries in the 20th century, there were absolutely no explanations for the creation of the universe and everything in it other than the supernatural. Thus, the Norsemen, like every other ancient culture before them, had their own explanation as to how the world came into fruition, and it involved supernatural and otherworldly powers wrapped in myths and epic tales.

Many of the aspects regarding the creation of the universe from a Norse mythological perspective seem familiar and are shared to an extent among other mythological beliefs. However, some of the myths and aspects of the Norse creation myth are especially fantastical and surprising.

The Creation of the Universe, the Gods, and Man

According to Norse mythology, the cosmos began with an empty void of magical power known as Ginnungagap (as mentioned in Chapter 1). In the north of Ginnungagap, there was a well-known Hvergelmir, which was the sole water source of the universe and streamed directly into the great world tree, Yggdrasil. The northern region of Ginnungagap was extremely cold and was known as the coldest region of the universe. While the water from Hvergelmir flowed into Yggdrasil, there was an excess amount of water that was not being absorbed by the world tree. Thus, the water that was not being absorbed by Yggdrasil quickly froze, and gradually grew en masse. This mass of frozen wasteland created a world of ice and frost, which formed the world of Niflheim (Greenberg, 2020).

However, at the same time, the southern region of Ginnungagap was extremely hot, and as time went on, the southern region grew hotter and hotter by the day. The heat led to a landmass of lava, flames, and fire, and the world known as Muspelheim was formed. The intense heat that radiated from Muspelheim rose and made its way to the frosty land of Niflheim. The heat from Muspelheim caused the ice to melt from Niflheim, and water droplets from the ice began to drip down to the land below. When the water droplets from the ice voyaged all the way from Niflheim to Muspelheim, the drops caused sparks to shoot up from below (Greenberg, 2020).

When the extreme cold and extreme heat from Niflheim and Muspelheim mixed and collided with one another, the start of life was birthed. The water droplets from Niflheim began to melt and drop down to the fiery depths of Muspelheim; a phenomenon occurred within Ginnungagap. As the two climates mixed with one another, steam began to be produced and rose. The mists formed and began to swirl in Ginnungagap until it was concentrated. Humanoid form took shape. With everything working in synergy, the steam, the heat from Muspelheim, and the melted ice droplets from Niflheim, the birth of Ymir commenced, and the first living creature and giant was born.

However, Ymir was not the only giant that was birthed from this phenomenon. Another giant by the name of Auðumla was also created. Auðumla was a giant primordial cow. Although Ymir was born first, he was trapped in an icy prison deep in the walls of the ice of Niflheim. Centuries passed, and Ymir remained trapped.

Over the years, Auðumla would lick the frost off of t Ymir's skin, eventually freeing the giant from his icy prison. According to the myth of creation, Ymir would feed on Auðumla's milk, and Auðumla would feed off the salt that had gathered on the icy rocks of Niflheim. For centuries, all that was in existence in the universe was Ginnungagap, Niflheim, Muspelheim, Ymir, and Auðumla. Many years passed, and Ymir and Auðumla would live together peacefully. However, that would change as time went on, and as Ymir fed off the milk of Auðumla, Auðumla fed off the ice of Niflheim. As the cow would do this, a large dent of Niflheim would be lost. Where Auðumla licked, the ice would take shape, and eventually, the land formed the shape of Búri, the first god of the known universe (Greenberg, 2020).

Búri was born, and because of this, so was the bloodline of the gods. Búri would go on to have at least one more child; however, even amongst experts, it is unknown how Búri conceived the child or how the child was born. Regardless, Búri had a son, and his name was Borr. The accounts differ, but it is said that Búri had another child, a daughter named Bestla, who was the first-ever goddess. Borr would go on to marry Bestla. However, other accounts say that Bestla was formed from the sweat of Ymir and was the first frost jotunn (giant).

Just as Búri had children, so did Ymir. It is said while Ymir slept, he would perspire from the heat that radiated from Muspelheim; two beads of sweat fell from his arm, creating one male and female jotunn, and from his legs, he produced a six-headed son (Geller, 2016). Ymir's male and female offspring would procreate, resulting in the next generation of frost jötnar. Ymir also sweated out his son, Surt, who was an evil flaming giant who traveled down to Muspelheim, whose fire made Surt feel welcome (New World Encyclopedia, 2020). Surt would go on to become the ruler of Muspelheim and the other fire giants that would be born in later generations (Greenberg, 2020).

However, whether Bestla was a daughter of Ymir or the daughter of Búri will always be a debate amongst experts in mythology. Although, what is not a debate and is agreed upon by the university is that Búri's son, Borr, married Bestla, and they had three sons. The three sons that Bestla gave birth to were considered gods, and they were named Odin, Vili, and Vé.

Centuries passed, and Ymir had now become the father to and ruled an army of frost giants. Ymir and his army were considered incredibly cruel and evil, and as a result, the three sons of Bestla and Borr planned to eliminate Ymir and all those that followed him, as he was perceived as a great threat to the cosmos.

Odin and his two brothers carried out their hunt and successfully slew Ymir. Many experts debate that the reason Odin and his brothers slew Ymir was so that they could use his bodily remains to create other worlds; others debate that they killed Ymir because he was an evil entity in the universe. However, the motives behind Odin and his brothers' crusade will remain a mystery and be a topic of debate for eternity.

However, it is said that when Odin and his brothers killed Ymir, the amount of blood the giant spewed out was so immense that it drowned all the jötnar but two. The only two surviving frost jötnar were Bergelmir and Ymir's wife, whose name is unknown. These surviving frost jötnar would repopulate and wage lifelong warfare and hatred among the Aesir gods (Learn Religions, 2016).

Odin, Vili, and Vé left Ymir's corpse in the center of Ginnungagap and then used the remainder of Ymir's rotting body to create a new world known as Midgard, which would be placed in the center of the Yggdrasil. The brothers made use of Ymir's body to act as the surface of the world and his blood to form the oceans, seas, and rivers. Odin used Ymir's bones and his teeth to make the mountains and fjords.
To make the sky, the brothers placed Ymir's skull over the new world of Midgard and used his brains to create clouds. Every part of Ymir's body created Midgard, and eventually became home to the mortals and animals. Midgard is Earth as we know it as human beings. Midgard was placed in the central region of Yggdrasiland and is often referred to as Middle Earth, due to its location in the cosmos.

However, Odin and his brothers did not stop there. They went on to capture all of the sparks that shot up from Muspelheim and place them within Midgard's new sky. These sparks brought light to the new world and were used to create the sun, the moon, and the stars.

Ymir's remains were fully utilized, and Midgard was complete; however, Odin and his brothers knew that the jötnar would want revenge for what happened to their ruler and father, thus they recognized that the jötnar would pose a threat to the Aesir and humanity. To counteract this, Ymir's eyebrows were used to form a protective wall that encircled Midgard and kept this new world safe from any attacks initiated from the jötnar (Greenberg, 2020).

Odin, Vili, and Vé were incredibly pleased with the new world they had created, and decided they wanted to bring life to their new world by creating new people and animals to inhabit Midgard. Odin and his brothers went on to create the first man and woman; they were known as Ask and Embla. They were given life by the brothers as a result of being carved out of the branches of trees in Midgard.
Odin and his brothers went on to create six new realms, bringing the total number of realms in the universe to nine. Odin, Vili, and Vé settled in Asgard, and the realm of the Aesir gods came into existence.

As the myths progressed, and over time, Vili and Vé became absent and were no longer mentioned; however, Odin went on to become the chief and ruler of the Aesir. Odin married Frigg, the goddess of fertility, marriage, and family. Odin became the All-Father of the Norse world and the most powerful god of them all (Greenberg, 2020).

Chapter 3: Norse Traditions, Worship, and Sacrifice

The Vikings of Scandinavia at the time were pagans. This ultimately means that Vikings practiced polytheism, and thus worshiped multiple gods as opposed to one god, such as how it is done in Christianity. Within Norse mythology, there are numerous gods and goddesses; however, unlike other ancient civilizations at the time, the Vikings had not organized a conventional priesthood or instilled a hierarchy of religious leaders. The Vikings were, for the most part, an oral civilization, and thus were not a civilization of people who tended to document their history, as most Vikings were largely illiterate. The pagan Vikings also did not build grand temples or religious buildings in honor of their religious views, unlike other beliefs and religions at the time. The lack of documentation and concrete evidence on how the Vikings worshipped their gods is a difficult puzzle to piece together.

Norse Mythology Religious practices and Rituals Practiced by Vikings

Norsemen, or Vikings, are well-known for the exploits in battle, voyages, and raids. However, according to Norse mythology experts, it is believed that the Vikings were also known for adopting religious and ritual practices as an important part of their culture and everyday lives. The Vikings' religious beliefs incorporated the worship of many different gods and goddesses; as a result, it is considered that the Vikings believed in a non-doctrinal community religion. What this means is that the Norsemen's beliefs and rituals varied among different regions of Scandinavia.

Although all the regions of Scandinavia worshipped the same gods and held similar beliefs, there were no exact principles in place or set practices that had to be followed by the book...as there was no book. Vikings worshipped the gods they felt were most relevant to their lives and who they believed would bestow them with good fortune.

Vikings were also believed to have worshipped their ancestors, many of which had fallen in battle. According to experts, Vikings largely partook in attempting to communicate with their ancestors' spirits, practiced in the arts of divination and sorcery. The Vikings also practiced a wide variety of different burial practices. These various rituals would often occur within and between various Viking communities.

Due to the Vikings largely being an oral community and very rarely documented their rituals and practices on paper, the accounts of the Viking era were largely written by outsiders rather than firsthand accounts from the Vikings themselves. What we understand today regarding Viking worship and traditions may not be fully understood with complete accuracy, as they are written based on the accounts of witnesses, hearsay, or written many years after the Viking era had occurred.

Thus, as a result, Norse worship and rituals are often conflicting, relatively inaccurate, or even made up by enemies of the Vikings, such as the British, to paint the Norsemen in a bad light, or sometimes to simply tell a more tantalizing story of the mysterious Vikings.

However, according to Norse mythology experts, these seven rituals are generally considered to have been traditionally practiced by the Vikings during the Viking Age. These rituals include the blot sacrifice, human sacrifice, Yule celebration, burial traditions, warding off draugr, wedding ceremonies, infant rituals, and naming rituals (Esser, 2018).

Blot Sacrifice

The blot sacrifice was one of the most highly respected traditions in Viking society. The purpose of the blot sacrifice was to secure the good faith and goodwill of the gods for you and your family. This ritual would be carried out with a large group of people on the estate of the local chief of the region. The chief would act as the 'priest,' or commissioner of the sacrifices during the ceremony. The blot sacrifice was an opportunity not only for the public to honor the gods with sacrifices they felt fitting, but also acted as an opportunity for the chief of the region to show off their wealth to the community.

According to Norse mythology experts, a blot sacrifice would happen four times in a year. It would occur at the close of the winter solstice, spring equinox, summer solstice, and autumn equinox. However, certain years had exceptions, and there would be more than four blot sacrifices if the community was experiencing problems such as a bad harvest.

One of the very few detailed descriptions of the blot sacrifice ritual was written by Snorri Sturluson in the 13th Century. The detailed account of the ritual stated that all the local farmers of the region would come forth to the chief's temple and sacrifice many animals. The animals that were sacrificed the most were horses. The chief would use twigs to spray blood across the temple, as well as spray blood on the faces of the farmers who offered sacrifices (Esser, 2018).

It was customary to bring with you your own cooked meat and beer, which would be blessed by the chief of the blot sacrifice. When everybody gathered together after the sacrifices had been made, they would drink beer and toast to Odin, the other gods, and their ancestors.

Human Sacrifice

Human sacrifices were not a common occurrence within Viking life, but they were practiced from time to time. As stated earlier, many stories regarding the Vikings are often fabricated and told in such a way as to portray the Scandinavians in a negative light; however, archaeological remains that have been found from expeditions indicate that, on occasion, the Vikings did occasionally partake in human sacrifice (Esser, 2018).

One source of a secondhand account of human sacrifice in the Viking age was written by Adam of Bremen in the 11th Century. Adam writes about the tradition of human sacrifice that would be practiced at Uppsala, Sweden at the beginning of spring once every nine years. According to the account, the ritual was meant to last nine days, and every day, nine sacrifices were made and a feast was enjoyed. That is a total of 81 sacrifices during the festival's ritual.

On each day, one human male would be sacrificed along with eight male animal sacrifices. It is said that the bodies were hung from trees just outside of the temple in which the ritual had occurred. The purpose of this ritual was to honor the All-Father Odin and secure victory in all of the Vikings' battles in the coming year.

According to experts, it is said that the sacrifices were normally criminals or slaves; however, one year a king was sacrificed at Uppsala as a sign of good faith to Odin to bring an end to the extreme famine that the region was experiencing. According to Snorri Sturluson's saga, it is said that the previous two years before the king was sacrificed, the Vikings sacrificed a group of oxen to bring an end to the famine. When the group of oxen failed the following year, they sacrificed a group of men, but still, the famine persisted. The public blamed the king for their misfortune, and thus sacrificed him to Odin and covered the altar in the king's blood (Esser, 2018).

Yule Celebration

Believe it or not, the Vikings celebrated a festival that has incredible similarities to the Christian holiday of Christmas. There are a lot of differences, but there are some interesting similarities. This is largely due to the fact that many Christmas and Christian traditions were borrowed, or born, out of Pagan traditions and were reframed for a Christian audience in mind. What is most similar about these two holidays is the tree. The Vikings' Yule celebration implemented a tree that symbolized Yggdrasil (the world tree), and Vikings all over Scandinavia would decorate their houses with trees known as Yule trees this time of year. According to experts, it is believed that the Yule tree actually inspired the Christmas tree that is ever present in millions of family homes across the globe come the 25th of December (Ancient Pages, 2020).

The Yule tree to the Vikings was not only symbolic of the world tree that connects the nine realms together, but it was also a symbolic reminder to the Vikings that even during the dark and cold winters Scandanvia experiences, the sun will return and provide great harvests for the Vikings in the months to follow.

To highlight even more similarities between the Christmas tree and the Yule tree is that the Vikings were believed to have decorated the Yule tree with a little statue carved to look like the Norse pantheon. Sounds familiar to Christmas trees being decorated with candy canes, bells, socks, and stars, right? The Vikings were also known to leave out food and clothes by the Yule tree as they attempted to call the spirits of the forest. This is similar to how Christans leave out milk and cookies for Santa Claus. The spirits of the forest that the Vikings were trying to invite into their homes with food and clothes were known as vættir (vättar in Swedish). These were woodland creatures that were believed to live in trees. However, it was a common belief among Vikings that the small creatures would freeze in the forest due to the harsh icy conditions of winter during the time of the Yule celebration. The Vikings did not want the vættir to meet such a grim end, thus they took the trees inside (which were the Yule trees) so that the vættir could have a home in the Vikings' houses during the treacherous winter. Thus, the Vikings opened their homes to the vættir and provided these spirits a warm and cozy atmosphere. This showed a very different side of the Vikings' general perceived nature.

For a civilization of people considered to be savages and ferocious brutes, this was a very human and empathetic emotional side of the Vikings that is too often ignored. It is important to remember that Vikings were humans too and not just blood-thirsty warriors.

The actual celebration of the Yule holiday was celebrated by the Vikings on the winter solstice, which begins on the 21st of December. What's interesting is to note how closely the holidays of Christmas and the Yule celebration are celebrated on the annual calendar. Yet another similarity between the two holidays. What's more is, while Christians celebrate Christmas in remembrance of Jesus Christ, the Vikings celebrate Yule in honor of Odin and the Norse gods. Funny enough, Odin has many a time been compared to Santa Claus. Perhaps this is due to Odin's elderly appearance and long flowing white beard.

The word Jól in Old Norse can be translated to a feast, and the word Jólablót, which was the traditional name for the Yule festival, means midwinter festival and is associated with the rebirth of the sun. This is because the Yule festival happened on the shortest day of the year. The sun would only be visible for a few hours, and in some parts of Scandinavia, it could barely be seen at all. Thus, the festival was centered around the rebirth of the sun, and that from here on out, the light would be more frequent (Ancient Pages, 2020).

The Yule celebration was a day that was keenly awaited by all Vikings, and was a day marked on every Viking's calendar. It was a special tradition to the Nordic people and was practiced in Iceland, Denmark, Norway, and Sweden. According to scholars and extracts from the famed Icelandic Sagas, the Yule celebration was meant to last three full days and nights.

During the Yule celebration, Vikings would get together for a massive feast and would invite their friends, families, neighbors, and whoever else wanted to join in the festivities. It was a time for good company, good food, and worship to the Norse pantheon. Everybody would gather around a long table, known as the Yule table, to eat and engage in lovely conversation. Everybody would bring with them a variety of different foods, from fish, to meat, to beer; you name it, the Yule table had it. It was a time for good wholesome fun. During the Yule celebration, entertainment was a must and the Norsemen would generally participate in singing, dancing, playing games, and telling captivating stories. It is important to note that during the Yule celebration, everybody was invited to participate, even foreigners and travelers from distant lands. In fact, Vikings actually loved when travelers from other parts of the world would join in the festivities. The

Vikings enjoyed hearing stories from these travelers about their foreign lands and voyages. For a Viking, travel was key, and thus, they were always fascinated with the ins and outs of what was happening across the world.

Burial Traditions

During the Viking Age, the dead were generally honored in one of two ways when they were sent to the afterlife. For most Vikings, the dead would be given a ceremony to help guide their souls to the afterlife either in the form of cremation or burial. The ceremony was thought to help guide the souls of the fallen Vikings either to Valhalla (the home of Odin and the Norse version of heaven) or Helheim. However, where the fallen Vikings ended up after their life on Midgard (Earth) would be determined by their actions when they were alive. Those pure of heart would be rewarded by spending the rest of eternity within Valhalla, although it was also believed if a Viking died a warrior's death, they would have a better chance ending up in Valhalla . However, those who had committed horrific acts of injustice or had a corrupted soul would spend the rest of eternity in the depths of Helheim.

Cremation was generally used as a means to honor the dead of early Vikings, as they were fiercely paagan, and the act of cremation was practiced upon a funeral pyre. The reason for being cremated instead of buried was because it was believed that the smoke from the fire that scorched their lifeless bodies would act as a carrier to guide their souls to the gates of Valhalla. Once the deceased Viking's corpse had been devoured by the flames, leaving nothing but ash and bones, the remains would be placed in an urn and the rest would be buried in the ground.

When the Vikings honored the dead, whether it was in relation to burials or cremated remains, the location ranged widely. Locations of the burial generally consisted of shallowly-dug graves and large burial mounds that were dug with the intention of holding multiple corpses. There were also groupings of mounds known as grave fields, which served the purpose of what could now be understood as a cemetery.

These Viking cemeteries were specifically designed to resemble the shape of a ship. This was because ships were regarded as incredibly sacred symbols and were considered to be the apparatus that would guide the fallen Vikings safely to Valhalla, similarly to how the smoke from cremated bodies would guide the souls of the dead to the afterlife. This was done by placing stones, or systematically burning graves in the outline of a vessel's shape
The common Viking could not be buried with their actual boat, as ships were far too valuable, thus against popular belief; boat funerals were extremely rare. However, the grave mounds that were made to symbolize a ship were the alternative for almost every Viking that was buried. Boat funerals, as depicted in media such as *History Channel's* highly esteemed TV series *Vikings* were solely reserved for very highly-ranked warriors and Norsemen.

Only a very select few Vikings were granted the honor of being buried with their actual boats (Morgan, 2018). What was even rarer was for Norsemen to be cremated at sea with their ship, which would be set on fire due to a fiery arrow being shot from the shores from the hand of an archer. What is interesting is that boat funerals were not reserved solely for males;boat funerals were a tradition practiced for both male and female deceased Vikings.

According to a report from Ahmad ibn Fadlan, a middle ages-traveler, one instance of the notorious boat funeral was for a Viking chieftain, which included a female slave as a sacrifice who would be cremated at sea with her master. The scenes that were said to follow were truly horrific and unimaginably barbaric. According to Ahmad, the female slave was forced to drink alcohol to such levels of severe alcohol poisoning. However, the alcohol would not be what killed her, as immediately after she was raped by every man in the village in the name of tribute for the deceased chieftain. After being raped countless times, she was strangled and stabbed to death by the deceased's wife, who at the time was known as the "Angel of Death." Finally, the slave would be placed on the vessel with her master and set alight from a fiery arrow shot from an archer's hand (Morgan, 2018).

There were many variations in the Viking Age when it came to disposing of and honoring the dead; however, regardless of how the dead were to be honored, the fallen Vikings would still practice a few rituals that would remain untouched no matter how the body was disposed of. One of these practices included dressing the deceased in brand new clothes that would be created specifically for the funeral. Another tradition was that at the funeral service, a ceremony was always held, which would always include food, alcohol, chants, and traditional songs.

At these ceremonies, gifts were also ever present, and they were offered as tribute in honor of the fallen Vikings. These gifts were known as 'grave goods' and generally consisted of items that were equal to the dead Viking's economic status. These would often include things such as garments, weapons, jewelry, and occasionally, slaves. The 'grave goods' would either be buried with the deceased or burned at the pyre if the Viking was cremated.

Recently, a Viking site was discovered in Flakstad, Norway. At this gravesite it was found that there were multiple bodies laid to rest together in a single grave. Some of these were even decapitated. After studies and a DNA analysis had been done, it was determined that the bodies were in fact slaves who had been sacrificed to spend their eternal slumber with their owner even in death. (Morgan, 2018).

Warding Off Draugr

Just as the Vikings would honor the dead and assist the dead on their travels to Valhalla, the Norsemen were also wary of the draugr. Draugr, also known as aptrgangr in Old Norse, were the equivalent of modern-day zombies at the time of the Viking Age. According to experts, it was believed that once a person was buried, it was possible that the departed corpse could be reanimated again. The corpse was believed to live innocently in its grave, protecting the goods and treasures they were buried with from grave robbers. These innocent undead corpses were known as hangbui. However, if the hangbui's goods were stolen by grave robbers, they would turn into a draugr. When a hangbui turned into a draugr, they would borrow out of their eternal resting spot into the world of the living and harm any man, woman, or child that crossed its path (Esser, 2018).

In order to prevent this catastrophe from unfolding, the Norsemen took many precautions when burning the deceased's body. The Vikings would place many pieces of straw in the shape of crosses under the shroud, as well as a pair of scissors that were opened across the chest on those who had since passed. The Vikings were believed to have tied corpses' big toes together and hammer nails into the soles of their feet so that if the dead were to arise and go on a rampage, they would not be able to walk.

How the coffin was carried and lowered into the grave was also significant. When the Vikings carried the coffin out of the deceased's house, the coffin bearers would cautiously come to a halt. Before exiting the door of the deceased's house, the bearers would lower and raise the coffin in three movements in different directions, creating the shape of a cross. According to experts, sometimes the body would be carried out through a specific door known as the 'corpse-door,' which was a hole in the wall covered in bricks. The corpse door was specifically designed to only be exited once someone had died and would be torn open to remove the dead and then be put back together once the deceased had been buried.

The corpse-door may seem incredibly unnecessary without context; however, according to experts, it is believed that Vikings thought that the deceased could only return into a building in the same entrance they came out of. Due to this logic, once a corpse-door had been reassembled, the draugr wouldn't be able to enter the house again. The Vikings' fear of the draugr went even further. The deceased's corpse would carefully be carried out with their feet coming out of the door first so that its head would be facing away from the path the coffin bearers took to the burial mound. This was done so the corpse would not be able to memorize the path back from where it came if the deceased were to turn into a ferocious draugr. Once buried, a magic spell was meant to be said at the gravesite to bind the deceased to their eternal grave.

Lastly, once the coffin had safely and cautiously been moved out of the house, then every jar, saucepan, cutlery, crockery, chair, and stool recently used by the deceased were to be turned upside down (Esser, 2018).

Wedding Ceremonies

The Vikings believed in holy matrimony and the sacred bond between man and wife. Just like Christians and other religious followers, the Vikings also partook in the act of marriage and was practiced by almost the entire adult population of the Norsemen. Before a woman was to be married to a male Viking, they would wear a kransen. A Kransen was a gilt circlet that was won by all unwed Viking women, along with their being worn loose. However, during a wedding ceremony, the bride would remove her kransen and would replace it with a Viking wedding crown. The bride's kransen would then become a family heirloom. The kransen would be passed down to her future daughter, then to her granddaughter, and eventually be passed down from generation to generation to all the women of the bride's bloodline (Esser, 2018).

With regards to the groom, he would acquire a sword from one of his ancestors that had been passed down from generation to generation. Some experts believe that there was a possibility that the sword had been recovered by breaking into the grave of their dead ancestors and taking the sword that they had been buried with. Other opinions on the matter suggest that a fake grave was prepared for occasions like a wedding, which would be broken into to obtain the sword the groom would be presented with. However, regardless of the methods of how the groom obtained the sword, the protocol at the wedding ceremony was the same. During the wedding ceremony, the groom would carry the sword and sometimes even a hammer to symbolize the god of thunder, Thor. What is interesting is that neither the groom nor the bride had special clothes allocated for them to wear for the wedding; they wore the same clothes they would have worn on a regular day.

A Viking wedding was always held on a Friday. Friday was Frigg's day; Frigg was the wife of Odin and the goddess of fertility. The ceremony would always begin by attempting to garner the attention of the Norse gods by dedicating a sacrifice in the form of an animal in honor of Frigg, Odin, and the other gods.

After the sacrifice, the bride and the groom would meet at the altar. The groom would present the sword of his ancestors to his soon-to-be wife as an heirloom that would be passed on to their firstborn son. The bride would give the groom another sword as a token of their marriage to be used to protect their future family from any danger. Once the bride and the groom had exchanged swords, it was time for the soon-to-be newlyweds to exchange rings and vows (Esser, 2018).

The bride and the groom would exchange a kiss, and the two would officially be named husband and wife in the name of the gods. After the ceremony, all who had attended would make their way to the hall to feast on a seemingly endless supply of meat, fish, alcohol, and all sorts of delicious food. It would be here in the hall where everyone was feasting that the groom would assist the bride over the threshold and thrust his sword with all his strength into a pillar. It was believed that the deeper the groom managed to plunge his sword unto the wooden pillar, the more children and luck would be bestowed upon the married couple by the gods. Furthermore, it was customary that the newlyweds would share bridal ale, which was usually mead, every night for the next month.

Lastly, after everyone had eaten and the ceremony had come to a close, one last tradition needed to be upheld. The couple would be accompanied to bed by a few of the guests who attended the wedding to act as witnesses so they could testify that the union between husband and wife had been consummated. The morning after the marriage had been consummated, the bride would tie up her hair and would cover it with a cloth to showcase her new status of being a wife to the rest of the village. The groom would finally hand over the keys to his house to his new wife and they would continue their lives as a happily married couple (Esser, 2018).

Infant Rituals and Naming Ceremonies

Within Norse mythology, when a baby was born, there were a handful of rituals that needed to be practiced before the infant child could be considered a real person in Viking society. Before these rituals had been completed, the baby Norseman could not be considered a human being yet. According to experts, it was likely a defense mechanism that the Vikings had adopted to protect themselves emotionally, as the infant mortality rate was dangerously high. If the infant wasn't considered human yet, then the death of a baby was far less emotionally taxing in the minds of the Viking parents at the time.

So in order to emotionally protect the parents, infant rituals were put in place. When a Viking baby was born, the infant would be placed on the ground until his/her Viking father picked up the child and placed the infant inside of his coat. Placing the child inside of the father's coat would symbolize that the father had accepted the infant as his own child. Once the father had done this, he would then inspect if the infant had any physical problems. If the child was found to have any problems from birth, the child would be left exposed and unattended until the baby died. However, if the child was found to have no birth defects, a ceremony would be held known as ausa vatni. During ausa vatni, water would be sprinkled over the baby, similar to baptism in Christianity (Esser, 2018).

Once the ceremony had concluded and the baby was found to be healthy and accepted by its father, a naming ceremony would commence known as nafnfesti. During nafnfesti, the father would provide his newborn baby with a gift and name the child. The gift that most infants received during nafnfesti would generally be a ring, a weapon, or a farm/land deed that they would receive when the child grew older. Once the ausa vanti and nafnfesti ceremonies were completed, the child was accepted by the Viking community and was officially considered a human being. The child could no longer be subject to harm or exposure to the elements, as this would, from this point on, be considered murder (Esser, 2018).

Chapter 4: The Gods of Norse Mythology

The Aesir gods made up a large portion of the Norse pantheon. The word pantheon can be understood as a collective group of gods within a particular culture; for example, there would be the Egyptian pantheon or the Greek Pantheon that would consist of those regions' collective gods. The word pantheon comes from the Greek words pan (all) and theoi (gods), thus suggesting all the gods of a particular group or belief system. The Norse pantheon consisted of the Aesir, Vanir, jötnar, and many other minor deities and demigods. Thus, the Norse pantheon consisted of a wide range of deities and divine beings who were responsible for and controlled different sections of the nine realms of the cosmos.

However, the list of the Norse pantheon is incredibly lengthy and is made up of many different bloodlines and races, making it difficult to single out every Norse god of the time. Thus, in order to truly grasp the Norse pantheon, it is best to highlight only the most important gods and goddesses that the Norsemen worshipped during the Viking age.

The Norse pantheon can be divided into three major groups. These groups consist of the Aesir (the newest generation of gods), the Vanir (the old gods), and the jötnar (the giants who inhabited the universe first). However, only the most important of these gods will be discussed. After years of bloodshed between these three groups, the Aesir would come out victorious and be the most powerful gods who would rule the cosmos (Gill, 2019).

Odin

Odin, also known as Woden in Old English, is the father of all the gods and mortals and rules over Asgard, home of the Aesir. Odin is married to Frigg, the goddess of love and war, and has many children, most notably Thor, Baldur, and Vidar. In the Marvel comics, Loki is his adopted son, but in mythology, Loki is occasionally referred to as his half-brother.

Odin would sit on his throne, known as Hlidskjalf, inside the safety of Valhalla's gates, where he would observe tirelessly over the nine realms of the cosmos. Odin is the god of war, however, he is also associated as the god of magic, wisdom, poetry, and the runic alphabet (Gods and Goddesses, 2017).

Odin often appears in many heroic pieces of literature, written at the time of the Vikings, as the protector of heroes. What this means is that Odin admired and protected warriors who had fallen in the name of battle and would welcome them into the gates of Valhalla, Odin's palatial home with 640 doors. Odin and his wife Frigg would possess the souls of the warriors who had been slain in battle. The half that belonged to Odin would enter Valhalla for their final resting place, where they would feast, indulge in fornication, and engage in as much battle as their heart's content. The fallen warriors would be met by Odin's daughters, the valkyrie, and would be transported to the heavenly realm of Asgard; those who were not worthy would be transported to Helheim (Britannica, 2018).

Odin valued knowledge and always sought out ways to further it. He was intently captivated by the runes, the letters of the runic alphabet. Odin was so interested to seek out further knowledge from the ancient runic alphabet that he hung himself from a tree with a spear impaled in his side for nine days and nine nights with no food or water and vowed to himself that he would only come down from the torture until he unlocked the secret of the runes. Eventually, after nine full days and nights, the All-Father unlocked the secrets of the runes and would often use them to practice his wizardry, for which he was highly esteemed for.

However, Odin's quest for wisdom and knowledge never ceased, and he would search for new ways to improve upon these qualities no matter the cost. Odin even lost his eye in search of true never-ending wisdom. Odin sacrificed his eye so that he could drink from Urd's (well of wisdom located by Yggdrasil). His eye was the price he had to pay to convince the giant Mimir to provide him with a drink from the well out of a horn. However, Odin's sacrifice did pay off, and he profited with eternal wisdom. Odin would also steal the head of Mimir, the giant that offered him the drink from Urd's well when Vanir decapitated the giant, as Odin believed that Mirmir's severed head would tell him the secrets of the universe and provide him with advice (Gods and Goddesses, 2017).

In art, Odin was depicted as a tall, old man with a full white beard and would always be shown as having only one eye, as his other eye was traded for enhanced wisdom. Odin would normally be seen wearing a cloak and a large wide-brimmed hat. The god of war would generally be depicted with a spear, known as Gungnir, which he received from his adopted son Loki, the god of mischief, after he stole it from a group of dwarves who created it.

Odin sometimes was depicted with two ravens by his side who were known as Hugin (thought) and Munin (memory). These ravens were Odin's companions, and he would send them across the nine worlds to bring back intel and stories of what they saw in the rest of the cosmos. In art, Odin is also often accompanied by his two pet wolves Geri and Freki. Odin created these wolves due to being lonely. Odin would send Freki and Geri to bloody battlefields to feed off the corpses of the fallen warriors. Odin is the god of all gods in Norse mythology, and was generally honored above all the other gods (Gods and Goddesses, 2017).

Frigg

The word Frigg can be translated to 'beloved' in Old Norse, which is incredibly fitting, as the goddess of love was definitely the most beloved goddess of the Norsemen, as she was the Queen of the Aesir and the loving wife of the All-Father Odin. Frigg was a goddess considered to represent many aspects of the human condition and reality, and the Norsemen believed Frigg to be the goddess of love, fertility, marriage, and war. However, it does not stop there.

In many regions of Scandinavia, Frigg was also considered to represent fate, foresight, and wisdom. It was often believed that Frigg could see one's fate and could see into the future. Frigg was also a sky goddess and was responsible for weaving the clouds, as well as weaving the fates of mortals. It is believed that Frigg would use the clouds to weave garments for the Aesir gods. Frigg was a motherly figure to all the Norse pantheon, as well as to the Vikings that worshiped her. What is interesting is that Friday is named after the goddess, Frigg, and Wednesday is named after her husband the All-Father, Odin (Woden in Old English), and to this day, the names have never changed and the origins of these days of the week remain true. What's more, the god of lightning, Thor, also has a day of the week named in his honor, which is Thursday, also known as "Thor's day." This shows how renowned these gods were even outside of Scandinavia, and that the name of these days was used even in England, the nation that hated the Vikings more than anybody.

Frigg had many responsibilities, which was to be expected with a goddess of her stature. One of the goddess's most important duties was to oversee all of the mortal marriages sanctioned in society, and was a beacon of shining light to the Vikings and highly admired and worshiped during matrimonies. In fact, during the Viking Age, it was sanctioned that you could only be married on a Friday. This was because Friday, as mentioned earlier, was the day that was specifically reserved in honor of the goddess Frigg. Due to this, Frigg was seen as the protector of the Norsemen's homes and families, and brought good fortune to those who were married.

As Queen of the Aesir and Asgard, it was only natural that the Norse women of Scandinavia would view the goddess of love, marriage, and fertility as their role model and a figure they strived to imitate in their daily lives. Frigg was often called upon by her female followers for aid in the domestic arts and cottage industry, as it was believed that the goddess herself would partake in these activities due to her perceived kind, gentle, and loving nature.

Another responsibility of this goddess was to ensure that peace and social order in the cosmos was maintained. According to legend, whenever the Aesir gods had a feast, Frigg would be present and she would always be carrying a horn filled with mead. At these feasts, she would do one of two things: she would either welcome warriors back from battle or she would give them one last meal before sending them off to battle. Thus, Frigg was sometimes referred to by her nickname 'lady of the hall,' which led to the goddess of marriage being associated as a patroness of diplomacy (Ancient Origins, 2019).

However, as Frigg was the goddess of fertility, she was also a mother herself. In Scandinavia at the time of the Vikings, the longest night of the year was known as 'Mother Night,' and was believed to be the night that the goddess Frigg gave birth to her son Baldur, the god of light and joy (Ancient Origins, 2019). Frigg was a fantastic mother and was incredibly loving and nurturing to her son; however, ill fate awaited Baldur, and Frigg knew this. As mentioned earlier, Frigg is also the goddess of prophecy, and as such, she foresaw in a dream that her child would have an untimely death. Unfortunately, she could not save her son, and Baldur lost his life, regardless of her multiple efforts to try and avoid it. Frigg was believed to never be the same after her son's death, but remained the goddess of love, marriage, and fertility to the Norsemen and was beloved and honored by all.

Baldur

Baldur is the god of all that is good and is associated with all that is beautiful and joyous in the cosmos. Baldur was the second son of Odin and Frigg and the younger twin sibling of his blind brother Hodr. Like his mother Frigg, Baldur was a very friendly, kind, and loving god; however, he was not particularly mighty or powerful, nor was he bestowed with the great strength and physical prowess like his half-siblings, such as Thor, had been gifted with (P. Geller, 2016b).

However, despite this, everybody loved Baldur, and he was one of the most loved gods in all of Asgard. Whoever Baldur spent time with, or wherever the son of Frigg went, joy was inevitably going to be experienced by all.

As said earlier, it was prophesied that Baldur would meet an untimely demise, and no matter how hard his parents tried to prevent it, the result would end in tragedy. However, this was not with a lack of effort. Odin and Frigg would not accept this fate, and thus, Odin took it upon himself to seek out a solution. Odin traveled to Helheim (the underworld) where a deceased female seer resided. Odin would disguise himself, but would find that Helheim had been decorated for an event of celebration. It turned out that the seeress that resided in

Helheim was aware of the prophecy regarding Baldur's death, and that the residents of Helheim were preparing a party in Baldur's honor, as they wanted to welcome the arrival of such an esteemed guest of Baldur's divine status.

Horrified from what he witnessed, Odin told Frigg about what had been prophesied in Helheim and what would befall their son. Frigg was terrified, and she visited every living thing in the cosmos and got an oath from everybody that no harm would befall her son.

With this new collective oath, Baldur was considered essentially invincible. The other gods of Asgard found this incredibly amusing and decided to play a game. The game entailed throwing all sorts of things at Baldur to watch them bounce off the god of joy harmlessly.

Loki, the god of mischief, saw this as an opportunity to bring upon chaos. Loki lived for chaos and mischief, as it entertained him immensely. Loki disguised himself and went over to Frigg and asked the goddess if she truly got an oath from EVERY living thing in the universe. Frigg carelessly let slip that she failed to gain the oath from the mistletoe, as she could not see any harm that it could bring upon her son.

Armed with this new and exciting knowledge, the god of mischief went over to Hodr, Baldur's blind brother, and asked if he wanted to join in throwing objects at his now invincible brother. Hodr accepted and Loki gave the blind brother a sharpened branch of the mistletoe that Frigg failed to get an oath from and pointed Hodr in the right direction of his brother. Hodr launched the branch and struck Baldur dead on the spot (P. Geller, 2016b).

Thor

Thor is the son of Odin and is the god of thunder. Thor was one of the most popular gods in Norse mythology, and was even more popular than Odin himself in some regions during the Viking Age. Thor's popularity grew in stature at the expense of his father Odin in the 9th century. This is because many farmers would flee Norway for a safer life in Iceland in order to escape the tyrannical and oppressive rule of the Norwegian king, who worshiped Odin. Due to this, Thor's popularity reached its peak from around the years 790-1066 during the Viking Age (Gods and Goddesses, 2016).

Thor has become widely popular in the modern era through his portrayals in pop culture, most notably his depiction in Marvel comics and the Marvel cinematic universe. However, with regards to Norse mythology, Thor was the god of thunder. He was also associated as being the protector of mankind. Thor is widely recognizable for wielding his hammer Mjölnir (Mjǫllnir in Old Norse), which he used to control the lighting, thunder, and storms. Thor was regarded as the most powerful of the Norse gods and was renowned for being incredibly strong. Due to this, he was feared by many. Many mortals feared Thor due to his immense power, but had the utmost admiration for him, as they knew he was interested in preserving the wellbeing and happiness of mankind.

Thor represented many aspects of the human condition. It is believed that the god of Thunder symbolized the three main pillars of manhood, as well as being associated as being the god of fertility. These pillars included the ability to provide for your loved ones, protect those who are dear to you, and procreation. Thor was not necessarily known as a god who was loving or gentle, but it was a collective belief that Thor had a good heart and always had pure intentions.

Thor would use his overwhelming strength to protect the people around him. Thor was known to be a prideful god, and thus would protect his own honor, as well as the honor of others. Thor was the ultimate defender of justice and balance of the cosmos, unlike his half-brother Loki. Thor was married to the goddess Sif. The exact details of Thor's lineage are blurry; however, based on accounts, it is evident that Thor had at least three children, Thrud, Magni, and Jarnsaxa, and was a supportive and nurturing father (Geller, 2017).

Thor's greatest enemies were the jötnar who lived in Jotunheim, as well as the ginormous sea serpent known as Jormungand. Jormungand represented all that was evil and was a beast that needed to be slain. According to Edda, which is a body of ancient Icelandic literature that has served as the primary source and basis of what the modern world knows of Norse mythology, Thor and Jormungand fought on two occasions. The most notable of the two was a battle that depicts a scene where Thor virtually pulls the sea serpent straight out the ocean; however, at the last minute, Thor was stopped by the jotunn Hymir, who believed that if Thor plucked Jormungand from the ocean, it would lead to the end of the cosmos. Thor listened and restrained from slaying the sea serpent. According to legend, Thor and the Jormungand will fight again during Ragnarok and both will end up killing one another (Gods and Goddesses, 2016).

Thor's appearance is actually much different from that of his modern portrayal in Marvel comics and films. Thor was believed to have long flowing red hair and a full red beard. He was always portrayed as a very strong and muscular man, leaving no secret of his immense strength based on his build. Most artistic representations of the god of thunder depict him with a ferocious appearance, yet despite his intimidating stature and aesthetic, he remained among the gods of the Norse pantheon. Unlike Odin, Thor did not accept any human sacrifices. This only added to the Norse god's lovable reputation.

Heimdallr

Heimdallr, or Heimdallrr in Old Norse, was considered to be the watchman and messenger of all the gods. Heimdallr is often described as being the fairest or whitest-skinned of all the Norse pantheon, and is why he is sometimes referred to as the Shining God. Heimdallr dwelled at the entry gates of Asgard and guarded over the Bifrost bridge, which was a rainbow-colored bridge that connected Asgard to all the other eight realms of the cosmos. Bifrost was so enormous that it could be seen from anywhere in all the realms of the cosmos. In Old Norse, the word bifask can be translated to the English word 'tremble,' and the röst can be translated to mean 'mile.' Thus, Bifrost directly translates to the 'trembling mile' (Skjalden, 2020b).

Heimdallr was tasked to guard Bifrost with his life and keep Asgard safe from any enemy frontiers or intruders. Due to Heimdallr guarding the Bifrost, he was also regarded as the symbol of the preservation of the cosmos and acted as the communication link between the gods, goddesses, and mankind.

Heimdallr was an incredibly powerful god and possessed heightened physical abilities that surpassed almost all of the gods; this is why he was entrusted to guard something as important as the Bifrost to ensure the safety of Asgard. Heimdallr was believed to need less sleep than a bird and possessed the ability to see his surroundings from hundreds of kilometers away. His hearing was as impressive as his sight, as it was said Heimdallr could hear grass that was growing in meadows and hear wool that grew on sheep.

These were excellent qualities to have and perfectly suited for the guard of Asgard. Heimdallr would sound his horn, known as Gjallarhorn, if he felt Asgard was being ambushed or the kingdom of the Aesir was in danger. However, he would only sound Gjallarhorn when he felt it was absolutely necessary. If a jotunn were to be so foolish as to launch an attack on Asgard or sneak into the realm of the Aesir, then Heimdallr would use his sword, known as Hofund, to slay the enemies and intruders. However, it was extremely unlikely that the jötnar would be able to launch an attack on Asgard, as they were unlikely able to make their way up the Bifrost anyway. The rainbow bridge was constantly on fire, and thus, it was too hot to be on the bridge itself. It is said that the Bifrost always had a red glow to it due to the heat radiating off of it (Britannica, 2019a).

It is believed that when Heimdallr blows on Gjallarhorn, it can be heard throughout heaven, earth, and the lower realms. According to legend, Heimdallr will sound Gjallarhorn to signal the beginning of Ragnarok and use it as an alarm to summon the Aesir to form an army to fight their enemies to the death. It is said that during Ragnarok, Heimdallr would engage in battle with Loki, and the two gods would wind up killing one another.

Loki

Loki was the god of mischief, but is also sometimes considered the god of fire. Loki was a trickster god by nature and was never considered to be either good or evil, as although he caused terrible trouble for both mortals and the gods, he would also sometimes use his cunning, wits, and slyness for the wellbeing of the gods and mortals. Loki would often be represented as the trusted companion of the great gods Odin and Thor; however, Loki's main ambition in life was to create chaos. No matter who was affected by his schemes was irrelevant to him.

Unlike many other gods in the Norse pantheon, historians have managed to decipher the meaning of Loki's name and its origin. In Old Norse, the noun 'loki' can be translated to the English word 'tangle.' This is significant, as tangle had the connotation of knots, chaos, and scheming, which would symbolize Loki's ability to tangle up the lives of others and rope them into his treacherous and mischievous plots.

Loki was not your typical god and he was not a blood relative of the Aesir tribe. This is because Loki's father was actually a jotunn known as Farbauti, and his mother was Laufey, who is sometimes considered a god and other times considered a jotunn herself. However, Loki was astray from his parents, was known to spend most of his life in the realm of Asgard, and was even often considered an Aesir, despite his jotunn heritage. Some believe that Loki was even the adopted son of Odin; however, some sources deny this claim.

Loki had a romantic relationship with the jotunn Angrboda and had three children with the giant. Their children included Loki's daughter Hel, who rules over Helheim (the underworld), the enormous sea serpent Jormungand, who was prophesied to kill Thor during Ragnarok, and their third child Fenrir, who was a ferocious wolf.

However, Loki would go on to marry the goddess Sigu, and the couple would have a son named Nari. Loki also had the power to shapeshift, and as expected, he would use this ability to scheme cunning plans and cause immense chaos in the cosmos. On one occasion, Loki even shapeshifted into a beautiful woman and seduced Odin, and he would go on to become the mother of Sleipnir, who was Odin's trusted horse.

As mentioned earlier in the chapter, Loki was responsible for the death of Aesir's favorite son Baldur. The gods of the Aesir found out that Loki was indeed the schemer behind the murder. When Baldur died, Loki immediately began to laugh, which was a testament to his guilt and role in the death of Odin's son. Loki knew immediately that the Aesir knew he was to blame, so he began to flee; however, he was caught and the gods came up with a fitting punishment. The Aesir removed the intestines of one of Loki's sons and used those intestines to tie the god of mischief to a rock. Loki would be sentenced to spend the rest of eternity tied to this rock while a cobra would spit burning venom on his face for the rest of his days.

In art, the god of mischief Loki would generally be portrayed as donning a jester-like appearance, with many artistic representations depicting Loki dancing and sneering. Loki's nose is generally represented as being unusually large; however, what is interesting about Loki is that you will find many depictions of his appearance, as Loki could shapeshift and alter his appearance as he pleased.

Freya

Freya was one of the principal goddesses of the Norse pantheon; however, she was not born an Aesir goddess but instead of the Vanir tribe. Although she was born of the Vanir tribe, she lived in harmony with the Aesir in Asgard for most of her life. Freya was the goddess of blessings, lust, love, beauty, and fertility. Due to Freya being born from the Vanir tribe, she shared her tribe's penchant for magical arts. Freya was the goddess that introduced the magic known as *seidr* to the Aesir gods, which would eventually lead to the Vanir and Aesir war. The Vanir and Aesir war will be discussed in Chapter 6. Freya's seidr magic would allow their practitioners to have knowledge of the future, and armed with that knowledge, the future could be changed (Mythopedia, 2018).

In nature, Freya was more agreeable than other Norse gods and goddesses. For example, where Thor would achieve his goals through brute strength and Loki would achieve his ambitions through trickery, Freya would achieve her objectives through gentler persuasion with the help of her beauty, offering sex, and gifts. Frey was generally considered as being an unselfish and helpful goddess; however, she also had a dark side. Similar to the males of the Norse pantheon, Freya had a taste for blood and was said to be a fierce warrior who would fight valiantly in battle. According to myths, it is said that Frey took countless lives of warriors in battle (Mythopedia, 2018).

While Freya was not known to typically fight with weapons, she was known to possess countless spells and powerful magi to aid her in battle. On top of that, Freya possessed many assortments of various different types. One of the most significant of these assortments included a cloak made out of falcon feathers, which would allow the goddess the gift of flight; however, the cloak did not just give Freya the power. Anyone who wore it would have this power also. It is said that when Freya was not using this cloak, she would lend it to many companions and collaborators who agreed to her bidding. However, although this cloak was extremely powerful, it was not her most prized possession.

The possession that Freya considered to be all-important was a necklace known as Brísingamen. Brísingamen was forged by dwarves, and the goddess purchased this necklace at a dear price. It is said she would constantly guard this necklace and would kill any soul who dared take it from her. However, Brísingamen and the cloak made of falcon wings were not the only possessions she cherished. This included the goddess's glittering chariot, which was pulled by two black domesticated cats. Freya would also generally be accompanied by an animal familiar, which was a boar known as Hildisvín, which translates to battle swine. Freya was a significant goddess in the Norse pantheon and was loved by many (Mythopedia, 2018).

Chapter 5: The Poems of the Poetic and Prose Edda

The poems of Edda are a godsend for historians, and are the primary sources in which historians have been able to piece together the Viking era and Norse mythology as we know it today. Due to the Viking culture being one of an oral society rather than that of a written one, a lot of the secrets, customs, and beliefs of the time have been lost to history due to the lack of documentation. However, thanks to the Prose Edda and the Poetic Edda, some light has been brought on the history of the Vikings.

The Prose Edda was a text of old Norse Poetics, which was written around the year 1200 by an Icelandic poet by the name of Snorri Sturlson. Snorri compiled an anthology of poems that provide the world with a large variety of lore, which shed light on what life in Scandinavia during the time of the Vikings was like.

The text itself is incredibly beneficial from an educational standpoint as it provided a consistent narrative of many of the plotlines of Norse mythology that had been lacking before the introduction of the poems of Edda. Snorri did not believe in Norse mythology himself; in fact, he was a Christian.

However, he treated the ancient pagan mythology with the utmost professionalism and respect. Thanks to Snorri, a quasi-historical backstory of the Norse pantheon was developed. What was so significant about the Prose Edda was that Snorri documented one of the first attempts to devise a rational explanation from the supernatural and legendary events that unfolded from the perception of mythology (Sacred Texts, 2019).

The Poetic Edda was written slightly later than Snorri's Prose Edda and is dated back to the second half of the 13th century. However, the Poetic Edda contains even older materials than the Prose Edda, and as a result, is sometimes known as the Elder Edda, even though it was written after the Prose Edda. The Poetic Edda is a collection of epic poems that highlight the mythological beliefs of the Viking age between the years 800-1100; however, the authorship of the Poetic Edda is unknown, unlike the Prose Edda (Britannica, 2019a).

Nevertheless, the Poetic Edda is the collection of evidence that historians of today rely on to a larger degree, as it is the largest source of information regarding Norse mythology to date. The revolutionary poems that are found in the pages of the Poetic Edda usually consist of short dramatic dialogues and simple archaic writing styles, which beautifully portray the poetry of the skalds (poets) of ancient times. The poems in the Poetic Edda highlight the iconic stories of Thor, Odin, Loki, Frigg, and the other Norse gods and goddesses, the jötnar, Vanir, and other magical creatures.

The Poem of Vafþrúðnismál (Vafthundnir's Sayings)

This poem of the collection of the Poetic Edda in the *in-Codex Regius,* the All-Father Odin's obsession for knowledge is truly highlighted. In the poem of Vafþrúðnismál, Odin sets forth to search for further knowledge about himself and the cosmos by venturing to the home of the jotunn Vafthundnir. Odin's wife Frigg is frightened and tries with all her effort to persuade Odin to give up on his venture for knowledge as she fears the jotunn Vafthundnir may be too dangerous and too powerful for even the All-Father to handle alone. However, Odin refused to listen, dismissed all of Frigg's claims, and left to go and test the jotunn's wisdom.

Upon Odin's arrival at the hall in which **Vafthundnir** resides, Odin cleverly disguised himself as a man known by the name as Gagnrad, so that the jotunn would not be able to recognize the mighty god of war. Gagnrad asked Vafthundnir if he was merely wise or very wise and challenged the jotunn to a game of wits. Vafthundnir accepted and invited the stranger in to entertain his request. Thus ,Odin and the jotunn began their battle to see who was wiser (Book Rags, 2018).

Odin originally planned to simply have a friendly Q&A with the jotunn; however, Vafthundnir was far too prideful and competitive for that. Instead, Vafthundnir proposed that the two engage in a game with much higher stakes. The jotunn proposed that the loser of this battle of wits should be decapitated and disposed of. However, Vafthundnir did not realize he was dealing with Odin, and to little surprise, the god of war accepted the jotunn's terms.

Odin suggested that, as Vafthundnir's guest, he should be asked the questions first. The jotunn agreed and asked Odin a series of questions. The two would go on and ask each other questions one after the other and both of them would continue to get them correct. However, after some time, Odin found the answer that he had been searching for, which was how he was prophesied to die.

Now that Odin was armed with this knowledge, he grew bored and would ask a question only he knew the answer to. The question he asked was, "What did Odin whisper to his dead son?" At that point, Vafthundnir knew he was not playing a game of wits with Gagnrad, but with Odin instead. The jotunn could not answer Odin's question, and as agreed upon earlier, the loser would be decapitated. Odin had gained the knowledge he had been searching for and Vafthundnir lost his life (From Baker to Edlund, 2014).

The Poem of Þrymskviða (Thrym's Poem)

The poem of Þrymskviða, also known as Thrym's poem, is a comical one and a very interesting take of the Norse pantheon, who are so often associated with blood and warfare. There is still death in this poem; however, it is a rather amusing and charming part of Norse lore.

The poem begins with Thor's iconic hammer, Mjölnir, being stolen by the jotunn Thrym, also known as Þrymr in Old Norse. The jotunn tells Thor that the only way he will return Mjölnir is if the goddess Frigg is offered to him in marriage as payment for it.

Thor, desperate to get the all-powerful Mjölnir back in his possession, tries to convince Frigg to marry Thrym; however, unsurprisingly, the goddess refuses. Thor needed to get creative and sought help from the god of mischief, Loki. Loki found this hilarious, but nonetheless provided Thor with an 'ingenious' scheme to get Mjölnir back. Thor agreed and went along with Loki's ridiculous plan. Instead of Frigg being offered to Thrym, the Aesir would trick the jotunn and offer Thor in an Aesir dress. Thor would act as the bride, and Loki Thor's bridesmaid. The two gods would travel to Jötunheim for the wedding, starting their quest to retrieve Mjölnir. Thor's identity is hilariously hinted at throughout the reception.

Thor was not shy at the reception either; it is stated that he ate an entire ox on his own. Loki somehow managed to cunningly provide very shallow explanations to the giants regarding the odd behavior of the soon-to-be wife 'Frigg,' and miraculously, the giants accepted these explanations to be true.

It is stated that Loki claimed that the bride's unimaginable hunger was due to her not eating for seven days because she was simply too excited for the wedding that she couldn't stomach anything. However, the wedding ceremony continued and Mjölnir eventually landed in Thor's hands. This was part of the tradition in which the bride and groom are meant to present one another with a weapon. Now that Mjölnir was safely given back to the thunder god, he used it to strike down the jotunn and return back home to Asgard (The Honest Modern Heathen, 2020).

The Poem of Hymiskviða (The Lay of Hymir)

In the poem of Hymiskviða, an epic story of Thor's acquisition of the jotunn Hymir's cauldron is told. This type of poem is the stuff of legends and is the kind of story you would tell your children at bedtime.

The poem begins with the gods of Asgard searching for an eternal source of mead in which they demanded to be provided to them by Aegir (Ægir in Old Norse), the god of the ocean. However, Aegir was not impressed with the tone of the request from the gods, and thus, the god of the ocean would supply the gods with endless mead if they could supply Aegir with a cauldron large enough to hold their unimaginable request.

This enormous vessel was incredibly scarce, and very few were known to be in existence. However, Tyr, the god of war and justice, knew how they could obtain this enormous cauldron. According to Tyr, his father Hymir, who was an enormous jötunn, owned a cauldron that was described to be a 'league deep.' To put that into perspective, that would mean that the cauldron was three and a half miles in size, which would be the perfect vessel to entice Aegir to supply the Aesir gods with an endless supply of mead. Though Tyr knew his father Hymir would not be so willing to hand over his enormous cauldron without a fight. The god of war enlisted Thor to aid him in tricking Hymir into handing it over through deception.

Thus, Tyr and Thor began their quest and ventured forth to pay a visit to the jötunn, Hymir. The journey to Hymir was long and full of adventure. The two gods even participated in a fishing trip in which Thor caught two enormous whales he planned to give Hymir as a gift. However, even though Thor presented his gift to the jötunn, Hymir still was not warming up to his guests. Hymir tells Thor, "Sure, you may be able to row a boat well, but if you are really strong, you should be able to prove it by breaking this glass goblet." Hymir would offer his enormous cauldron as a prize if Thor could break the goblet.

Thor accepted Hymir's proposal. He took the goblet from the hands of Hymir and smashed it with all his strength against a stone pillar. However, the glass goblet was still completely intact without a scratch while the stone pillar crumbled to pieces.

It is said in the poem that Hymir's wife provided Thor with some advice and told the thunder god to instead smash the goblet on Hymir's head, as it was far harder than the glass goblet. Thor accepted the advice he was given and the goblet shattered on the jötunn's head. Hymir was saddened that his prized goblet had been shattered; however, he stuck to his word and rewarded Thor with the cauldron that the Aesir gods were searching for. However, Hymir said, "You may only take the cauldron if you can carry it."

Tyr could barely make the cauldron budge; however, Thor managed to carry it with ease, so the two gods left Hymir's palace. Tyr and Thor did not get very far before Hymir had a change of heart and decided he wanted the cauldron back. Having just taken a few steps, the pair of gods looked behind them only to see Hymir and troops of his multi-headed henchmen coming to reclaim the jötunn's prized possession by force. Thor put down the cauldron steadily on the floor, pulled out his trusty hammer, and dispatched all of the pursuers and Hymir with relative ease. Once the pair of gods knew that the cauldron was safely in their possession, they would journey back home to Asgard.

Tyr and Thor returned, and the rest of the Aesir gods were extremely pleased with the pair and the successful quest of obtaining the cauldron needed for the mead the gods so desired. Even the god of the ocean, Aegir, was overjoyed and full of praise. Aegir changed his tone towards the Aesir's initial request and began to cheerfully brew up an unimaginable quantity of mead to last the Aesir through the winter (Kissell, 2018).

The Poem of Skírnismál (Skirnir's Journey)

This poem is a story of love, and unrequited love at that. The poem begins with Freyr, the god of kinship, good harvest, sunshine, peace, fertility, and prosperity. Freyr decides it upon himself to take a seat on Odin's throne within the gates of Valhalla, even though he knows he is not supposed to. On the throne, Freyr is able to view all the nine realms of the cosmos. Freyr's gaze is drawn to North Jotunheim, in which the god of peace and prosperity feasts his eyes on the great jötunn, Gymir.

As Freyr casually gazes upon Gymir's halls, he sees Gymnir's astonishingly beautiful jötunn daughter by the name of Grid, who is exiting the hall. She is described in the poem as almost seemingly made of light and that when she lifted her arms to close the door of the hall, the realm of Jotunheim became brighter. Freyr was fixated by Grid and could not take his eyes off of her. He watched as Grid made her way to her own palace and began to pay the price for sitting on Odin's sacred throne, for he longed to be by the side of the beautiful jötunn. Freyr eventually left Odin's throne; however, he was sorrowful and did not talk to anybody. Freyr would not eat, and would simply do nothing else but think of the beautiful Grid. Freyr's father Njord was concerned for his son and could see that something was not right; thus, Njord sent Freyr's servant Skirnir to find out what was wrong with his son. Freyr told everything to Skirnir about his longing for Grid. He told Skirnir about how much he loved the beautiful jötunn and how much the other gods of the Aesir would never approve.

At that moment, Freyr asked Skirnir to fetch Grid for him, regardless if his father approved of this voyage or not. For Skirnir's quest, Freyr provided his servant with his horse that was trained to travel through the most severe darkness and was fearless in the face of fire and magic. To further aid Skirnir on his venture, Freyr provided his servant with his sword that could slay even the fiercest of jötunn. He would hand over these items as payment for the dangerous quest he was sending Skirnir on, and these items were Freyr's two most prized items. In hindsight, the god of peace and prosperity would regret losing his sword when he is to face Surt in the midst of Ragnarok.

Skirnir humbly accepts Freyr's request and ventures forth on his quest to Jotunheim. Skirnir arrives at the home of Gymir, where he is faced by ferocious hounds chained at the enclosure that surrounds the jötunn's great hall. However, Skirnir continues his journey and rides towards a cowherd sitting on a mound, and he begins to ask the herder several questions. However, their conversation is being overheard, as Gymir can hear every word. Gymir is intrigued and sends over one of his slaves to invite Skirnir into his home. Skirnir enters the jötunn's home and sees that Grid is present. Grid asks what the reason is for his unannounced visit. Skirnir goes on to explain the nature of the situation and that he had been sent by Freyr to court her.

Skirnir offers a proposal to the beautiful jötunn in order to entice her to accompany him back to Asgard. Skirnir offers Grid eleven golden apples; however, Grid outlandishly refuses as she states she would never accept these apples for any mortal pleasure. Skirnir proposes another alternative and offers the ring Draupnir (the ring Odin laid on Baldur's funeral pyre), but yet again, Grid refuses, explaining that there is no lack of gold in the halls of her father's court. Skirnir is incredibly frustrated and threatens the jötunn with death and that he will decapitate her father Gymir if she refuses to accompany him back to Asgard, but this too has no effect. At his wit's end, Skirnir tries one last time and threatens to curse Grid with his magic wand Ganbantein. The thought of this terrifies Grid and she finally agrees to meet with Freyr at a secluded place called Barri for nine nights. Skirnir, pleased with himself, returns home to Asgard to tell Freyr he was successful in his mission (Encyclopedia Mythica, 2018).

Chapter 6: The Myths of Norse Mythology

The world of Norse mythology has so many myths and fascinating tales that it is sometimes overwhelming to know where to begin. Up until this point, many of the epic tales and stories of the Norse pantheon have been discussed and highlighted. However, even so, there are so many more tales to be told; each one is as fascinating as the last. Norse mythology never fails to captivate the reader, and provide us with stories that capture our wildest imaginations. Our interest has always piqued from the whimsical tales of the Norse pantheon. There are so many myths to uncover, and so many that have withstood the test of time.

The Creation Myth of Thor's Hammer, Mjölnir

This myth tells the tale of how the most sacred symbol of Norse mythology was created: Thor's hammer, Mjölnir. The story begins one day with the god of mischief, Loki, who found himself in a particularly mischievous mood, more so than usual. Loki decided that he would cut off all of Thor's wife, Sif's, gorgeous golden hair. Thor learned of Loki's blatant disrespect and was quickly fueled with rage. In a raging temper, Thor seized the mischievous Loki and threatened to break every bone in his body. In an attempt to spare himself from unimaginable pain, Loki pleaded with Thor to allow him to go down to Svartalfheim (the realm of the dwarves) and convince the dwarves, who were master craftsmen, to fashion Sif a new head of hair. Loki tells Thor that the dwarves of Svartalfheim would fashion a new head of hair that was even more beautiful than the hair he cut off. Thor listened to Loki's plea and allowed him to venture forth to Svartalfheim on his quest (McCoy, 2012).

Loki did what he did best and convinced the dwarves to forge a new head of gorgeous blonde hair for Sif. Ivadi's (the dwarf who forged Sif's new hair) sons would also forge two other marvels for the god of mischief to present to the god of thunder. The first of these additional gifts included the Skidbladnir, which was the best ship ever created and could be folded up to a size that would allow the ship to fit in one's pocket. The second gift the dwarves presented was Gungnir (Odin's spear), which was the deadliest spear ever forged. Loki had accomplished his task, as well as secured two very powerful gifts on top of what he had originally come for; however, Loki was overcome by an overwhelming urge to remain in the caves of Svartalfheim and revel in more recklessness. Loki decided to approach two dwarf brothers whose names were Brokkr (a metalworker) and Sindri (a spark-sprayer) and began to taunt the pair. Loki began saying to Brokkr and Sindri that they did not have the skill to forge three new creations that could parallel the might of the gifts that the sons of Ivandi managed to create. Loki was so confident that Brokkr and Sindri would never live up to the level of craftsmanship of Ivadi's sons that he even wagered his head on their lack of ability. Brokkr and Sindri were not ones to step down from a challenge and they accepted Loki's wager.

As the two dwarf brothers worked, Loki disguised himself as a bee and stung Sindri's hand. When the dwarf pulled his creation out of the burning fire, an unusual sight was seen. The dwarf pulled out a living boar with golden hair; this boar was known as Gullinbursti. He gave the dark room light and had the ability to run faster than any horse in the cosmos. Gullinbursti was said to even be fast enough to run through air and on top of the water. Thus, Sindri had created the first of three marvels that the brothers would forge for Loki.

However, the brothers were not done. Sindri laid down yet another piece of gold in the raging fire as his brother Brokkr worked on the bellows. Loki, still disguised as a bee, stung Brokkr on the neck. However, this did not phase Brokkr and the dwarf pulled out the magnificent ring, Draupnir, from the forging fire. This ring was instilled with magic and had the power that every ninth night, eight new golden rings of equal weight would fall to the beholder. Thus, the second of three magnificent marvels had been forged by the dwarves.

The brothers were on a roll. Sindri would go on and put new iron on the hearth. Sindri tells his brother Brokkr that they need to be extremely meticulous for their next creation, as a single mistake would prove far more costly than their previous two.

Loki overheard the brothers speaking and believed this was a great opportunity to sabotage the dwarves' work. Thus, once again, Loki took the form of a bee, except this time, he stung Brokkr in the eyelid. The metalworker's eye was incredibly swollen and blood blocked his vision, preventing the highly talented dwarf from properly seeing what he was forging. However, that did not stop the brothers from producing a hammer of unsurpassed quality. A hammer that's power had never before been seen. The dwarves named it Mjölnir, and designed the hammer so that it would never miss its mark and would boomerang back to its owner after every throw.

However, the dwarves saw one flaw with Mjölnir: the handle was too short. Sindri believed this blunder ruined the piece; however, he still viewed the finished product as acceptable. The dwarves were pleased with their astounding work and were sure in themselves about the great worth that their three treasures held. The two brothers would make their way to Asgard and claim the wages that were due to them (McCoy, 2012).

However, Loki returned to the halls of Asgard before the dwarves did, and thus presented the many gifts he had acquired from Svartalfheim to the gods. Loki would give Thor Sif's new beautiful head of hair and the almighty hammer, Mjölnir. The god of mischief would give Odin the mighty spear, Gungnir, and the ring known as Draupnir. Lastly, Loki would give Freyr the boat, Skidbladnir, and the golden-haired boar, Gullinbursti.

The Norse gods were incredibly grateful and were truly delighted with their gifts from the dwarves, especially with Mjölnir, as the gods foresaw that the mighty hammer would be extremely helpful in battling jötnar during Ragnarok. Although the gods were truly grateful to Loki for securing these gifts for them, they concluded that Loki still owed the dwarf brothers his head. The gods were a race that was true to their word, after all. When Brokkr and Sindri approached Loki with knives, Loki, being as cunning as he was, pointed out he had promised them his head, but he did not promise the dwarves his neck. The brothers, unfazed, decided that instead of taking Loki's head, they would be content with sewing Loki's mouth shut and to their forge (McCoy, 2012).

The Myth of Brunhilde

Brunhilde is a character in both German and Norse mythology, and her story has been encapsulated as a common trope among many fairytales and princess stories alike. The story of how a prince awakens a slumbering princess with a kiss. Her story is told in both the poems of Edda as well as the German epic of the 1200s. However, we shall discuss the Norse origin of the legendary princess.

According to Icelandic legend, Brunhilde was a valkyrie. This means Brunhilde was a maiden warrior to the All-Father Odin. Some consider the valkyries to be the daughters of Odin himself. However, Brunhilde was not an obedient valkyrie and was rather brutish by nature. Due to this disobedience that Brunhilde showed to Odin, she was punished, and Odin sentenced her to an eternity of everlasting sleep. Brunhilde was left to slumber in a castle surrounded by a wall of fire. However, the hero of the story was a prince by the name of Sigurd, and according to legend, he would slay a dragon that circled around the fiery fortress and cross through the flames of the castle that imprisoned Brunhilde and finally awaken the valkyrie with a kiss.

Brunhilde, forever grateful for Sigurd's bravery, is indebted to the brave prince and falls in love with her knight in shining armor. Sigurd too falls in love with Brunhilde, and the two become engaged. However, time passes, and Sigurd continues with his duties as a prince and travels without Brunhilde. On his travels, Sigurd is given a magic potion that makes the prince forget about his love for his valkyrie lover, and thus, Sigurd goes on to marry a woman by the name of Gudrun. However, this complicated love triangle does not stop here. Gudrun's brother Gunnar falls in love with Brunhilde at first sight and decides he wants the valkyrie to be his wife. Gunnar schemes to pursue his new love interest and persuades Sigurd, Brunhilde's former lover, to help him win over her heart. Sigurd agrees, as all his love for Brunhilde has vanished. Gunnar disguises himself as Sigurd in an attempt to win over Brunhilde's heart. The deceit works for a short period of time; however, Brunhilde would realize that she had been made a fool and was tricked by her former lover.

The valkyrie, consumed with rage, would arrange to have Sigurd murdered. The deed was done and Sigurd was killed for his deceit and utter disrespect. However, as the rage in Brunhilde's heart began to fade, she felt overwhelmed with grief and sadness as the act of what she had done hit a nerve. Brunhilde could no longer live with herself knowing that she had been responsible for her lover's death and commits suicide by throwing herself on Sigurd's funeral pyre. In Valkyrie's mind, she could join her lover once again in death.

The Aesir vs Vanir War

Within Norse mythology, there are two major tribes of gods and goddesses. These tribes include the Aesir and the Vanir, and throughout the myths, the two tribes have had many encounters. In later myths, the Vanir and the Aesir have generally gotten along; however, in early myths, this was not the case and the two tribes were bitter enemies.
The myth of the Aesir vs Vanir war began when the Vanir goddess Freya was the foremost practitioner of the terribly powerful magic art known as seidr. Like many other practitioners of the arts of seidr, she would wander from town to town offering her talented craft for hire.

Freyr eventually ventured forth to Asgard on her travels and offered her talents to the Aesir. The gods and goddesses of Asgard were greatly intrigued with Freya's abilities, and zealously acquired her services for personal gain. However, it didn't take long before the Aesir realized that their values of obedience to law, loyalty, honor, and faithfulness were being ignored. Their values were slowly being replaced with selfish desires as they obsessively desired the Vanir goddess's magic more and more.

Soon, Freya became a scapegoat and was blamed for the Aesir's shortcomings. The gods of Asgard labeled the Vanir goddess as a 'gullveig,' which translates to gold-greed, and due to her perceived deceitfulness, the Aesir gods tried to murder her. However, Freya would not die. They tried to burn her three times, but each time she would rise up once again from the ashes (McCoy, 2012a).

Due to these attempts, the Aesir and Vanir gods became bitter enemies and the two tribes began to fear and hate one another. The tension was ripe and the bitter hostilities of each tribe erupted into full-blown war. The two sets of gods fought with two very different styles. The Aesir gods were known to engage in battle through brute force with the use of plain combat and weapons, while the Vanir gods were known to fight with magic and curses. The war between the Aesir and the Vanir raged on for many years; however, it is difficult to pin down how long the warfare actually went on. The war was long, and throughout the battle, both the Aesir and the Vanir would gain the upper hand at different periods of the war. It was a stalemate, and neither tribe seemed to have been definitively winning the war.

After many years of fighting, both tribes grew tired and decided to call a truce. Calling a truce was customary during ancient Nordic times, as well as a regular occurrence with the Vikings. Thus, the Vanir and the Aesir agreed to send over hostages to live in each other's respective realms as a sign of peace. The Vanir tribe's hostages who would go on to live in Asgard were the gods and goddesses Freya, Freyr, and Njord, while the Aesir hostages who would live in Vanaheim were Hoenir and Mimir (McCoy, 2012a).

It was believed that the Vanir hostages who lived in Asgard would live more or less in peace under the watchful eye of the Aesir; however, the same could not be said for the Asgardian hostages living in Vanaheim. According to legend, the Vanir gods began to notice that the Aesir god Hoenir was able to provide incredibly wise advice to the Vanir tribe on any problem they faced; however, he was only able to do so when he was in the presence of Mimir.

The fact was that Hoenir was actually rather dim-witted and was considered a simpleton who would on many occasions be at a loss for words when he wasn't around the other Aesir hostage, Mimir, to counsel him. The Vanir gods grew tired of Hoenir's simple, slow-witted replies. After Hoenir responded to the Vanir's questions with yet another unhelpful response such as, "let others decide," the Vanir believed that they had been cheated in the hostage exchange. The Vanir were furious, as they believed that they were made a fool of by the Aesir, and as a result, they beheaded Mimir and sent the hostage's severed head back to Asgard. Odin was absolutely distraught, as he loved Mimir like a brother. Odin tried his very best to revive Mimir by chanting magic poems over the head of his dead friend, and embalmed the head in herbs. Odin managed to preserve the head of one of the wisest beings in all the cosmos, and Mimir's severed head would continue to provide the All-Father with indispensable advice in times of need.

Both the Aesir and the Vanir gods were still wary of fighting a war that in the past had been so evenly matched that they feared losing too many gods through casualties.
Thus, instead of engaging in battle once again as a result of this misunderstanding, the two tribes would come together on neutral ground and spit into a cauldron. Within the cauldron lay the saliva of both the gods of the Vanir and the gods of the Aesir, and through this mixture, the wisest of all beings was created, Kvasir.

The creation of Kvasir was a way of symbolizing and pledging a sustained harmony between the two tribes; however, both the Aesir and the Vanir were still not fond of each other, and tension still remained in the air for many years to come.

The Binding of Fenrir

As mentioned several times before, Fenrir is the monstrous wolf child of Loki. Fenrir posed great power and possessed a violent and brutish temperament. As such, the Aesir gods of Asgard feared the power of Fenrir. The gods would desperately look for a way to subdue the beast, as they knew the son of Loki was capable of causing great destruction in the cosmos.

When Fenrir was no more than a young pup, the Aesir gods decided to keep the beast in Asgard, however, as the monstrous wolf grew at an extraordinary rate, they realized they would need to find another solution to subdue the beast from unleashing chaos upon the cosmos. At first, they tried to bind him with incredibly powerful chains by tricking the wolf into thinking the chains were a test of Fenrir's ferocious strength. However, as powerful as these chains were, they were no match for the unimaginable might of Fenrir, and he broke them with ease. No chain in the Aesir arsenal could subdue the beast, and thus, the gods decided to venture forth to Svartalfheim to garner the assistance of the master craftsman of the dwarves.

As usual, the masterclass forging talents of the dwarves did not disappoint, and they created a set of chains that could subdue the monstrous Fenrir. The dwarven chains would be forged from the sound of a cat's footprint, a fish's breath, the beard of a woman, a mountain's roots, and even the saliva of a bird. These components in unison would create the strongest chains in all the known cosmos.

The gods once again told Fenrir that the chains were just to test his strength; however, this time, Fenrir was suspicious. Fenrir said that he would only agree to wear the chains if one of the Aesir gods was willing to put their hand in the beast's mouth as insurance. The gods were hesitant until Tyr, the god of war and justice, stepped forth and was willing to sacrifice his hand if it meant that it would chain the beast once and for all. The chains would hold Fenrir, and as he said he would, he bit off Tyr's hand. Fenrir was safely subdued until the final cataclysm of the universe known as Ragnarok (Eskify, 2017).

Asgard's Wall

The myth begins one day when a highly skilled blacksmith traveled to the gates of Asgard and offered the Aesir gods his assistance in building an impenetrable wall around the realm to protect the gods from their many enemies. The gods were intrigued with the smith's offers, and listened to him intently. The smith promised that he was capable of building this indestructible wall in only three seasons; however, there was a catch. The smith said that he would only consider building Asgard's unbreakable wall if he would be duly rewarded with the goddess Freya as his wife.

The gods were angered by the smith's absurd request and turned the smith down immediately. However, Loki did what he did best and managed to convince the gods to accept the smith's terms on the condition that he completed the indestructible wall in only one season instead of three. The condition would also mean that the smith could not get anybody to help him build the wall and that he and his horses were the only ones allowed to work on his proposed project.

The smith was unphased and he accepted this deal suggested by Loki and the gods. The smith began working on forging this wall with extraordinary speed, and he even managed to get his horse to help build the wall with him. The horse was said to be able to work twice as fast as the smith could. The smith was making great haste on the wall and was close to completing it. As a result, the gods watching over his progress began to panic.

The gods were famous for being true to their word, and they had promised the smith no harm, as well as offering him Freya as a wife. The gods were furious and they knew exactly who was to blame. They approached Loki and commanded him to find a way to clean up the mess that he had made. Loki quickly thought of a plan and he shapeshifted into a female horse so that he could seduce the smith's horse. Loki was successful, and the smith's horse refused to carry on working, as he was smitten with Loki. The smith did not manage to finish the wall in time without the aid of his horse, and as a punishment for his failed promise, the gods killed the smith (Eskify, 2017).

Chapter 7: Ragnarok Explained

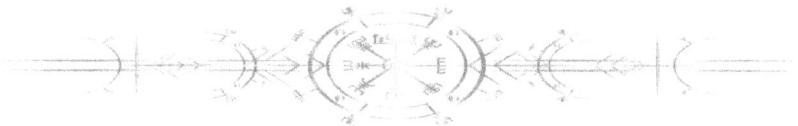

The word Ragnarok can be translated as the 'fate of the gods.' However, in old Norse literature, the meaning of Ragnarok has been played with and is also sometimes referred to as Ragnarøkkr, which means the 'twilight of the gods.' Ragnarok was given a host of other names, such as Aldar rök, which means the 'fate of mankind' (McCoy, 2018).

In Norse mythology, Ragnarok is the cataclysmic destruction of the entire cosmos and all the nine realms in it. Not even the immense power of the Aesir gods are safe from its destruction. As history can be described as linear, so can the chronological events of Norse mythology, and Ragnorok is considered the end of the set of tales the Vikings passed down to one another for generations. In respect to the Vikings, the time in which the prophecy of Ragnarok was to occur was an unknown and unspecified period of time in the future. Although the Vikings did not know when Ragnarok was to occur, it had profound ramifications regarding how the Norsemen lived their lives and how they understood the world around them.

How it's All Meant to Unfold

Some day in the future, whenever that may be, the world will experience an icy winter like no other winter that has come before it. This winter is known as Fimbulwinter, also known as *Fimbulvetr* in Old Norse. The icy winds will be so intense that snow shall be blown from all directions across the globe, and the warmth and presence of the sun will cease, plunging the world as we know it into a frozen wasteland, crushing the flourishing of life. Fimbulwinter is prophesied to last for the equivalent length of three normal winters, with no warmth from the other seasons in between the bitterness of the snow (McCoy, 2018).

Life will not be able to grow, and thus livestock and grain will become almost nonexistent. Due to the lack of food and other essential resources, mankind will succumb to collective desperation for food and other necessities to survive; all laws and morals shall fade away and chaos shall prevail. According to experts, Ragnarok for mankind is described as an age of swords and axes, a time where lover will slay lover, brother will murder brother, the father will kill son, and son will take the life of his father. Utter barbarism and disorder shall take over as the guiding force of mankind.

The wolves known as Skoll and Hati are wolves who have dedicated their existence to hunting down the sun and the moon since the beginning of time, and will finally catch their prey. The sun and the moon will disappear, along with the stars, leaving nothing but a pitch-black void in the heavens, similar to that of Ginnungagap. Yggdrasil, the world tree that holds the cosmos together, will crumble, and as it falls, so will all the trees and mountains (McCoy, 2018).

The chains that have imprisoned Loki's monstrous wolf son, Fenrir, will shatter and the ferocious wolf will run free, issuing terror among the cosmos. Loki's other son and Fenrir's enormous sea serpent brother, Jormungand, will rise up from the murky depths of Midgard and spill all the oceans onto the earth as the treacherous sea serpent makes his way to land.

The convulsions created from the escape of Fenrir and Jormungand will shake the Nail Ship known as Naglfar. Nagalfr is a ship made entirely out of the fingernails and toenails of every dead human on the earth. Naglfar will easily sail over the flooded earth, and it will be captained by Loki, the traitor of the Aesir, who managed to break free from his confines the Asgardians bound him to. Loki would be accompanied by an enormous crew of jötnar, as well as all the forces of destruction and chaos at his disposal. Loki would marvel at the chaos the cosmos had fallen victim to.

According to legend, Fenrir will have blazing fire bursting from his eyes and nostrils and will destroy the earth as we know it. Fenrir will sprint across every inch of the earth with his lower jaw planted in the surface and his upper jaw clenched on the top of the sky, devouring everything in his way. The very little that Fenrir doesn't destroy, the sea serpent Jormungand will. Jormungand will spit venom into the oceans, onto the remnants of the land, and poison the air to make sure that no entity could ever inhabit the earth again. The dome of the sky will be split into pieces, and from the cracks will emerge the fire jötunn from Muspelheim led by their brutal leader, Surt. Surt will enter the scenes of destruction with his flaming sword that is believed to be even brighter than the rays of the sun and begin marching his men towards Asgard. The fire jötnar will march across the rainbow bridge, Bifrost, and as they march, the Bifrost will crumble behind them.

Heimdallr will spot Surt and his endless troops of fire jötnar marching towards the gates of Asgard, in which the gatekeeper Heimdallr will blow his horn, Gjallarhorn. Heimdallr's Gjallarhorn will be heard throughout the cosmos, signaling the end of existence is near. The All-Father Odin will hear Heimdallr's warning and will realize his fear of Ragnarok has come to fruition. Odin will anxiously seek council from the wisest of all the known entities in the cosmos: the head of Mimir (McCoy, 2018).

Once Odin has sought counsel from the head of Mimir, it is clear to him what it is he needs to do. Odin declares war and rallies all of the Aesir to go to battle, despite knowing what fate has in store for them, as they are aware from the prophecies that the Aesir will meet their demise during the cataclysmic eclipse of Ragnarok. The Aesir, warriors from Valhalla, and valkyries will arm themselves with all the firepower they can muster, even joining forces with their sworn enemies, the Vanir gods. The gods will meet their jötnar foe on a battlefield called Vigrid, also known as *Vígríðr*, which translates to the 'plain where battle surges.'

The Final Battle

The battle between the gods and the jötnar will be one of epic proportions, leading to unthinkable bloodshed and destruction. The All-Father Odin will battle the blood-thirsty wolf Fenrir. By Odin's side will be the einherjar, who were the many chosen mortal warriors Odin selected from Valhalla to aid him in battle. Many believe that these mortal warriors were kept in Valhalla for this very moment.

It is said that Odin and the warriors of Valhalla fought more valiantly than any warrior has ever done so before; however, their bravery and valiant efforts will go unrewarded and prove to not be enough. Odin and the einherjar will fall in battle, as Fenrir will devour them whole. However, Odin's death would not be done in vain, as one of his sons, Vidar, witnessed his father's death and would charge at the wolf, burning in rage to avenge Odin. Vidar wore a shoe that was crafted for this very moment, as it was prophesied to the gods that this would occur. The shoe was crafted from all of the discarded leather mortals threw away. Odin's son would use this shoe to hold open the blood-soaked mouth of Fenrir and stab the beast in the throat with his sword. Vanir avenged his father and Fenrir was dead (McCoy, 2018).

However, the battle between Odin, Vidar, and Fenrir is only one of many epic battles that will commence on the battlefield of Vigrid. In another event, the Norse god of war, Tyr, will battle another ferocious wolf by the name of Garm. It is prophesied that Tyr and Garm will both end each other's lives in this battle. While that battle commences, the gatekeeper of Asgard, Heimdallr, will engage in battle with the god of mischief, Loki. Much like the battle between Tyr and Garm, both Loki and Heimdallr will kill each other.

However, Heimdallr is said to have taken delight just before he died for being the one responsible for finally putting an end to the trickster Loki's treachery. While Loki may have finally been silenced after all these years, the Aesir take a heavy loss by losing one of their greatest ever warriors in Heimdallr.

The battles continued to commence, and the next battle to be highlighted is the battle between the god Freyr and the brutal leader of the fire giants, Surt. The theme of Ragnorok's epic battle remains true, and both Surt and Freyr would be responsible for ending one another's lives. The last major battle to be highlighted during the battle of Ragnorok is between Thor and his lifelong nemesis Jorgmumgand; however, there were still plenty of other battles all unfolding at once. Thor and Jormungand have waited for almost eternity to end one another's lives, and during Ragnarok, both mighty beings will have their wish granted.

Thor would ultimately win the fight with his brute strength and would beat down the enormous sea serpent with vicious and deadly blows with his hammer, Mjölnir. The battle looked like it had been won, Jormungand was dead, and Thor would be seemingly unscathed. However, Jorgmumgand would cleverly smother himself in so much poisonous venom during the battle that even though Thor bested the beast, he would die from severe poisoning. Thus, once again, both foes would take each other's lives (McCoy, 2018).

No warrior would be left alive during the battle of Ragnorok, and Vigrid would be a sight of countless dead bodies in which blood would saturate the soil the bodies rested upon. Once the battle is over, the remains of the cosmos will sink into the sea and there will be nothing left but an empty void of nothingness. Creation, and everything that had occurred prior to Ragnarok, will be completely nullified, and it would be as if the cosmos were never created in the first place.

The Rebirth of the Cosmos

According to some myths, it is said that Ragnarok is not the imminent end of the cosmos, and although certain scholars and mythologists will argue that Ragnorok is the perpetual end of life as we know it, some argue that Ragnorok will birth a new world. The new world that shall commence as a result of Ragnarok will be a world that is green and beautiful and will arise out of the waters of the fallen cosmos.
As some myths believed all gods were to die in Ragnarok, other myths believed that there were a few survivors. According to these myths, the son of Odin, Vidar, and a handful of other gods shall survive the brutal battle at Vigrid such as Vali, Hodr, and Thor's sons Modi and Magni. These few gods will survive the downfall of the cosmos and live joyously in the new world.

The gods were not the only ones to survive, as there were two mortals, a man, and a woman, by the names of Lif and Lifthrasir, who survived the disastrous effects of Ragnarok as well. The man by the name of Lif translates to 'life,' and the woman by the name of Lifthrasir translates to 'striving afterlife.' Both Lif and Lifthrasir would have managed to hide from the cataclysm in a place of safety known as Hoddmímis Holt. The surviving mortal man and woman will rise from the ashes and surface from their place of hiding to repopulate the luscious green land in which they now call their new home. A new sun will arise who will be the daughter of the previous sun that was devoured and will bring an end to Fimbulwinter. A new almighty ruler of the Aesir will take over the mantle left by Odin, and the cosmos will begin to be rebuilt again slowly but surely to its previous glory (McCoy, 2018).

The Meaning of Ragnarok to the Vikings

As mentioned before, the myth of Ragnarok has two conclusions to the epic cataclysm that is present in various Norse sources. The one conclusion hints at the destruction of the cosmos and everything in it with nothing left but an empty void with no mention of a rebirth that follows the tragic events. However, the other conclusion hints at rebirth and how the cosmos will rebuild itself and rise from the ashes.

It is believed that the conclusion where no rebirth is hinted at is the older version of the epic tale of Ragnarok and constitutes a greater pagan perspective of the cataclysm.

However, the conclusion that states that rebirth is to occur is an addition to the original tale, and one that was developed later on in the Viking Age under Christian influence.
The rebirth of the cosmos after the events of Ragnarok is considered a reinterpretation of the cataclysm and describes the religious transformation the Viking world was undergoing at the time. The Vikings were beginning to be influenced by Christianity, much of which had to do with the lands in which they were pillaging and raiding. Thus, this Christian influence had an effect on the Vikings, and their pagan gods were beginning to slowly be phased out and were gradually being replaced with other beliefs.

Evidence of this is based on the fact that the mentioning of the rebirth is only discussed in three very late sources of the Viking Age. One of these sources was completely dependent on the other two while every other source that speaks of the events of Ragnarok does not mention a rebirth, and rather speaks of the complete destruction of the cosmos with no chance of rekindling (McCoy, 2018).

What Ragnarok Meant in the Minds of the Vikings

The question is how did the idea that the world would eventually come to an end with no chance of rebirth affect the minds of the Vikings? Well, to fully understand this, we need to put ourselves in the shoes of a Viking during the Viking Age. Picture this, you are a Viking, and you live in a world that you have been led to believe throughout your existence will be obliterated with no chance to rekindle. The very gods in which you have believed in all your life to be incredibly powerful and all protective of you will perish, and their fate of demise has been set in stone. You as a Viking would believe that nothing will be spared, not your children, your wife, your belongings, or anything that holds value to you. Now that you understand that the thinking of the Vikings was about the inevitable fate of the cosmos, you must ask yourself how that would make you react.

How does such a fate sit with you? In the present moment, how does the world look to you, knowing that everything you know has been decided to be stripped away from you and the seeds of destruction have already been sown?

In your mind, your world as you know it is coming to a final conclusion of nothingness, and there's nothing you, or even the gods you believe in wholeheartedly, can do to stop it. Fate seemed incredibly gloomy as a Viking, and as such, in their minds, it seemed incredibly difficult to escape the conclusion that Ragnarok would be the demise of everything. This is how the Vikings saw the world, and this is why the Vikings were a brutal, coldhearted, and ruthless civilization that took what they wanted when they wanted, as they believed that Ragnarok would do the same to them when the time came (McCoy, 2018).

How the Thought of Ragnarok Influenced the Vikings

Although Ragnarok weighed on every Viking's mind and brought an air of despair to the Norsemen of Scandinavia, it is important to remember that the Vikings were warriors and some of the bravest humans in history the world has ever known. Ragnarok carried various other meanings to the Vikings, one of which completed yet altered the Norsemens' tragic view of life. Although Ragnarok served as a prophecy for the Vikings' inevitable future, it also served as a paradigmatic model for human action among the mighty Vikings.

The tale of Ragnarok may have sealed humanity's fate in the minds of the Norsemen, but it did not produce hopelessness. In fact, it often served as a means of inspiration and invigoration. The Vikings believed that just as the fate of their gods was sealed, so was humanity, and just as the gods would face their gloomy fate with honor, courage, and dignity, so too would the humans. Believing in this logic, the Vikings were fearless and were not afraid of death. They knew death was inevitable, and thus, they would go into every battle fearless, face all challenges head-on, be ready to face misfortune, and be spurred on to hold noble attitudes (McCoy, 2018).

Chapter 8: How Norse Mythology Influenced Modern Pop Culture

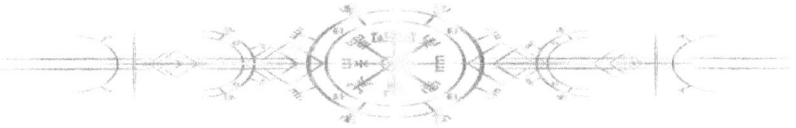

In the last 100 years or so, Norse mythology has made a resounding comeback and has become relevant in the minds of the world's populace once again. Much of this resurgence of the old Norse beliefs regaining popularity has to be credited to its resounding influence over various properties in pop culture. By now there isn't a single medium where Norse mythology hasn't played a part in influencing some sort of portrayal of the ancient Norse pantheon. Whether it be books, movies, TV series, video games, board games, music, or even advertisements, the Norse gods are back and they are back with a bang. Some incredibly notable franchises and pop culture properties that the Norse pantheon and Vikings have influenced include *Game of Thrones*, Marvel's comic line *Thor*, *The Lord of the Rings*, the video game *God of War*, the introduction of Viking metal, and many more.

Norse mythology is incredibly fascinating, and it is no wonder Hollywood, writers, and game studios have jumped on the bandwagon. The tales are epic, the battles are fierce, the drama is plentiful, and the whimsical appeal of the Norsemen and Norse pantheon sure know how to reel in a crowd. Norse mythology, especially in recent years, has been oversaturated with pop culture references and portrayals of ancient legends.

Whether it be Thor, Odin, Loki, Heimdallr, Fenrir, and the nemesis of the Aesir, the jötnar, they are all fascinating and deserve the attention of the world once again. The stories and tales are here to stay, and the world cannot wait to see what pop culture has in store for the notorious Vikings and legendary Aesir.

Marvel's *Thor*

Perhaps the most relevant Norse mythological portrayal of all modern pop culture can be credited to Marvel's highly successful comic line *Thor*. It is also largely credited for the overwhelming resurgence of Norse mythology becoming a part of the public's collective consciousness once again.

The god of thunder has captivated the imaginations of millions with his countless adventures across the nine realms on the panels of comic books, as well as on our movie screens. Thor has been a staple character of the Marvel universe since the 1960s, in which fans all over the world have enjoyed reading about his many adventures in Midgard, Asgard, Jotunheim, and more. The Marvel comics do not only portray the god of thunder, but pretty much all the Norse pantheon. After over 60 years of comics, we fans have been entertained by stories of Thor, Odin, Loki, Heimdallr, Frigg, Helheim, Fenrir, and many more.

There have been countless epic battles between Thor and the jötnar, Thor and his nemesis Loki, and many other tales influenced by Norse mythology. Although Marvel's depiction of the god of thunder is not a perfect portrayal of Norse mythology, it is definitely a love letter to ancient mythology. Marvel has taken some liberties with retelling the epic myths of the much-loved mythology, but it is incredibly clear the influence that these ancient tales played in inspiring this beloved comic line.

However, Marvel did not stop at comics alone, and have released three extremely successful blockbuster hits, which were widely popular and well received. Thor has also played a massive role in Marvel's cinematic universe, appearing in many of their other movies, most notably the three beloved *Avengers* movies that the public adore. Marvel's extensive comics featuring Thor, and Chris Hemsworth's portrayal of Thor in the cinematic releases, has truly captured the embodiment of the Norse god of thunder and provided a generation with an appreciation for the ancient Norse gods once again.

How the Vikings and Norse Mythology Influenced J.R.R Tolkien and *The Lord of the Rings*

J.R.R Tolkien was an incredibly talented author who wrote a franchise of fantasy books that took the world by storm; those books were none other than the famed *Lord of the Rings* series. *The Lord of the Rings* franchise consisted of three books, three movies, and would be the inspiration to the spin-off franchise *The Hobbit*, which had the book and three movies.

It was an insanely popular cultural phenomenon that encapsulated the imagination and interest of millions of fans. However, what most people don't know was that the Vikings and Norse mythology played a significant role in inspiring the esteemed author Tolkien into creating the franchise we all now know and love.

J.R.R Tolkien was incredibly fascinated with Scandanavian culture, and much of that had to do with his Icelandic nanny, who lived with Tolkien and his family in Oxford, England, in the early 1930s. It was through the tales that his nanny told him as a child that made the author further acquainted with Norse folk tales and the mythology attached to those very stories. Tolkien incorporated those stories into his writing, and it is evident regarding the aspects of the landscape, the language, setting, and plot aspects that helped him shape the legendary fantasy world of Middle Earth.

Due to Tolkien's fascination with Norse mythology and the culture of the Scandinavian Vikings, he began to become increasingly familiar with the texts of the Prose Edda and the Poetic Edda. The writings within the Eddas also helped inspire the famous opera *Der Ring des Nibelungen.* An all-powerful ring and a broken sword are both crucial elements of both Wagner's famous opera and Tolkien's iconic *Lord of the Rings* series, and both were inspired by the accounts in the Eddas.

As evident in the title, *The Lord of the Rings*, the ring in the novel is the crucial aspect that ties everything together, and what the story revolves around in Tolkien's novels. In Norse mythology, rings and swords were incredibly significant symbols and were prevalent throughout the poems found in both the Eddas. However, according to Norse mythology, the most powerful and magical of the rings were Odin's ring and the rings of the Niflungs (any race of dwarf who possessed a treasure, generally a ring, that would provide the wearer with unlimited power). Both Odin's ring and the rings of the Nifling were forged by dwarves just like the rings forged in *The Lord of the Rings* franchise. What is also significant to note about the rings in *The Lord of the Rings* is that nine of the twenty power rings were given to the mortals. This is noteworthy, as the number nine holds significant value in

Norse mythology, as mentioned in previous chapters. In Norse mythology, rings were used as a metaphor to symbolize power, thus the idea that the power rings of *The Lord of the Rings* were all-powerful. During the Viking age, when you owned a ring, it symbolized that you were powerful and strong, and when you would share a ring with somebody else, it meant you shared property together; thus, this tradition has become a universal sentiment in modern marriage ceremonies. What also needs to be noted is that in

Norse mythology, all famous swords were named and given a back story, which is evidently similar to the swords that belonged to the main characters of *The Lord of the Rings,* such as Gandalf's sword Glamdring.

However, it is not just the element of the power ring that is heavily inspired by Norse mythology. Other aspects of Tolkien's fantastical world of Middle Earth draw similarities from Norse mythological beliefs such as the elves and dwarves who are heavily inspired by the poems of the Prose and Poetic Edda. Gandalf, who is arguably one of the most popular and powerful figures of the entire franchise, is often associated with a connection with the All-Father Odin, especially in his appearance and design. Gandalf, much like Odin, sports a long white beard, wears a wide-brimmed hat, uses a staff as his weapon of choice, and is clothed in a white cloak. If Gandalf's appearance wasn't enough to showcase Odin's influence on the character, there is also the fact that Gandalf is also often associated with spreading wisdom, truth, and knowledge throughout Middle Earth.

Tolkien even took inspiration to help shape the geography and setting of his fantasy world of Middle Earth. Not only is Middle Earth the direct translation of the mortal realm Midgard in Norse mythology, but Midgard was also known as only one of three realms that were home to mortals, dwarves, elves, and giants just like in *The Lord of the Rings'* Middle Earth.

The only other two realms other than Midgard that the mortals could live in were in Valhalla (Asgard) and Helheim. However, it was not only Middle Earth that shared similarities to locations described in Norse mythology. In *The Lord of the Rings,* there is a realm known as Valinor, which is described in an incredibly similar manner to the realm of Asgard, home of the Aesir gods. *The Lord of the Ring's* Valinor is described as being home to the Valar, who are the equivalent of the gods in Tolkien's novels, and instead of being located above Middle Earth, it is located to the far west of it. Valinor's described appearance and nature of ambiance also inherits various similarities.

Thus, with all these similarities that are evident between Tolkien's novels and that of Norse mythology, it is fair to say that the esteemed author was definitely influenced by the tales his Icelandic nanny told him as a child.

Viking Metal

Norse mythology did not only play a part in influencing many books, TV series, films, and video games, but also played a role in music and birthed the musical genre known as Viking metal. Viking metal is a genre of music that is a subgenre of heavy metal. Viking metal is characterized and grounded by a lyrical focus on the Norse gods, myths, Nordic legends, Nordic pagan beliefs, and the Vikings. The genre itself is a relatively diverse one and inherits various musical styles and backgrounds; therefore, many people and music lovers consider the genre of Viking metal to be a cross-genre rather than a stand-alone genre. However, Viking metal is more often than not believed to have been born from the influences of black metal and Scandanvian folk music. There are many common traits and artistic music choices that are present in the Viking metal genre that are also found in other musical genres; these include a slow-paced and heavy-riffing style of music.

The genre was founded in Scandinavia around the late 1980s-early 1990s and has shared many opposing views of

Christianity, much like that of the musical genre of black metal and other heavy metal genres. However, Viking metal is not Satanic and, in fact, rejects Satanism and occult themes, and alternatively, creates music in favor of paganism, the Norse gods, the Nordic myths, and the notorious Vikings. The lyrics, sound, and imagery used by Viking metal bands are often similar and fall in line with that of other pagan-themed metal bands, although there are slight differences between pagan sub-genres in music, especially surrounding the imagery of the Norse gods and Nordic myths. The genre of pagan metal is often associated with a broader focus on mythological influence than other pagan bands, and uses folk instruments more extensively, while Viking metal distinctly focuses only on Norse mythology/paganism as opposed to paganism as a whole (Wikipedia, 2021a).

Many scholars view Viking metal to be a genre that forms part of a modern pagan movement known as the neo-völkisch movement. This means it is a genre that is trying to renew the interest in and celebration of Vikings and Norse mythological beliefs to the greater public through a resurgence of the ancient religion through music and artistic expression.

God of War

The fourth canon installment of the much-loved video game series of *God of War* is heavily rooted in the influence of Norse mythology. The majority of the Playstation 4 exclusive release is set in Ancient Norway in the mortal realm of Midgard. The video game actually predates the Viking Age, and instead of being set during the age of the Vikings, it takes place during a time where Midgard was supposedly inhabited by mortals, jötnar, elves, and other magical creatures. Other realms that can be found in this *God of War* installment include Alfheim (home of the light and dark elves), Helheim (the icy Norse equivalent of Hell), and Jotunheim (the realm of the ferocious jötnar). These are just realms part of the main storyline of the fourth *God of War* video game.

Other realms that the player has options to explore if they want include Niflheim (the icy realm and coldest region of all the cosmos) and Muspelheim (the realm of fire ruled by Surt). However, the other realms in the cosmos have been blocked off, and thus Kratos, the main protagonist, cannot enter. This is because Asgard, Vanaheim (home of the Vanir gods), and Svartalfheim (the realm of the dwarves) have been blocked off due to the wrath of the All-Father Odin (Kumar, 2020).

As Kratos, you are able to travel from each realm that is accessible to you thanks to the Bifrost, which is connected to the world tree Yggdrasil at the center of the realms that connects each realm together in the cosmos. In the game, the Bifrost is located within a temple at the center of a lake known as the Lake of Nine, in which Kratos can travel to and from realms as he pleases. According to the *God of War*, the temple was created by the god Tyr, who was a peaceful god of war.

However, he was killed by the hand of Odin, as he was believed to be aiding the jötnar and was scheming to try to overthrow Odin to become the new king of the Aesir.
In *God of War* 4, Kratos comes across many iconic figures in Norse mythology on his quests, such as Loki's son, Jormungandr (also known as the Midgard sea serpent) Thor, Odin, Heimdallr, and many more. There were also many iconic boss battles in this installment that Krotos has to defeat, which include Baldur, the valkyries, many jötnar, dark elves, Magni, and Modi (Thor's sons), and Matturgr Helson (the gatekeeper of Helheim) (Sayers, 2018).

This installment of the *God of War* franchise takes further inspiration from Norse mythology, as much the game focuses on runestones and runic symbols. This is significant, as Odin was considered the god who discovered the secrets hidden within the ancient rune alphabet. A runestone was typically a raised stone that was inscribed with letters of the rune alphabet. However, the runic inscription on the stone does not necessarily have to be on a runestone, as the term can also be implied as a runic inscription on boulders and on bedrock.

The tradition of inscribing messages on a runestone began in the 4th century in Scandinavia and survived way into the early 12th century. However, most runestones can be traced to the late era of the Viking era from around the 9th-11th century. Runestones are significant to the Vikings as they generally were not a literate culture, and thus, they never left the world with much of a literary legacy. However, the Vikings did have an alphabet known as the runic alphabet and would describe themselves and the world around them on stones using the alphabet they believed was gifted to them by the All-Father Odin (Kumar, 2020).

Hellblade: Senua's Sacrifice

The video game *Senua's Sacrifice* is a dark fantasy action-adventure game that was influenced by Norse and Celtic mythology. This video game installment was released in 2017 and was developed by British video game development studio Ninja Theory. The game's story follows the adventures of the female protagonist Senua, a Pict warrior that ventures forth on a quest to Helheim. Senua's mission is to rescue the soul of her dead lover from the clutches of Loki's daughter Hel, who is the goddess of Helheim. On her journey to Helheim, Senua must defeat various monsters, creatures, and otherworldly entities in order to rescue her lover from spending the rest of eternity in Helheim (Kumar, 2020).

Ragnarok

Ragnarok is a Norweigan Netflix original series grounded in the genre of fantasy drama which has been largely influenced by Norse mythological beliefs. Firstly, it is evident in the title *Ragnarok*, which is the Norse equivalent of the apocalypse, that this series was inspired by the ancient beliefs of the Vikings. There are more references by name to Norse mythology as the setting the story takes place in is known as Edda, which is in reference to the Poetic and Prose Edda.

The plot takes place in Edda, which is plagued by the ferocious effects of climate change due to the pollution that is being excreted by the surrounding factories of Edda. The large majority of these factories causing this accelerated wave of climate change are owned by the antagonist family known as the Jutul family, who is the fifth-richest family in all of Norway. The Jutuls all turn out to be jötnar who are posing as mortals.

However, the protagonist of the story is a teenage boy by the name of Magne who has just recently moved to the town of Edda with his family due to his father recently passing away. Magne recognizes the pollution in Edda and comes to the realization that the Jutul family is responsible for the accelerated climate change effects. Thus, Magne challenges the powerful jötnar family for their blatant greed and disregard of the world around them. It turns out that Magne is actually the embodiment of Thor and comes into his newfound power through puberty. Magne, armed with all the powers of Thor, begins to fight anybody who shows blatant disregard for the planet, and he has his eyes set on taking down the Jutul family of jötnar (Kumar, 2020).

It is an interesting take on Norse mythology and it is quite amusing to see how the themes of Norse mythology and modern-day issues such as climate change interconnect in a cohesive narrative together.

Game of Thrones

Game of Thrones is considered by many to be one of the greatest TV series of all time, and even in all of its glory, it was largely inspired by Norse mythological events, tales, and symbolism. However, due to the immense influence that *Game of Thrones* took from Norse mythology and the immense length and universe of *Game of Thrones* we will highlight only a few similarities and symbolisms that connect these two cultural phenomena together

From the very first episode of *Game of Thrones,* fans from all over the world would be warned that "winter is coming." This phrase would become the catchphrase of the monumental series. Since the start of the series, the White Walkers were growing in numbers on the other side of the Wall of Westeros. White Walkers were humanoid supernatural beings with frosty skin, eyes like ice, and were nearly indestructible beings. They were represented with many similar characteristics as the frost jötnar in Norse mythology (Sons of Vikings, 2019).

The White Walkers symbolized the jötnar and they were growing in numbers to attack one day to end the world, similar to that of Ragnarok. While on the other side of the wall, the living were embroiled in civil war, intrigues, and accelerated chaos, mostly unaware of the danger that would eventually unravel.

This is very similar to the civil war between the Aesir gods and Vanir gods who engaged in civil war amongst one another for countless years while the jötnar army was preparing for all-out war on Asgard and the cosmos. While we as the audience do not know what is going to happen come the final season of *Game of Thrones,* it has been made very clear to us that the series was headed towards a great cataclysm that would result in the destruction of everything the world had ever known.

This all ties into Norse mythology because the Vikings believed that the world would come to an end as a result of a tremendous battle of epic proportions between the gods and the jötnar, in this case between humanity and the White Walkers.

This battle would be known as Ragnarok and would occur when a brutal winter engulfs the Earth and the jötnar breach the gates of Asgard. The barrier that separates the jötnar and the Aesir is the Bifrost bridge; however, the equivalent in the *Game of Thrones* series was the wall of Westeros. To fight against the onslaught of the jötnar, Odin would source the bravest warriors in all of the cosmos and Valhalla, even if they had been enemies of the Aesir in the past, in order to fight as an impenetrable unit to defeat the jötnar during Ragnarok. Similar scenes and story arcs are present in the award-winning series *Game of Thrones* (Sons of Vikings, 2019).

In Norse mythology, jötnar could only truly be harmed by the gods. The gods would often have to rely on their sacred magic weapons (Odin's spear, Gungnir, or Thor's hammer Mjölnir) to kill the jötnar. Similarities to this can be seen in *Game of Thrones,* as the White Walkers are only susceptible to damage if they are struck down by Valerian steel or dragon glass. It is also important to note that when the White Walkers would kill somebody, their victim would be resurrected as a wight, which is a zombie-like creature. It is possible that also drew inspiration from Norse mythology, as according to the legend, the jötnar who are slain during Ragnarok will be brought back to life as an undead warrior to continue their battle due to the help of the goddess of Helheim, Hel, and her undead hordes. These are just some of the many similarities between the extremely well-received TV series *Game of Thrones* and Norse mythology (Sons of Vikings, 2019).

Conclusion

Norse mythology is a truly fascinating pagan belief system filled to the brim with exciting tales, myths, gods, goddesses, customs, traditions, and stories. Throughout our read, we have peeled back the many complex layers of history that surround the Vikings and their Nordic beliefs. We have learned so much and have truly encapsulated what life was like for a Viking, how their belief system shaped their lives, and how their many gods shaped society and everything in it. Everything we need to know about the Norse pantheon and Norse mythology has been neatly wrapped in one read that provides us with a beautiful window to view what the world was like over a thousand years ago.

We covered it all, starting with the geography of the complex structure of the cosmos in which the universe coexisted with nine realms. How these realms such as Niflheim, Muspelheim, Asgard, Midgard, Jotuneheim, Vanaheim, Alfheim, Svartalfheim, and Helheim all had their own specific geographic composition and were the allocated homes of the various characters of Norse mythology.

How all these realms were connected by Yggdrasil, and how all these realms were connected to Asgard through the Bifrost. We unpacked the origin of the cosmos and how all life began with Gunningagap, a black empty void of magical power that led to the creation of the first realms made of fire and ice, Niflheim and Muspelheim. We covered that from the creation of the realms of Niflheim and Muspelheim the giants Ymir and Auðumla were created and how their existence was incredibly vital for all that was to unravel in the cosmos. Ymir gave birth to the race of jötnar and Auðumla would give birth to the first gods. The creation of the jötnar and the gods would go on to form a fierce hatred between the two races and lead to unimaginable bloodshed for years to come.

We learned how the creation of the other seven realms was from the help of Odin and his brothers in defeating the evil Ymir who posed a threat to the gods and all of the cosmos. We unpacked how Odin and his brothers created mortals out of tree bark to inhabit Midgard and how the world as we know it was created by the remains of Ymir and his decaying corpse. From Ymir's death, we learned how the Asgardians ruled over the cosmos and how Odin, the All-Father, would watch over all of the nine realms from his throne in Asgard.

However, just as the creation of the universe and the gods needed to be discussed, so did the Vikings of the Viking Age and how they worshipped these very gods. The Norse gods and goddesses played a significant role in the lives of the Vikings and were responsible for shaping their society and how they lived their daily lives. The Vikings worshipped their gods and goddesses in many ways. The Vikings adopted many customs and traditions in which they would practice to honor, respect, show admiration, and attempt to secure favor from the gods. The Norse pantheon was to be respected and honored in plenty of customs and traditions, such as blot sacrifices, human sacrifices, wedding ceremonies, infant ceremonies, burial traditions, Yule celebrations, and even ward off evil spirits.

The Vikings wholeheartedly believed in and worshiped the Norse pantheon and much of their life was centered around the gods and goddesses they believed were protecting them. They knew the gods were not all-powerful and had their faults, however, the Vikings placed great trust, respect, admiration, and honor to their name. The traditions, customs, and beliefs of the Vikings were collectively practiced throughout Scandinavia and were a great part of a Viking's identity and general lifestyle.

There were many gods and goddesses who were worshiped by the Vikings, most of which belonged to the tribe of gods known as the Aesir. However, there were exceptions, and sometimes gods of the Vanir tribe were also worshiped, such as Freya and Njord. More surprisingly, gods who belonged to the jötnar race like Loki would also be worshiped by the Vikings, as they lived in Asgard on occasion. There were many gods and goddesses of Norse mythology who were worshiped, including Odin, Frigg, Thor, Baldur, Heimdallr, Vanir, Tyr, Loki, and many more. All these gods and goddesses represented the human condition and played a role in the greater cosmos. These gods were extremely powerful, but not all-powerful, as they had faults and weaknesses and felt human emotions, often succumbing to them.

The gods and goddesses were ever-present in the myths of Norse mythology, and were ever-present in the minds of the Vikings, thus leaving a significant legacy in history. The myths and tales of the Norse gods and goddesses were well known among the Norseman and they would be passed down from generation to generation keeping the legacy of the gods alive. The gods were ever-present in the minds of the Vikings and helped the Norseman understand the world around them.

Thus it is fair to say the Norse pantheon left an enormous legacy behind for the Norse populace of Scandinavia. Almost all of that legacy can be found in two sources, which make up the overwhelming majority of what we know in the 21st century about the Norse pantheon and the Vikings. These sources are known as the Poetic and Prose Edda. The Eddas are full of epic poems that highlight the myths and tales of the gods and provide us as historians with the much-needed insight to understand the Viking mind and what it is the pagan Vikings believed in. Poems such as the Poem of Vafþrúðnismál (Vafthundnir's Sayings), the Poem of Þrymskviða (Thrym's Poem), the Poem of Hymiskviða (The Lay of Hymir), and the Poem of Skírnismál (Skirnir's journey) all give us invaluable insight into the adventures that the Norse pantheon experienced. The poems of Edda also highlight many other interesting myths, such as the creation myth of Mjölnir, the myth of Brunhilde, the Aesir vs Vanir war, the binding of Fenrir, and the myth of the Asgard wall.

These poems and myths found in the two Edda's are not simply tales meant to entertain per se, but they are also stories full of life lessons and interesting facets of the human condition. These myths give depth to the Norse pantheon and provide us with knowledge about the gods for who they are. It is important to note that in these myths the gods are not all-powerful and have their own faults and challenges they need to overcome.

However, one myth in the Eddas is truly significant and is the myth that ends all myths. This myth is known as Ragnarok, and is the cataclysmic tale of the end of the cosmos and everything in it, including the fate of demise for the gods and goddesses. It is the tale of the final battle between the gods and their greatest enemy, the jötnar, as well as the Fimbulwinter that will wipe out all of humanity.

The final battle is one of epic proportions where all the Norse gods will fight with all their might, but in the end, they will not be able to escape their bloody fate. It is a truly grim tale that will leave nothing left in existence; however, it is believed in later Norse myths that Ragnarok will lead to the rebirth of the cosmos and that life as we know it will rise from the ashes once again.

As we have said before Norse mythology is truly fascinating, and as such, it is no surprise that this ancient mythology has received a resurgence in popularity in the form of pop culture. By now, there is no medium that has not been influenced by the Nordic beliefs and the Vikings, whether it be films, TV, literature, video games, or music. Some of the most famous portrayals and re-telling of the Norse myths include Marvel comics' *Thor*, *Game of Thrones*, *Lord of the Rings*, *Ragnarok*, Viking metal, the fourth canon installment of *God of War*, and *Hellblade*; however, there are many more examples.

It would not be surprising to see the media flooded with more and more retellings of Norse mythology through being inspired by the epic tales the mythology of the Vikings has to offer.

If there is one thing we can take away from this book it's the immense influence the Norse pantheon played in Viking society and how the Viking age was inherently influenced by the epic tales and myths that surround this fascinating pagan belief system. What's more, is how the Vikings were truly governed by their many gods. A large part of a Viking's daily life during the Viking Age was centered around their gods. The gods would influence their actions, thoughts, and lifestyle to a great degree. Vikings would also often honor and respect their gods as they believed the gods were always protecting and watching over them, thus they would often worship their many pagan gods to gain good favor from them and protect them from ill fate. Norse mythology is here to stay, and it is back with a bang through the legacy that these myths have stamped on modern society. Many portrayals of Norse mythology in pop culture will ensure that the Nordic belief system from over a thousand years ago will stay fresh in our minds. The Vikings may be dead, but their customs, traditions, and beliefs are as strong as ever.

References

Ancient Origins. (2019, July 16). *Frigg: Queen of Asgard, Beloved Norse Goddess, Mother*. Ancient-Origins.net; Ancient Origins. https://www.ancient-origins.net/myths-legends-europe/frigg-queen-asgard-beloved-norse-goddess-mother-009707

Ancient Pages. (2016, August 7). *Asgard: Enter The Ancient Kingdom Of The Powerful Norse Gods*. Ancient Pages. https://www.ancientpages.com/2016/08/07/asgard-enter-the-ancient-kingdom-of-the-powerful-norse-gods/

Ancient Pages. (2020, December 17). *How Did Vikings Celebrate Yule - The Winter Solstice?* Ancient Pages. https://www.ancientpages.com/2020/12/17/how-did-vikings-celebrate-yule-the-winter-solstice/

Book Rags. (2018). *Elder Edda Summary*. Www.bookrags.com. http://www.bookrags.com/studyguide-elderedda/chapanal003.html#gsc.tab=0

Britannica. (2018). Odin | Myth & History. In *Encyclopædia Britannica*. https://www.britannica.com/topic/Odin-Norse-deity

Britannica. (2019a). Edda | Icelandic literature | Britannica. In *Encyclopædia Britannica*. https://www.britannica.com/topic/Edda

Britannica. (2019b). Heimdallr | Norse mythology. In *Encyclopædia Britannica*. https://www.britannica.com/topic/Heimdallr

Britannica. (2019c). Midgard | Norse mythology | Britannica. In *Encyclopædia Britannica*. https://www.britannica.com/topic/Midgard

Britannica. (2019d). *Muspelheim | Norse mythology*. Encyclopedia Britannica. https://www.britannica.com/topic/Muspelheim

Encyclopedia Mythica. (2018). *Skírnir | Facts, Information, and Mythology*. Pantheon.org. https://pantheon.org/articles/s/skirnir.html

Eskify. (2017, January 6). *10 Epic Tales From Norse Mythology*. Eskify. http://eskify.com/10-epic-tales-from-norse-mythology/#:~:text=In%20norse%20mythology%20the%20Gods%20Odin%20and%20his

Esser, J. (2018, August 6). *10 Interesting Viking Rituals - Listverse*. Listverse. https://listverse.com/2018/08/06/10-interesting-viking-rituals/

From Baker to Edlund. (2014, December 5). *Vafthrudnir's Sayings*. Frombakertoedlund. https://frombakertoedlund.wordpress.com/2014/12/05/vafthrudnirs-sayings/

Geller, P. (2016a, October 23). *Ymir - The First Giant in Norse Mythology*. Mythology.net. https://mythology.net/norse/norse-creatures/ymir/#:~:text=Ymir%20did%20not%20marry%2C%20or%20have%20children%20in

Geller, P. (2016b, November 6). *Balder - Norse God*. Mythology.net. https://mythology.net/norse/norse-gods/balder/

Geller, Prof. (2016, November 6). *Frigg - Norse Goddess and Wife of Odin | Mythology.net*. Mythology.net. https://mythology.net/norse/norse-gods/frigg/

Geller, Prof. (2017, January 3). *Thor - Norse God of Thunder, Lightning and Strength | Mythology.net*. Mythology.net. https://mythology.net/norse/norse-gods/thor/

Gill, N. S. (2019). *10 Important Norse Gods and Goddesses*. ThoughtCo. https://www.thoughtco.com/gods-and-goddesses-in-norse-mythology-120007

Gods and Goddesses. (2016). *Thor • Facts & Mythology about the Norse god of Lightning and Thunder*. Gods & Goddesses. https://www.gods-and-goddesses.com/norse/thor/

Gods and Goddesses. (2017). *Odin • Facts & Mythology about the Norse god of Creation and Wisdom*. Gods & Goddesses. https://www.gods-and-goddesses.com/norse/odin/#:~:text=Odin%20is%20the%20Norse%20king%20of%20the%20Aesir%2C

Greenberg, M. (2020, November 9). *The Norse Creation Myth*. The Norse Creation Myth. https://mythologysource.com/norse-creation-myth/

Kissell, J. (2018). *Hymir's Cauldron | Interesting Thing of the Day*. Itotd.com. https://itotd.com/articles/4375/hymirs-cauldron/

Kumar, A. (2020, May 7). *How Vikings & Norse Mythology are making its way into the modern entertainment*. Medium. https://medium.com/nerdvolume/how-vikings-norse-mythology-are-making-its-way-into-the-modern-entertainment-f148c15c1d52

Learn Religions. (2016). *How Did the Norse Believe the World Was Created?* Learn Religions. https://www.learnreligions.com/creation-in-norse-mythology-117868

McCoy, D. (2012a). *Freya - Norse Mythology for Smart People*. Norse Mythology for Smart People. https://norse-mythology.org/gods-and-creatures/the-vanir-gods-and-goddesses/freya/

McCoy, D. (2012b). *The Creation of Thor's Hammer - Norse Mythology for Smart People*. Norse Mythology for Smart People. https://norse-mythology.org/tales/loki-and-the-dwarves/

McCoy, D. (2018). *Ragnarok*. Norse Mythology for Smart People. https://norse-mythology.org/tales/ragnarok/#:~:text=Ragnarok%20is%20the%20%20cataclysmic%20destruction%20of%20the%20cosmos

Morgan, T. (2018, November 28). *How Did The Vikings Honor Their Dead?* HISTORY. https://www.history.com/news/how-did-the-vikings-honor-their-dead

Mythopedia. (2018). *Freya*. Mythopedia. https://mythopedia.com/norse-mythology/gods/freya/

New World Encyclopedia. (2020). *Norse Mythology - New World Encyclopedia*. Www.newworldencyclopedia.org. https://www.newworldencyclopedia.org/entry/Norse_Mythology#The_beginning

Norse Mythology for Smart People. (2018). *Alfheim*. Norse Mythology for Smart People. https://norse-mythology.org/cosmology/the-nine-worlds/alfheim/

Sacred Texts. (2019). *The Prose Edda Index*. Sacred-Texts.com. https://www.sacred-texts.com/neu/pre/index.htm

Sayers, S. (2018). *God of War PS4 Bosses – The Complete List*. PlayStation Universe. https://www.psu.com/news/god-of-war-ps4-bosses/

Skjalden. (2011, June 1). *The Nine Realms in Norse Mythology*. Nordic Culture. https://skjalden.com/nine-realms-in-norse-mythology/

Skjalden. (2020a, July 22). *Ginnungagap - The Yawning Void - Norse Mythology*. Nordic Culture. https://skjalden.com/ginnungagap/

Skjalden. (2020b, September 7). *Bifröst - The Rainbow Bridge - Norse mythology [FACTS]*. Nordic Culture. https://skjalden.com/bifrost/

Sons of Vikings. (2019, April 17). *Game of Thrones and Norse Mythology*. Sons of Vikings. https://sonsofvikings.com/blogs/news/game-of-thrones-and-norse-mythology

The Honest Modern Heathen. (2020, February 24). *Þrymskviða – The Lay of Þrym*. The Honest Modern Heathen. https://thehonestmodernheathen.com/codex-regius/in-codex-regius/the-poetic-edda/thrymskvida-the-lay-of-thrym/

Wikipedia. (2021a, March 4). *Viking metal*. Wikipedia. https://en.wikipedia.org/wiki/Viking_metal

Wikipedia. (2021b, March 14). *Fafnir*. Wikipedia. https://en.wikipedia.org/wiki/Fafnir#:~:text=F%C3%A1fnir%20then%20killed%20Hreidmar%20to%20get%20all%20the

The Vikings

Who Were The Vikings? Enter The Viking Age & Discover The Facts, Sagas, Norse Mythology, Legends, Battles & More

History Brought Alive

Table of Contents

Introduction 165

  Author Bio 168

Chapter 1: The Age of the Vikings—A Timeline 170

  The Beginning of the Raids 170

    Further Expansion 174

    Europe Resists 175

  The Influence of Christianity 178

  The Last Years 179

Chapter 2: Culture And Customs 181

  Common Misunderstandings About the Vikings 181

    Horned Helmets 181

    Unified Viking State 182

    Being a Viking Was a Career 182

    The Vikings Were Barbarians 183

  Truth Is Stranger Than Fiction 184

    Viking Funerals 184

    The Vikings Were Only In Scandinavia 185

  Customs in Viking Culture 185

    Social Structure 185

    Birth 187

    Marriage 188

    Death 191

    Ancestor Worship 196

    Viking Clothing 196

    Women's Clothing 199

Slave Clothing 200
Making of Clothing 201
Viking Architecture 202

Viking Art 206
Oseberg 209
Borre 210
Jellinge 210
Mammen 211
Ringerike 212

Daily Viking Life 214
Everyday Life in Viking Times 214
Viking Appearances 217
Sports and Recreation 218
Social Activities 220

Chapter 3: Geography and Regional Cuisine 221

Where the Vikings Lived 222
Terrain 222
Natural Wilderness 223
Climate 223
Ocean 224
Plants and the Environment 225
Viking Foods in Different Regions 226
A Typical Viking Meal 228
The Benefits of a Viking Diet 233

Chapter 4: Beliefs, Myths and Mythology 234

The Beginning of the Universe 235
Viking Gods and Goddesses 236

Paganism in Viking Culture 242

Christian Beliefs in Viking Culture 245

The Sagas and What They Tell Us 246

    Accounts of Pagan Practices in Viking Sagas 247

Viking Mythology and Folklore 250

    Thor Against the Frost Giants 255

    The Apples of Iduna 259

Chapter 5: The Viking Army and Famous Battles 262

How Did the Vikings Fight? 262

    Vikings on the Ocean 264

    The Great Heathen Army 264

Famous Viking Warriors 273

    Ragnar Lothbrok 273

    Rollo of Normandy 274

    Egil Skallgrimsson 274

    Cnut the Great 275

    Harald Hadrada 275

    Bjorn Ironside 277

    Erik the Red 277

    Ivar the Boneless 278

    Famous Viking Battles 279

    Englefield 280

    Ashdown 280

    Edington 281

    Maldon 281

    Stamford Bridge 282

Chapter 6: Viking Language 283

What Was the Viking Language Like? 283

    Old Norse 285

The Viking Language Throughout History 289
Runestones 291
Poetic Edda 291
The Uses of Viking Language 292
Chapter 7: What Happened to the Vikings? 294
Factors Leading to Viking Decline 295
Strengthened Opposition 295
Weakened Viking Army 296
Changing Viking Mindset 296
The Impact of Christianity 297
Changes in Social Structure 298
The Final Years of Viking Dominance 299
Absorption Into European Culture 299
The Aftermath of Viking Expansion 300
Where Are the Vikings Today? 302
Conclusion 304
References 307

Introduction

In the centuries following the fall of the Roman Empire, many civilizations, nations, and kingdoms came and went. But in 700 AD, a tribe of warriors left their homeland and struck out for glory and for conquest. They came to take no prisoners. Their eerie horns made a distinctive sound, and their fearsome longboats struck from out of nowhere; out of the fog and the gloom from the North leaving devastation in their wake. They were the Norsemen, more commonly known as Vikings, a group of men dedicated to expansion and conquest. However, the Vikings were not all about raping and pillaging. Their impact and legacy can be seen in every facet of the cultures they encountered. Many people misunderstand their cultural and historical significance in light of modern society. There is a tendency to view them as backward, unsophisticated, or mindless killers. Nothing could be further from the truth. This historical guide to the Vikings will examine what they contributed to the cultures they came into contact with, and the biggest impact that they had on European medieval society and beyond.

The name Viking comes from the Old Norse for "pirate raid." Although many did indeed raid the coastlines of European countries, they did not all have the same purpose. Some simply wanted to trade and settle in these more southern regions. Many settled in the European countries that they landed in and became citizens of those countries. They both took on the cultures of those countries and imparted their own ways and mannerisms onto these cultures. This book aims to focus on who these men and women were, and what their lives were like.

What did Vikings eat, and what did they think about the world they lived in? Food was central to the Viking culture. It formed the basis for their celebrations, rituals, and their daily lives. One could never say that they were ever timid around their food. They needed all the energy they could get in order to keep up with their daily activities, which included travelling, farming, working on the land harvesting crops, hunting, fighting, and many other activities. The Vikings, as is well-known, were seafaring people. It is important to know how their diet was impacted by their trade, industry, and expansion into other parts of the world. Vikings saw the world through the perspective of their current needs and desires. They were focused on subsistence and expansion.

What did they believe? The Vikings had their own set of beliefs and different deities that they worshipped. The worship of these gods and goddesses formed the basis of their activities as a society. Their beliefs affected their perspective of birth, death, and the afterlife. It is interesting to see what the Vikings believed about the world because it shows how their beliefs impacted the collective consciousness of Europe at the time. Traces of their systems of living and seeing the world still persist, even to this day. Much like the Vikings themselves, their legacy was built to endure throughout generations.

What was their culture like? Viking culture was intertwined with their belief systems. How they chose to live their lives was determined, to a large extent, by how they saw the world. Different times of the year were dedicated to different feast days. In battle, their warrior spirit shone through because of their emphasis on a proud and fierce patriotic sense of camaraderie. Different seasons were seen as either bountiful or cursed by the gods in times of plenty or in times of scarcity. The Vikings viewed the world in an almost mystical sense and were always on the lookout for omens and signs. This guide will dive into the vast and complicated network of their mythologies, beliefs, and ideas about the natural and spiritual world.

Most importantly this book looks to answer the question: What happened to the Vikings, and where did they go? If you go to Scandinavia today, you might find traces of the old Viking culture still there if you look hard enough! There are ancient ruins, buildings, books, and literature that testify to the great and glorious past of the Viking people. In fact, the people are the most interesting products of this era. You can learn a lot by talking to passionate Scandinavian historians themselves. But by and large, society has moved on from the age of the Vikings. Or have they? This book illustrates the ultimate fate of this richly nuanced—and often misunderstood—society.

If you want to find out more about the Vikings, this book is the definitive guide for you. It will look at the culture, life, and practices of the Vikings in a new and refreshing light. It will challenge you to see things from their perspectives. Moreover, it looks at their legacy and what we can learn from their lives.

Author Bio

History Brought Alive reveals new insights into this fascinating culture. If you want to discover more about this interesting civilization, look no further. This is the definitive guide for you.

This is a reference you will want to use over and over again. You will be amazed at the depth of knowledge present in these pages. It is a well-researched and thoroughly documented guide to the life and times of the Vikings, and puts forward the facts in a way that forces the reader to think differently about what is commonly known by Viking and Norse culture. Be prepared to tackle the subject of the Vikings with an open mind, and you'll be surprised at how much you can learn. Much like the Vikings themselves, the reader has to be prepared to expand their way of thinking in order to appreciate the intricacies of ancient and complex cultures.

Chapter 1: The Age of the Vikings—A Timeline

The Beginning of the Raids

The period of the Vikings is thought to have begun after the reign of Germanic warlords and barbarians in Europe, and about 200 to 300 years after the fall of the Roman Empire. The world had vastly changed at this point, after thousands of years of Roman rule. From around the year 793, bands of warriors began to make their way south, striking out from their native lands of what is today known as Norway, Sweden, Denmark, and the surrounding territories. Following the period commonly referred to today as the "Germanic Iron Age", people from the Nordic countries (known as Norsemen) made use of rivers around Europe to facilitate trade, travel, raids, and conquest. It was the latter of these activities that they would become most noted for.

Much of what is known about the Viking Age is based on what was written down during this period, and long after it as well, by ancient historians and experts on ancient cultures. What we learn from these records depends on who wrote down the tales of these people. If you only read the Viking records they wrote themselves, you'll get a one- sided view, as is the case if you consult the records of the people they attacked and raided. Everyone has a different view of events. It is only through a holistic view of events that the truth about this age can be properly realized.

The Vikings were not one unified group of people, although the all-inclusive term "Vikings magnat" seems to categorize them all into a single ethical or racial group. The truth is that they were a group made up of a myriad of smaller ethic groups from various Scandinavian countries such as Norway, Denmark, Sweden, and other surrounding regions. Vikings did not only come from Scandinavia, however. There are historical records of many other kinds of Vikings, such as people from Finland, Estonia, and Lapland, along with the Kola peninsula of Russia.

Let's look at where these various groups went when they left their homeland in these territories. Bear in mind that these regions were not called by their modern names until very much later on.

The Danes struck out from Denmark and immediately travelled west along the North Sea to the coast of France. They landed in Spain and made sorties into the Mediterranean, and even raided a small territory in Italy called Luna, thinking that this was the seat of the Roman Empire. The Swedes sailed up towards the Baltic sea and established the Kievan Russian state, and also to the territory of the Byzantine empire and beyond, in the Orient itself.

The Norwegians sailed west towards British territory, the Scottish regions, and Ireland. Dublin itself was set up as a base for slave trading in 841. Overall, these men and women spread across much of the known world, taking whatever they wished, whenever they needed it.

Apart from trade, these groups of people had little to do with each other and certainly did not present a united front. In fact, they often fought each other over scarce land, spoils, and resources. However, the Vikings were united in the eyes of the people they attacked and conquered. They were a universally feared group.

They had learned the art of shipbuilding and sail-making by observing what the Romans did during the time of their empire many years before. Celtic and Germanic merchants interacted with the Romans in around 300 to 400 AD and studied their technology (Mark, 2018). It was this influence of the Romans which led the Vikings to try and grow their own navy many years later. From modern-day excavations, it is clear that the Vikings and their ancestors had held an interest in sea-related technology for a very long time. Their ancestral activities can be traced back many thousands of years before the Vikings even came to be, and this can be proven by examining the evidence of rock carvings from about 4000-2000 BC.

It is worth noting that trade between the European mainland and Germanic or barbarian traders had been taking place since Roman times. Viking furs, whetstones, and other resources had always been passing between the two groups. This, of course, led the would-be raiders to the European shores and the promise of new and fertile land for them. They saw the land they came into contact with as being ripe with opportunity for the establishment of a new civilization.

Further Expansion

In 791 AD, small raids on British monasteries began because these were often solitary and unprotected. In addition to this, these monasteries often contained a large amount of money or gold. One of the most significant of these raids was in 793 in a place called Lindisfarne. The monastery at Lindisfarne was considered to be the center of Christianity in the region of Northumbria. It was not, however, the first raid on British territories in the British Isles. In 787, three Viking warships appeared off the coast of Wessex travelling down from a place called 'Hørthaland', in what is known as modern-day Norway today. The men on the coast of Wessex who were there at the time had expected that these ships would be willing to engage in friendly trade, but they were sorely mistaken. Further attacks occurred at the monastery of Iona in Scotland, Jarrow in Northumbria, and at various locations off the coast of Ireland in the 790s.

The Vikings left no one that they encountered alive. Their objective was to gain as much loot as they could and get back to their ships. They often burned the buildings they encountered, which included the churches they came into contact with. This is documented in the account of the raid at Lindisfarne. Many other churches along the British coastline suffered the same fate. Such was the pattern of the Viking attacks during the early years of their reign of terror.

Europe Resists

The attacks didn't stop in the 9th century. In 840, the Vikings raided territories in Ireland and established the slave colony of Dublin. During this time, they set up camps in this region and began to establish a presence in the area. Paris, in France, was attacked by the Danes in 845 and sacked. It was attacked by them again in 860. In 844, the Vikings had relocated as far south as the Spanish coastline, where they came into contact with Muslims currently living there. Sailing up the river Guadalquivir towards Seville, they were attacked by Islamic troops there and forced backwards. After this reverse, Viking raids on the Spanish territories were few and far between.

In 866, Vikings raided the north of England and established the Kingdom of York. Unusually, though, the two kings of that region—Aelle and Osbert—were not harmed or captured. In 872, Harald Hårfagre became the first king of Norway according to Viking literature. He would rule until around 930 and is considered to be the king responsible for the unification of Norweigan tribes after the great battle of Hafrsfjord.

Following the traumatic earlier raids on their country and the overwhelming numbers of invaders running riot across their land, the English forces attempted to fight back at the battle of Edington in 878, and formulated what was known as the Danelaw in Northern England. This was an agreement allowing the Vikings to settle on various parts of English soil, where their customs took precedence over English statutes in those regions. Even in spite of their limited successes, the British Isles experienced tremendous hardship at the hands of the Vikings, and never gained true authority during these times. The Vikings eventually settled on foreign soil and established themselves there. However, more attacks from the invaders were still forthcoming.

In the year 900, the Vikings had moved as far east as they would eventually reach. On the way, they began to raid Mediterranean territories and came into conflict with the Byzantine army and navy. Under the leadership of Olef the Wise, they reached as far as Istanbul whereafter, having been paid a substantial sum of money, they decided to turn around and leave again.

Paris had been besieged in the 9th century, and it was attacked again in 911. Under the leadership of Viking Chief Rollo, they managed to forcibly gain territory in France. The descendants of Chief Rollo became the formidable force later known as the Normans. These warriors would play a huge role in shaping the outcome of English and British culture for centuries to come, although they didn't know it yet.

In 910, the Vikings were defeated at the battle of Tettenhall and Wedfield by the forces of Mercia and Wessex. In 915 and 918, the Viking King Ægnald defeated the Scots on the river Tyne. It was during these years that the Vikings began to move away from an expansionist mindset, and more towards a way of life that favored establishment of a culture and civilized life.

In the 11th century (around the year 1000), the Vikings strengthened their grip on mainland Europe, the British Isles, and made inroads into the Americas and the New World for the first time. At this time, the British tried to sue for peace with their oppressors, but they only ended up making a bad situation worse. This led to the massacre of many innocent people when they engaged in ethnic cleansing against the local population, who had settled on the coast after the arrival of the Vikings.

In 981, Erik the Red had discovered the New World after being expelled from Norway and settling in Greenland for a number of years. Within about 20 years of his landing there, about 3000 people of Norse descent now lived in this New World. They were mainly peaceful farmers and shepherds.

The Influence of Christianity

It was about the time of the turn of the millennium when the first seeds of Christianity began to be sown into the Viking culture. In 995, King Olav Tryggvasson constructed the first church on Norweigan soil. He survived being gravely injured in battle, and then returned to Norway where he attempted to introduce Christianity to the region. He might have been amongst the first Viking converts to the religion. In the year 1000, Christianity officially arrived in Iceland and Greenland when a chieftain known as King Olav took it upon himself to try and proselytize and convert fellow chieftains. He imposed trade embargoes upon those who refused to convert.

Christianity was one of the major issues that affected the development of the Viking way of life and way of thinking. A king named Haakon the Good attempted to spread Christianity to the mainland Viking community after his experiences in England, but he was unable to make much headway. King Harald Greycloak attempted to force the Vikings to acknowledge the Christian God by destroying all Viking pagan temples, but he encountered strong resistance from the people and communities that he tried to convert.

The Last Years

The age of the Vikings began to wane after the turn of the millennium due to their dispersal throughout the world and a change in their expansionist mindset. The settlement in the New World, now called 'Vinland', was abandoned due to the difficulty of receiving supplies from Europe, and the dangers of transporting goods while crossing the ocean from Scandinavia.

In 1066, the King of England at the time, Harold Godwinson, defeated the Norweigan ruler Harald Hardråda at the battle of Stamford Bridge while William, the Duke of Normandy, defeated King Harold at the Battle of Hastings. Such battles were indicative of the fact that the Viking order was drawing to a close, or at least changing in a significant way.

Gone were the days where the sight of their ships would cause chaos. At this time, other, more significant threats to Europe were becoming paramount. It is clear, however, that at this time, Vikings were becoming more and more integrated into European life as a whole. However, their practices and ways of living were still seen as crude and dirty by the people they came into contact with.

Chapter 2: Culture And Customs

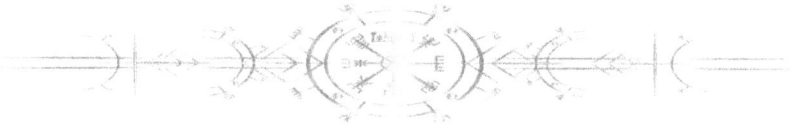

Common Misunderstandings About the Vikings

Horned Helmets

The Vikings did not often make use of horned helmets, as is commonly depicted in many forms of media. In fact, evidence of these horns has never been discovered, and Viking literature and the sagas make no mention of them at all. It is commonly believed that the idea behind horned helmets like this originated with an operatic work by Wagner in 1876 called *Der Ring des Nibelungen*. In real life, horned helmets would have made little sense in close combat. They could easily be removed and could be a danger to the wearer. In addition, they were unwieldy and likely to fall off during a fight. They would never have been used and were never used in any form of combat that the Vikings took part in.

Unified Viking State

There is the common misconception that the Vikings were part of one, large, unified state and that they all had a common goal. The reality of the situation was vastly different. There was no Viking Empire as there was with, say for example, the Romans. The Vikings were a group of people with similar interests from all over Scandinavia, who shared common customs and ways of thinking and living. There was unity of sorts when they formed the Great Heathen Army, but it seems as if such unity amongst various tribal groups was the exception rather than the norm. Their governments or leadership tended to operate on a more local level.

Being a Viking Was a Career

Many people misunderstand the nature of the Viking life. People were not born Vikings. They took this culture and way of life upon themselves when they decided to embark on a lifestyle of raiding and pillaging. They were Norse people, but Viking in occupation. Vikings themselves had their own specific cultural practices which weren't found in Norse culture, but on the whole, being a Viking was a way of life.

The Vikings Were Barbarians

A common misconception about Vikings is that they were uneducated, savage, or barbarian in nature. This is due to the fact that they (correctly) raided and pillaged, but this is not the only thing they did. Many were interested simply in finding places to live and to settle. They wanted to raise a family and survive as much of the rest of Europe was doing at that time.

The reason they raided and killed was because of a constant desire for conquest and expansion, so that they could form their own settlements in the places they conquered. The Vikings were practical people. They attacked the least defended places they could find, which included lightly-guarded settlements, small towns, monasteries, and other similar buildings. Monasteries were popular because they were filled with gold and other valuable materials. Many of the people who worked at these monasteries were some of the few people who were literate at that time. Therefore, the written records of Viking activity were generally of these raids and events. These records have contributed towards the overall image of Vikings as being fierce and doing nothing but raiding. Much less is said about their more peaceful activities.

Truth Is Stranger Than Fiction

Much of what is portrayed about the Vikings in TV and media is peculiar, and the reality is that their sagas portray a mythology that is much stranger than anything that could be shown on screen. For example, Loki is currently a popular character due to various movies and TV shows that have featured him. But his history and backstory is quite outlandish. He has been known to have given birth to an eight-legged horse, for example. He is also the father of a massive serpent and a giant wolf. None of this makes a great deal of sense to the uninitiated, but this is the strangeness, and the appeal, of Viking mythology in a nutshell. It is not to be understood, but experienced.

Viking Funerals

There is a common misconception that Vikings were always given the traditional Viking funeral, which involved placing the remains of the body in a boat and sending them off on the sea. This, however, did not take place that often. Viking ships were expensive and time-consuming to build, and they did not want to be breaking or destroying anything without good reason. It seems that Viking boat burials were instead reserved for the most important members of their societies. The Vikings had a variety of other funeral practices for others, which depended on their gender, social status, and military status.

The Vikings Were Only In Scandinavia

The Vikings travelled all over the world. They went to Canada, the United Kingdom, the British Isles, and all over Europe. There is no account that states that they were exclusively from Scandinavia, although this was where many Viking groups were active. Their presence in Europe was widespread.

Customs in Viking Culture

Social Structure

Viking society, depending on the region, was organized under more or less a strict social and patriarchal structure. There were three main classes in Viking society: Earls (*jarlar* in Old Norse), free men, and slaves. Earls were the upper class in society and received the greatest benefits. Many of these men were warlords and warriors who had obtained their success through being victorious in battle. When Viking territories became kingdoms, these earls became second only to the kings in these regions.

The majority of people fell into the second class, the free men (*karlar* in Old Norse). Most of these men and women were farmers and worked on the land. Others were content to labor for farmers within a kind of feudal system. Some worked at creating weapons, crafts, and other items. Free men on the land enjoyed the protection of legal systems, unlike those who were slaves.

Viking warriors often belonged to the free men. They were warriors who, although not at the very top of the social hierarchy in Viking society, enjoyed reasonable standing within the community. They had little wealth but were sometimes alloted portions of land that they could use to feed themselves and their families. Many, however, were unmarried. Due to their single status, they were able to act in whatever way they pleased without fear of social ostracization.

The final group were the slaves or the poorest class (*þrælar* in Old Norse). These men usually carried out the most menial of tasks and could be bought or sold. Female slaves were cooks, concubines and domestic workers. They lived in the houses of more wealthy people.

Slaves were often born into their status and remained there their entire lives. When a wealthier master died, their slaves were often sacrificed and then buried with them. Slaves were also made up of those who were captured during Viking raids. Because these men were not killed and were instead spared, they often had to pay back their captors by serving them their entire lives. Men could also become slaves through declaring bankruptcy as it was the only way they could survive and have somewhere to live.

Birth

The birth of any child within Viking society was a celebrated event, and was seen as a positive sign. The birth of sons was particularly auspicious. Before a child was born, songs were sung about the birth as a way of ensuring that the mother and child would remain safe and secure during the birthing process. Nine days after delivery, the father of the child would take the infant and place them on his knees, where water was sprinkled on the child's head. Guests were invited to the ceremony, and gifts were exchanged amongst the participants.

Marriage

Marriage was another celebrated event within Viking societies. A marriage could only take place if both the families of the bride and groom agreed on specific terms, such as property rights and a dowry for the bride. Viking weddings were meticulously planned events. A father would take his daughter around town so that she could be seen by other people and men in the town. Once they had gained the attention of a man, he would have to approach her family, and the two families would have to agree terms. Certain issues had to be worked out, such as the *mundr* (bride price), *heiman flygia* (dowry), and *morgedn-gifu*, which were morning gifts that were bestowed to the bride by the groom on the morning of the wedding itself. Once this contract was finalized, the marriage could proceed. A groom could be married to a bride after he proposed to her, accompanied by his family. When the proposal was accepted by the bride and ratified by the family, preparations for the event could start to take place. The day itself was accompanied by massive feasts and festivals that could last for days. Once vows were exchanged, it was considered customary for witnesses to accompany the newly-wedded couple to their bed on the wedding night.

Frigga was the Viking goddess of marriage, and it was considered to be lucky to hold the wedding ceremony on her holy day, known as "Frigga's Day" or Friday. Preparations for the wedding included gathering and preparing enough food and large supplies of alcohol for the celebration. A massive quantity of honey mead was consumed during the celebration along with the food. It was considered compulsory for the bride and groom to partake in the honey mead or ale at the wedding ceremony, and also during the month that followed the wedding. Weddings were also traditionally held after the harvest and before the long, cruel, and dark winter months where it would be considered to be difficult to be outside in any capacity. Guests would also not be able to travel during this period, so it was essential that wedding ceremonies be held when the weather was fine.

The bride would be prepared by her friends, bridesmaids, mother, and other married women. She would remove the *kransen*, or golden circlet, that she carried in her hair as a sign that she was ready to be married. This golden circlet would be worn her entire life and passed on to her daughter, if she had one, in order to maintain the family line. In such a way, this Viking tradition was maintained throughout the centuries. Following the ceremony, the golden circlet would be replaced with one made of silver or woven wheat or straw. The bride would bathe and be instructed in her new duties by her maids, servants or attendants.

As far as the groom was concerned, there were also ceremonies that needed to be carried out. One of the most interesting of these was that of breaking and entering the grave of an ancestor in order to retrieve a sword that belonged to a long dead relative. This symbolized his entering into the realms of death and emerging as a man, his boyhood left behind. He would then get dressed and be instructed by wiser and older men in his duties as a husband (Bartley, 2018). The ceremony itself was simple. The groom would present his bride with the ancestral sword he had retrieved, which she kept to pass along to her son in later years. She would present him with the sword of her own ancestors. Rings attached to the hilts of their swords were then exchanged between the couple.

After this, the groom would walk or ride to the feast venue and stand in the doorway with his sword across it, blocking the bride from entering. He would then carry her across the threshold himself. What followed were several days of feasting, jokes, laughter, drinking, and merriment. Wrestling contests also took place at the feast, and everyone had a good time.

The final part of the ceremony involved being parted for a short time on the morning after the wedding night. The bride was prepared and her hair was styled in a specific fashion by her attendants. She wore a linen head covering as a symbol of her new status in marriage. She was then escorted into a hall where a number of onlookers were waiting along with the groom. There, she would be presented with the morning gift from the groom. Before all the witnesses, the final act for the contract of marriage to be complete was performed. The husband then took the keys to his residence and gave them to her as a way of showing her authority over all things related to the home.

Death

Unravelling the way the Viking's responded to death in their culture is a complex matter. Inconsistency is abundant within their sagas and Viking literature of the time. Because written accounts span several centuries, opinions on this issue, the ultimate end of human life, tend to vary considerably.

However, there are certain patterns that we as amateur historians can use to draw certain conclusions. One thing is for certain, the Vikings did indeed believe in the existence of an afterlife, and this is evident throughout their literature. As for the beliefs of pagan Viking religion, they are difficult to decode, as little is written about them in Viking literature itself. It is therefore incumbent upon historians to try and piece together fragments of what we know about Viking life and their ways of thinking. How did they approach the issue of dying? What were their funerals like? What were their attitudes towards death?

From what we know of Viking religion, it was like a personal and private belief system which amounted to small groups 0f people who believed similar things, and families who had shared values of how they saw the world.

Vikings believed in cremating their dead, and this was an important process after death. When they died naturally or in battle, they were buried with the items that were most important to them while they were still alive. This included their weapons and jewelry. It was thought that they would need specific items when they went into the afterlife. Oftentimes, a Viking would be buried with the items that most represented who they were in life, for example weapons for warriors and clothing and other items for women.

The wealthiest of Vikings might be buried in a ship that they could use in the afterlife, or the outline of a ship would be drawn on the ground and the body placed in the middle of it. Other wealthy Vikings were often buried with their slaves as these were seen as being part of the wealthy Viking's possessions. Some outsiders and observers to Viking funerals have reported on the rare occasion that young women were sacrificed at the funeral of Viking chieftains, but little is known as to whether this was customary or even an accurate representation of what took place at that time.

Many people, when they hear the words 'Viking' and 'afterlife' together, think of Valhalla, and the famous stories of Viking warriors who nobly died in battle so that they could obtain the honor of going there. However, this is only one very small part in the much larger framework of what Vikings believed about the afterlife. The reality is a lot more complicated. In ancient Nordic beliefs, it was thought that a person was composed of four different parts: *Hamr* (physical appearance), *Hugr* (personality), *Fylgja* (essence or totem), and *Hamingja* (quality or inherent success throughout one's life). When a Viking died, it was thought that their *Hamr* passed away and disappeared, while their *Hugr* passed into the afterlife. Their *Hamingja* was what remained on earth after they were gone, and this was why the Vikings put such a great deal of emphasis on the need for retaining family customs throughout the centuries.

According to Viking literature and mythology, there were several places that the *Hugr* part of the person could find themselves after they died. By far the most well-known of these places was the legendary 'Valhalla.' Valhalla was considered to be a kind of hall in the mystical land of Asgard where the great Viking god Odin lived. Odin was the king of all the Viking gods, and he was also the god of war and of wisdom. In Valhalla, there would be constant feasting, fighting, and celebration for all eternity—or until the end of the world, when the great, devastating event would take place called 'Ragnarok' (the end of all things). Only the most famous and bravest of Vikings could end up in Valhalla, and one would have to perform certain feats of extreme valor during one's life in order to be allowed to enter.

The next realm was called 'Folkvangr', or the realm of the goddess Freya. She was the goddess of fertility and magic. It was her job to gather all the dead heroes from the battlefield and bring them to her realm. Although it is less well-known than Valhalla, Folkvangr seems to hold a higher prestige in Viking literature than Valhalla. Only the greatest of Viking heroes were allowed entrance. Like the Vikings in Valhalla, the men in this place would be allowed to take part in the final battle to end all battles at Ragnarok.

The next location is known as 'Helheim.' This was the region given to those who did not die in battle. It was located beneath the region of 'Midgard' and is also ruled over by the goddess known as 'Hel.' This realm is separated from the realm of the living by a river that cannot be crossed by those either living or dead. It is worth noting that this region was not for the souls of the wicked. That the region was known as 'Nastrond', or the realm of those who had no honor in life, and were rejected after death because of their actions.

'Ran' was the name of the next region. It was a special place in the afterlife reserved for sailors. Sailors who drowned would encounter the goddess known as Ran, after which the region is named. She kept large amounts of treasure there, and would capture the souls of dead sailors in large nets and imprison them.

The next region was known as 'Helgafjell.' This was a region located on top of a high mountain where the souls of the good sometimes ended up. Sometimes people going there would end up with their families, and it was considered to be a place of peace and serenity.

Finally, there were the traditional Christian views of Heaven (the abode of good people after they died) and Hell (the abode of the wicked). It is uncertain how much Christianity influences Viking beliefs as a whole. But one thing is for certain, Viking culture did believe in the afterlife, and as time went on, their beliefs evolved to become more like Christianity in many ways.

Ancestor Worship

The Vikings valued their ancestral ties, and their cultures revolved around the need to maintain them. It was believed that these ancestors were able to impact the lives of the living even after they themselves were dead. The family itself was a representation of all that the ancestors did in their lives in the past. It goes without saying that pagan religions within Viking culture tended to value the idea of ancestral worship more so than the Christian beliefs themselves.

Viking Clothing

Viking clothing was made for the climate in which the Vikings lived. It was designed to insulate the wearer against the harshest of climates. The warmest material that the Vikings had access to was wool. Hats were made of woolen materials or a fabric that kept heat in. Woolen socks kept cold feet warm in winter.

Belts were made of leather or another strong fabric and held an outfit together. Knives and other tools could be hung on these belts for easy access when they were required. Clothing was dyed using vegetable juices and other natural substances. Colors could be mixed with each other to create different shades. Silk and other more expensive materials were rarer in Viking culture, but the wealthier chieftains and members of society could still afford them.

Men commonly wore a tunic across the front of the chest and women tended to wear more traditionally feminine outer garments or longer dresses. Men usually wore trousers, which could be either tight or loose fitting. There are few examples of Viking clothing from archaeological sources. This is because what was preserved has not survived the hundreds of years post-burial. Fabric and other materials tend to disintegrate over time. Much of what we know about Viking clothing comes from their own sagas and literature of the time.
The Vikings made use of clothing in many ways, even if it was worn out or damaged. Old clothing could be coated with pitch or tar and reused or used for other purposes. A Viking overtunic was known as a *kyrtill* and was constructed from a number of woolen fabric pieces intricately woven together. It resembled a long-sleeved shirt without buttons.

Under the tunic, Viking men often wore an undertunic or vest. This provided an added layer of protection for them in the winter months. This second layer of clothing would sit close to the skin, wick moisture away from the body, and provide warmth by not allowing air to escape.

Vikings wore cloaks in colder weather and sometimes when they went into battle. It is considered to be one of the more distinctive parts of Viking attire. When one thinks of a stereotypical Viking warrior, they are usually depicted with these cloaks around them. So, how were these cloaks constructed? They were commonly made from animal skins—sheepskins in particular—as these were some of the warmest materials available at the time.

Viking trousers (or pants) had no fly and no pockets. This meant that if the wearer wanted to relieve themselves, they would need to drop their pants first. Pockets were non-existent, which meant that everything that needed to be stored on a person had to be carried by means of a belt. This could be loosened when the wearer wanted to remove the pants. Women also carried their items in this way—by wearing a belt.

In battle, clothes tended to be a lot more robust. A thicker cloak or tunic could be used to ward off lighter projectiles in a pinch. Overall, Viking clothing was designed to be practical and effective for the environment that it found itself in. Tight-fitting clothing was avoided amongst many Vikings, and is referred to as restrictive in some of their sagas. The reason for this is because it was difficult to remove when the occasion demanded it. When Vikings moved down and settled in the very different climates of Europe, their styles of wearing clothes changed because their needs were different. The warmer climates no longer necessitated the use of heavier cloaks and thick tunics, for example.

Women's Clothing

Women's clothing was similar to men's in terms of the basic material used. Women tended to wear a dress typical for women during the medieval period, in a style that was popular amongst many cultures or civilizations in Europe and the surrounding areas at the time. They wore a mid or ankle-length dress with the neck closed by a brooch. There is also evidence that Viking women wore a kind of overdress which required no brooches to fasten in place.

Oftentimes, women would wear brooches which were capable of carrying multiple items on them that were needed for work. These items included needles, scissors, pins, and more. A woman would also carry a whetstone and a knife on her belt. Women also wore jewelry, including beads, earrings, and necklaces of various kinds. Wealthy Viking women could afford the most costly jewelry available. Sometimes, they were gifted these items by their more wealthy husbands or suitors. It was for this reason that a wealthy Viking husband was highly sought after by many women because of the benefits that this could offer them, such as security.

Head coverings were sometimes worn by Viking women. These coverings included a knotted piece of square material. One special occasions, the headpieces might be more elaborate, such as when a woman got married. Sometimes, elaborate headdresses distinguished married women from unmarried ones.

Slave Clothing

Slave clothing was similar in terms of its constituent parts to that of wealthier Vikings but the nature of it was a lot simpler in style and fashion, and it was not as high in quality as the clothing afforded by wealthier people. The materials tended to differ as slaves could not afford the more expensive materials.

Making of Clothing

The making of clothes was a time-consuming process and had to be carried out by skilled members of the family. Depending on the materials being used, different processes had to be carried out. Clothes were made of natural fibres. These materials used for making clothes included the aforementioned sheep-skin, flax, silk, or various forms of linen. Women usually made the clothes, as Viking society dictated that this task would be entrusted to women, who were taught these skills from a young age. A well-made suit of clothes was considered to be costly and valuable. It would be carefully preserved and worn only on special occasions. Clothing could be dyed in various ways depending on what the need of the person wearing it was. It was considered fashionable to wear colorful clothing, and more expensive liquid could be used for dying clothes in certain colors. In many instances, dying clothes was an art form. Rich colors such as red, dark blue, purple, silver, gold, and even orange signified that the wearer was wealthy. If a garment was difficult to dye, it was left undyed. Patterned fabrics were popular throughout Viking culture and are mentioned in the sagas themselves, for example in the *Njáls* saga.
Furs

During the age of the Vikings, there was a roaring trade in furs. This is how they came into contact with people from Europe in the first place, amongst other reasons. These furs included mink, marten, bear, fox, bear, squirrel, and many other kinds of animals. Sable was also popular. It was seen as a symbol of power if one wore the skin of, for example, a bear, because it meant that you had killed that animal and you had power over it.

Viking Architecture

One of the lesser considered aspects of Viking culture and civilization is the way in which they created their buildings and edifices. Not much remains of Viking architecture these days, and what we know largely comes from the sagas and Viking literature. There are various buildings that the Vikings are most known for. We will examine two of these buildings, namely the Viking longhouse and the Viking stave church. Some of these iconic buildings are still standing today and can be viewed in Scandinavian countries.

Viking materials for building were primarily gathered from the forests of Scandinvian countries. Let us first look at the construction of Viking longhouses. These buildings were meant to be used by the community, and their design reflects this fact. According to Rouă (2016), Viking longhouses were made of wattle with thatched roofs with timber frames for support. These buildings were practical to design and easy to construct.

While wood was easy to come by in most Scandinavian countries, places like Greenland, Iceland, and the Faroe Islands found it harder to come by. These countries had to make use of alternative materials, such as turf, in order to construct warm, weather-proof houses. Sod, stone, and other materials were all used when wood wasn't available.

Longhouses were designed with a firepit in the middle and a hole above it so that the smoke could escape. In spite of the image of these longhouses as being dirty or crowded places, they were actually carefully constructed. Norse families lived in the central room of the longhouse where it was most snug. They cooked, slept, worked, and told stories in the warmest rooms. Viking longhouses were some of the cosiest places to be during the dark, cold winter months.

Some of these houses can still be seen standing today, while others have been reconstructed. These structures can be seen in places such as Borg in Norway, Hobro in Denmark, and Newfoundland in Canada. Some of these fascinating houses are considered to be world heritage sites by UNESCO and are considered to be culturally important areas.

Another noteworthy building in the context of Viking culture is the stave church, which of course, became more prominent with the advent of Christianity. These churches are interesting because of the unusual way in which they were constructed. There are many different kinds of stave churches, but what they all have in common are the fact that they are constructed with staves (posts) in the corners. The staves support a framework of timber beams, which in turn holds the plank walls upright. The walls are called stave walls and thus, this is how the church got its name. These buildings often feature ornate carvings of dragons and other animals which were commonly represented in Viking literature.

The dragon, in particular, symbolizes the ferocity of the Viking mindset before the advent of Christianity. These churches are dotted through Norway, Sweden, and Denmark and can be visited to this day, as they are not unlike museums. These buildings give us great insight into what Viking life was like during these years.

According to what is known through archaeological evidence and Viking literature, they did have an understanding of town planning and architecture. While not on the level of some of the more advanced civilizations, they did have a solid grasp of the basics needed to construct a network of roads and towns, and these things are evident in the historical evidence that has been left behind by them.

Examples of famous Viking towns included Hedeby in the German state of Schleswig-Holstein, Birka in Sweden, and Kaupang in Skiringssal in Norway.

These towns give credence to the idea that the Vikings not only had advanced technologies for the time, but that they were able to function in a coherent way as a society, while other societies might not have coped with the hardships they were faced with.

There is evidence that the Vikings or Norsemen built a ring of fortifications around the perimeter of their land in Denmark and southern Sweden. These fortifications were known as *trelleborgs*. These circular structures not only served as defensive barriers, but they could have also served as a base for launching raids on England and Europe during the 9th and 10th century. These could have also been used for trading and other important administrative activities. Let us look at what these fortresses were like, in more detail.

Each of these forts contained numerous houses within them that could have been used to accommodate troops, slaves, and chieftains. In addition to houses, they could also contain all the other elements of typical fortified defenses, such as watchtowers, storage space for supplies, areas where weapons could be constructed, and many other features.

Their uniqueness lies in the fact that they were circular, which was an unusual shape for a fortification during this era. Several of these constructions are still standing to this day and have been donated to UNESCO as a world-heritage site (Rouă, 2016).

In addition to the housing of warriors, slaves and other relevant parties, the *trelleborgs* also housed governmental officials and were a meeting point for royalty during Viking times. It was for this reason that they were heavily protected and were designed with this in mind. It was thought that the Vikings used these structures to launch attacks on the English coastline. For a long time, the English were unaware of their existence.

Viking Art

With all the talk of architecture, let us look at how this fits into the broader framework of Viking art. Architecture itself is considered a form of art, and it is interesting to see how the Viking view of the world was displayed in the way they expressed themselves through different mediums. It must be said the Viking art is amongst the most fascinating in the world, probably due to how little is known about it. Given the rough nature of Vikings, one would expect their art to be unsophisticated or crude, but the reality is very different.

Creation of highly developed and interesting objects was of great interest to the Vikings because of the nature of their mindset and civilization. Being as they were, an adventuring people, they were always trying new things and were always looking for new ways of accomplishing something. So, this is reflected in their art and creation of objects of rare sophistication and beauty. One must also remember that during this time, the Vikings were only a very small offshoot of a much larger Norse culture. The Vikings made extensive use of their resources to create these objects, making use of what they had available around them, and many of these objects still survive to this day.

One of the materials that they used most frequently was wood, as it was cheap and plentiful in the regions that they lived in. Unfortunately, wood has the tendency to disintegrate over time, and little remains of their work during this period. Stone and other similar materials are quite a bit more durable, and it is these items which we have many of today.

Metalwork, earthen vessels, and other items made of metal, clay, glass, and stone give us a great insight into the Viking way of viewing the world.

The nature of many of the items is utilitarian in nature, displaying the Viking propensity for items that could be *used*. They tended to view the world and art not through aesthetic means, but valued an item for its practicality. The more functional an item was, the more valuable it was. This does not mean that they did not value aesthetics, but that aesthetics played a secondary role in many respects.

According to Snow (2020), Viking art was made up of a number of different motifs, all combining together to form a continuous whole. It was difficult to tell the end from the beginning. Imagery in Viking art reflected the times that they lived in, their social practices, mythological beliefs, and daily life. As Christianity began to make its way into Viking culture, evidence of this was seen in Viking art. Instead of being mainly focused on pagan images, it began to incorporate more Christian themes.

Beasts were a common theme in Viking art, both mythological and natural. The most well-known of these was, of course, the dragon. It is abundantly used as a symbol throughout Viking literature, their sagas, and their art. There were two kinds of beasts that were quite common, namely the "ribbon beast" and the "gripping beast." The Vikings referred to the first beast as the "ribbon beast" because it had an elongated head and simplified features (Snow, 2020). The other was known as the "gripping beast" because it had well-defined limbs and detailed features.

These figures seemed to be most common in the most famous of Viking constructions, the longboat, carved in the prow of these legendary vessels. They not only struck fear into the enemy when they saw the ships coming, but they also marked the Vikings out as unique.

In order to understand a little more about how Viking art works, we can also examine the different styles into which their work is categorized. These styles are *Oseberg, Borre, Jellinge, Mammen, Ringerike,* and *Urnes*. Each of them is associated with a different time period starting from about 775 AD and ending in about 1125 AD (Snow, 2020).

Oseberg

This is a style associated with the early part of the Viking age. It was popular all over Scandinavia and not restricted to a particular localized area. One of the defining works of this period (775-875) is a specific longship, known simply as the *Oseberg* ship that was ornately carved featuring elements of the gripping and ribbon beasts in swirling motions. The burial mound where this ship was found has given rise to the name of the movement itself.

Borre

This is the second major style from the early Viking age period, and it overlaps with the first period. It lasted from around the year 850 to about 950. This style seems to have been focused around the British Isles and the Baltic region, as Vikings travelled in both directions. The *Borre* art period is characterized by the use of tightly-interlaced motifs that blot out the background, making it difficult to see. Animal motifs are more cartoonish, in a sense, than in other art styles, and classic ribbon shapes seem to be less conspicuous in this period. One of the most commonly known pieces from this period is that of a silver brooch from Gotland with a series of human and animal figures on it. The animals are portrayed as licking their backs with their tongues. Overall, the art during this period seems to focus on making its subjects appear with contorted bodies and triangular-shaped heads.

Jellinge

The next major art style has been placed at around 900 to 975. It combines many elements of the previous two styles and deals with a wide variety of subjects. The name of the style originated with the finding of a silver cup in a burial mound in Jelling, a region in Denmark.

In this style, backgrounds are lighter in color and more detailed, while the creatures themselves seem to be simplified. The ribbon beasts make a return during this period. Solid colors are used for images and geometric shapes are used to show the joints between their legs and arms (in the case of humans). This is in sharp contrast to *Borre,* where spiral shapes were used to depict the lines between leg and arms, and the bodies of the creatures.

Mammen

Mammen is a unique style of Viking art spanning the years 960 to 1000, known for being associated with the Viking king Harald Bluetooth. It comprises elements of *Jellinge* style, foliate motifs, and notable influences from the European continent. The name of this style originated from the account of a ceremonial ax head that was discovered near a village in Denmark. Loops, waves, and tendrils seem to be distinctive of this particular style, as is seen in the image of a bird created in the late 10th century. It is noted for having beaded ornamentation and wings which reflect this flowing style.

Another discovery in the *Mammen* style is a set of runestones in the Jelling region. It features a creature called a "great beast" (Snow, 2020). It is meant to reflect the conquest of a great ruler during that time, and his victory in a specific battle. It has been interpreted as a symbol of power and dominance.

These stones are meant to reflect the power and dominance of Harald Bluetooth at this time, hence why they were set up. These stones also contain images of Christ himself, wrapped in tendrils as typical of this style. It is a convoluted and complex technique to unlock given the varying influences that it had had over the centuries.

Ringerike

Ringerike is characterized by its whimsical nature and its ingenuity. It lasted from around 990 to 1050, just when the Viking age was entering its declining years—or changes were taking place within the culture and civilization as a whole. While being influenced by aspects of other art styles, *Ringerike* also tries to develop a unique style of its own. Gone are the beaded ornamentations from previous periods. European influences were beginning to take over at this point, and this is evident in the use of vegetal themes in the works. Tendrils continue to make an appearance, and the style is very much more reminiscent of other, popular European works at the time.

Urnes

In the final stage of the Viking age, there is a distinct move towards more elegant and classical European themes. The *Urnes* style lasted from around 1050 to around 1125, after which little is known of Viking art styles—at least that is recorded. It is commonly believed that even if the Viking age did not end at this point, something had been fundamentally altered in terms of their social and historical context. Europe was not the same place as it was 500 years earlier. With regards to the art style itself, it is known for its depiction of animals in a different manner. Animals were portrayed in regal poses, and anatomical features are more elongated. This style is associated with the Norweigan village of Urnes, where there is also a stave church located. Stave churches themselves, although around long before these techniques came to existence, seem to take on the artistic movements that were popular at the time.

Overall, Viking art styles demonstrate an unusual variety of color, variety, texture, and subject matter. From animal scenes to mythological beasts, to everyday living, Viking art seems to be noteworthy for its flexibility, creativity, and ingenuity. Looking at Viking art helps us understand that this society wasn't just about war, expansion, and conquest. They were people with keen and creative minds.

Daily Viking Life

Everyday Life in Viking Times

When Vikings weren't waging war in other countries, they were planting and harvesting their crops. They were primarily hunting, farming, and fishing people. Although they traded goods and services with Europe, most Norse people were subsistence farmers, which meant that whatever they grew, hunted, or killed, they used for themselves and their families. So given that their primary purpose was survival, for the most part, what did a typical day look like for someone living in Scandinavia during these times?

A day would typically begin early by getting up and milking the cows, feeding the sheep and goats, and getting the cattle out to pasture if they were wealthy enough to own a large amount of livestock. Men went to work in the fields or sent their servants to do this.

Women would work on chores around the house, which included cleaning, washing, dusting, preparing and cooking food, and taking care of children (if they had any). In the midst of all these activities, breakfast would be eaten. This was known as *dagmal*. It could consist of a small amount of meaty stew left over from the night before, bread, fruit, porridge made of wheat, barley or other grains, buttermilk, and cheese. Eggs would also be consumed if they were available. *Dagmal* was eaten two to three hours after waking up, and after they had done all their chores. Vikings did not eat much in the middle of the day.

The next meal they would eat would be in the evening, and it was called *nattmal*. It was a meal consisting of meat, fish, vegetables, bread, fruit, mead, and cheeses. In between these meals, Viking men would be working hard. There was not much time to do everything they needed to do, and so the daytime would be used for the most pressing of activities. When night fell, they could rest and socialize. During the day, however, farming activities such as ploughing and fertilizing would take place. This was backbreaking work, and everyone tried to do their best to contribute towards the labor effort so that the tasks could be done more quickly.

Tasks that were considered undesirable, such as constructing houses and buildings, flinging manure on fields, disposing of dead animal carcasses, old rotten food, waste from the house, and other negligible jobs were given to slaves to carry out. They were then afforded the generous protection of the household and allowed to live somewhere on the property and maybe partake in some of the food that was given out. Slave-holders did not pay their slaves any wages. However, if they sold some goods at market on the request of the master, they might be able to keep a little of the proceeds depending on the situation. These slaves were kept after raids or battles that were successful. They could earn their freedom if a master died or if circumstances changed. But usually, slaves were not sold once they were in the care of a master, unless he was somehow in financial trouble (in which case he would likely not have slaves—they were a sign of some kind of wealth).

The reality of everyday Viking life is that it was tedious and boring. The same kinds of activities had to be carried out every single day, and these tasks were time-consuming, arduous, and unexciting. Nonetheless, the Vikings had to do these things in order to survive, and it was a natural way of living for them. Famines, enemy raids, pestilence, disease, and many other dangers were also a part of their daily life, and they had to learn to cope with such situations as best they could when they arrived.

Famine and disease took their toll on the population, as did war. These elements of life were costly. The population had to adopt an attitude of acceptance when these things occurred because they understood that they had little power to stop them.

Viking Appearances

Vikings were Nordic people, often with characteristic blond hair and blue eyes, but this was not necessarily universal. Their skin was fair, and their hair color could vary between being blond, reddish blond, or extremely fair. Viking men had longer hair while slaves tended to keep their hair a lot shorter. The length of a Viking man's hair depended on what was practical or convenient at the time. For those in battle, it might not always be practical to have longer hair, so it was adjusted as needed.

Women tended to keep their hair up when working and when it was important to do so, only letting it down when they no longer needed to keep it tied up. Married women often wore their hair in a bun to differentiate them from those who were unmarried. The different classes of Vikings were easy to spot by their appearance.

Vikings who were more wealthy wore jewelry, ornate belts, and were well-groomed. Those in the middle class had similar tastes but expressed them in a less formal or ostentatious way. Slaves didn't have much of a choice about what to wear, and so were more simple in their manner of dressing and their appearance. The wealthiest Vikings would carry certain items with them with which to groom themselves, such as ornate combs and decorative items such as brooches. These would not be found on those who were less wealthy.

Sports and Recreation

Because physical fitness was important to the Vikings, they took part in many kinds of games and sports. These took place during the hours when they weren't doing work in the fields or whatever their daily occupation happened to be. Being a warrior culture, the Vikings took pride in their ability to overcome obstacles. Their sports reflected this. Games they played involved balancing, running, jumping over obstacles, swimming, rowing, and they had kinds of snow-related sports, such as ice skating and skiing. Mountain climbing was also popular as it built stamina and endurance.

During times when it was difficult to be outdoors, the Vikings loved board and dice games. Archaeological evidence supports this. The items used in these games were carved from wood, bone or tusks of animals such as walrus, and antlers from, for example, reindeer.

Vikings were rough during their games, and it was not uncommon for people to be hurt or killed during these rowdy activities. Vikings enjoyed a game played with a stick and ball. This game is known as *knattleikr*. It was a game popular across the region of Scandinavia and could be played in all kinds of weather if it was desired. It bears similarities to the modern-day game of hurling.

Few written rules about the game survive but from what is known, it seems that it was a game played on two teams. It was a spectacular game, played from the morning until evening, and much like our sporting events today, it was quite the spectacle. The ball was struck with a stick or any other part of the body. There were penalty boxes and penalties were given. It seems as if the more aggressive players tended to be more successful, and there are several instances where a war of words broke out in the game and physical fights occurred. A smooth surface was required to play the game, be it sand, dirt, or ice.

The game has been revived in modern-day society and is played amongst some adherents of Viking customs.

Social Activities

Social activities often revolved around food, as this was central to the Viking of thinking. Happy times were celebrated with feasting, drinking, and dancing. Storytelling, poetry, music, and other forms of visual or auditory arts were popular at social gatherings. Music in particular was an art form for the more wealthy in society, as only highly skilled people could play instruments, such as the lyre and lute. This was because only wealthy people could afford to be trained, or had the time for such activities. Those who were poorer could not because they had neither the money nor the time.

Chapter 3: Geography and Regional Cuisine

Viking geography might seem like a difficult or complex subject as it covers such a vast range of greatly-differing territories. However, it is vital to be aware of what impacted the Viking culture in terms of the climate, terrain, geographical features, and oceans that surrounded their home. These geographical factors played a crucial role in determining how the Vikings lived and how they impacted history. Each one of the different regions in Scandinavia and other places Vikings lived played their own role in determining how that culture thought and functioned. Most critical of all, perhaps, is understanding how the Vikings made use of sea routes in the expansion of their empire, and how this would lead them into contact with the rest of medieval Europe.

The ramifications were to be enormous not only for that time but for centuries to come. Let us start by familiarizing ourselves with the geography of the different regions where the Vikings lived, and the names of the important places and locations in their history.

Where the Vikings Lived

The Vikings were located all over the Scandinavian region at first. Their original territory stretched from Norway in the north and west (a larger region), to Denmark in the south (a smaller territory), and to Sweden further east. There were no major roads between these territories, and thus travel was severely hampered, as was trade.

Also included in the Viking territories were Iceland, the Faroe Isles, the Baltic coast, and Normandy. The Vikings travelled all over the globe: They invaded Europe, the British Isles, the Eastern half of Europe (modern-day Russia, Ukraine and these surrounding regions), the Middle East and Persia, North Africa, and even stretched as far as North America. One could say that their reach was truly global in this regard.

Terrain

The Viking's land was inhospitable and rocky. There was little welcome for travellers to that land. All around them was ice and snow, and also the unfriendly sea. Seeking a more fertile land, the Vikings decided to leave this desolate place and seek greener pastures further south. Better farmland was available in southern European countries and the British Isles.

Although wood was plentiful in Scandinavia, there was a lack of fertile soil that they could use to grow crops. Also, the climate wasn't ideal for growing the many types of crops that the Vikings needed. In these times, it must have been customary to make do with whatever one had, but it was hard to ignore the fact that there were more fruitful places elsewhere.

Natural Wilderness

The natural wilderness of these Scandinavian countries was rough and unforgiving, as mentioned before. There were many forests, icy caves, gorges, and ravines. It was a picturesque land, but it was not friendly to those unaccustomed to its ways. It was the ruggedness of this terrain that eventually convinced even the Vikings to move and search for better and more hospitable territory.

Climate

The climate in Scandinavian countries is widely familiar. Ice and snow dominated during the winter months, and even during summer there could be inclement weather. Viking people had to be prepared for anything, and they learned to endure the very worst of conditions.

This meant that when they migrated to the milder climates of southern European countries, they were accustomed to the weather that sometimes flared up in these places as well. The only thing that the Vikings needed to do was to adjust their culture and ways of living to suit the new climates and environments they found themselves in.

Ocean

The ocean played a vital role in the development of Viking civilization. It was used by them for numerous activities, namely the transport of their men on raiding missions. It was also an important facilitator of trade routes, and was an important way that the Vikings could migrate between the southern European countries to expedite their economic activities. The oceans bordering Viking territories in Scandinavia were the Arctic Sea to the west and the Baltic Sea to the east. Further to the south was the North Sea and even further south than that was the Mediterranean ocean. As the Vikings expanded further southward, they opened up new trade routes for themselves, and eventually ended up making the long trip west across the Atlantic to find the New World. Vikings also travelled as far as the Adriatic, the Black Sea, and even further to the Caspian Sea on the borders of the Asian continent. Elements of Viking culture continued to influence much of Eastern Europe for centuries to come.

Plants and the Environment

When speaking about the geography of Viking times, one cannot ignore the way in which the Viking people interacted with nature and their environment. What did they think about the world that they saw around them and the natural world specifically? Nordic people in general and Viking people in particular took great pride in their gardens, and they also took a great deal of interest in the environment itself. They tended to make use of whatever they could find to grow if it could benefit them in some way. A garden in a Viking town might have consisted of many different kinds of plants, herbs, and flowers depending on the social status of the people who owned the garden. The art of horticulture dates back many thousands of years and has always fascinated ancient civilizations. The Vikings were no exception.

With the constant back and forth movement of Vikings from their countries to Europe, they took back many herbs, seeds, and flowers. Some of the fruits and vegetables that Vikings used in their gardens included onions, cabbages, turnips, peas, beans, watercress, plums and apples, different kinds of flax used for making fabric, and many others.

Viking gardens are noted for their small, square shape. These tiny intimate gardens can still be seen dotting the Norweigan countryside as a long-forgotten sign of a bygone era.

Viking Foods in Different Regions

Viking civilization itself is a fascinating mix of traditions, rituals, and cultures. And no more is this more apparent than in their daily lives. What did the Vikings eat? How did they live? The answers to such questions are thought-provoking and offer an insight into the often-overlooked details of their lives.

Viking food was determined largely by where groups lived in the different regions of Scandinavia. Because there were people from such divergent regions spanning a landmass the size of a large country or a continent, foods would have differed substantially.

Due to the fact that the Vikings lived in a cold climate, they needed all the food they could get, so that they could maintain their body fat and stay warm during the cold, dark winters they faced. The Vikings cared little for what might be termed "fat free" food or "healthy food." They were not about dieting. Meat, fish, cereals, berries, milk, honey, alcohol, and fruit and vegetables were all part of their diet. Let us look at the way the Vikings ate in more detail to get a better understanding of how their culture worked. Why were mealtimes important to the Vikings?

Food wasn't always available to the Vikings. It had to be grown, caught, gathered, or hunted. Vikings needed to be self-sufficient. This could sometimes be difficult when resources were scarce.

We can tell a lot about what the Vikings ate by looking at the remnants of what were once their homes, in the fragmented bones and fragments left behind in the ruins of their towns and cities. We can also read the literature that they wrote and get a better understanding of what they ate.

According to Rouă (2016), the colder climates played a role in what kind of food was eaten. Vegetables are used to a lesser extent in Nordic cuisine and the preservation of meat is noted in some of their recipes, because it was easier to store. Norway was noted for this. On the other hand, in the Danish region, soils were far more effective for growing crops, and pork was eaten instead of fish.

A Typical Viking Meal

According to "Viking Food" (2019), a typical Viking meal is described in the poem about Hárbard and Thor, where Thor meets Odin who is disguised as a fisherman. He describes the meal of oatmeal and fish he ate before leaving home. This seems consistent with what we know about Viking food preferences. They ate a lot of berries and grains because these are the kinds of things they grew in the regions where they were living.

Let's look at other foods Vikings ate during their meal. It goes without saying that nuts and berries were the foundation of the Viking diet. Raspberries, bilberries, blackberries, plums, walnuts, hazelnuts, and wild apples were all gathered by them. Apples were considered to be particularly healthy ("Fruit and berries in the Viking age," n.d).

The Vikings kept much in the way of livestock. They usually would have pigs, goats, sheep, cows, horses, hens, geese, and ducks. All of these animals could either be used for their meat or eggs. Sometimes they would be used for their milk.

The Vikings made the best use of their animals. First, they would be used for their milk, or used as pack animals or for labor. Next, they would be slaughtered and killed, their bones, skin, and horns used for clothes, implements, and cutlery. If a cow was considered too worn out to work anymore, it would be slaughtered and its meat used for months in advance—depending on the size of the cow.

One of the problems that the Vikings faced during their time was the preservation of food. This could be overcome by salting meat or fish, thereby preserving for months or even years. Because the Vikings lived close to the ocean, they had their pick of many different kinds of fish. One of the most popular kinds of fish was herring.

The Vikings also made use of the offal of animals to make sausages, stew, and stuffings. Horses were also consumed on some special occasions. The Vikings drank milk and also made cheese or butter. Salt was added to butter to make it last longer.

One of the most common foods was, of course, bread. Bread formed the staple of life during the Viking age, especially the dark and coarse rye bread. Oats, millet, and barley were also considered to be of great importance, as they could be used in many different kinds of dishes. Wheat was a luxury to the Vikings due to the problem with growing it in their harsh climates. Flatbreads were made with a mixture of rye flour, honey, eggs, and water. These were grilled over the fire because ovens were an unknown invention to the Vikings at this time; they would only become popular much later on.

Porridge was a popular Viking food because it was easy to prepare, cheap, and nutritious. Various kinds of grains and cereals were used to make porridge and many different kinds of ingredients could be added. Buckwheat, oats, and millet could be combined with fruit to make a healthy breakfast. Berries and apples could be added to sweeten the porridge even further. Porridge was considered to be one of the foods that poorer people ate.

Alcoholic beverages were considered some of the most popular items in a Viking diet. Beer was one of these. It was created using barley. Water wasn't always safe to drink and thus it was avoided sometimes.

Watered-down beer was drunk by both children and adults, and those who were unused to drinking hard liquor. The Vikings were very fond of mead, and it played a large role in their culture and traditions. This spiced wine was mixed with honey and drunk in large quantities at weddings and other celebrations. Wine was made with fermented grapes. It was a luxury that only a few could afford.

Vikings loved hunting, and would hunt and kill many strange kinds of beasts for their food. When livestock was scarce, there were always other animals that they could use as food, such as wild game and wild birds. These birds included pheasants, partridges, and many other kinds of fowl. Wild game included elk, reindeer, and even bear. Their fur was made into rugs or used as clothing. The Vikings did not like to waste anything that they got from their kills while hunting.

A popular image of Vikings is that they cooked their meats over a large open fire using a spit. While this might have been the case in some instances, it is thought that the Vikings weren't overly fond of roasting or frying their food.

One of their favored methods of cooking was boiling. In fact, one of the most famous Viking dishes, called *skause,* was a combination of different kinds of meats and vegetables that were added day after day until the flavor was rich and intense. It was served with a coarse bread made of all kinds of grains, and even sometimes ground tree bark was added for nutritional value. The Vikings would make sourdough bread using old leftover dough mixes, and would even add buttermilk or fermented milk to their breads to give it a tangy flavor. By doing so, they enriched their breads greatly.

The Vikings grew many different kinds of vegetables. White carrots were added to the *skause* pot along with peas, beans, and endives. The Vikings grew cabbages and also grew herbs and spices. These included cumin and coriander. In the event that they were unable to grow something, they could obtain these spices from local trade and markets although at great cost. Condiments such as horseradish sauce and mustard sauce were also very popular amongst the Vikings.

Inspection of remains of Viking homes and sewers revealed that they also sometimes inadvertently ingested poisonous weeds and husks. Evidently, Vikings must have made themselves ill from time to time by eating whatever they could find, and from making bread from flour ground from these inedible weeds.

The Benefits of a Viking Diet

A Viking diet was high in essential fats, vitamins, and nutrients. It relied greatly on fish, red meat, and vegetables with an abundance of whole grains and alcoholic beverages, much the same as what is known as the "Mediterranean diet" today. It gave the Vikings plenty of energy for the tasks that they needed to carry out.

Chapter 4: Beliefs, Myths and Mythology

In order to understand how the Viking mindset works, one must understand that they viewed everything through a naturalistic and also a mystical perspective. The events in the natural world that they could not explain would simply be put down as the interference of supernatural origins beyond their ability to control. The following chapter is a brief overview of their basic understanding of the world as they saw it.

Some of the names may seem strange or unfamiliar, but bear in mind that these names are reflective of a language and a time period long ago forgotten. It is only through understanding these cultures that we ourselves can begin to connect to the past in a meaningful way and learn from it.

The Beginning of the Universe

The Vikings believed that the universe began with two distinct elements: Heat and cold. When these two elements met each other, the great frost giant, or titan, 'Ymir' was formed. 'Audhumla,' the primeval cow of Viking creation mythology, licked and suckled Ymir, and in the process created 'Buri', who would go on to be the father of the mighty Odin himself. Audhumla also created 'Vili' and 'Ve.' These three gods went to kill Ymir and use his body to create the earth and his head to create the sky. One of his eyebrows was used as a barrier to prevent the world of men, or Midgard, from interacting with the world of the giants (more commonly known as titans).

At the centre of all creation stood a grand tree known as 'Yggdrasill.' Its roots spread to all corners of the universe: One root spread to Asgard, or the home of the gods; the next root spread to Jotunheim, or the realm of the frost giants; and finally the last root spread down to Niflheim, or the realm of the dead. The tree connected all worlds in the Viking universe and was considered to be the most sacred of objects to the Vikings. It was populated by various strange beasts, birds, and animals that could talk to each other. In order to understand this world, it is necessary that we get acquainted with the main characters of the story: The Viking gods and goddesses themselves.

Viking Gods and Goddesses

The following is an account of the main players in Viking mythology. This list is by no means exhaustive and is meant to introduce the reader to the way which Viking mythology works. Everything is intertwined and so it is important to understand these basic characters. The story builds on itself. It is worth noting that there are two groups of gods: The *Æsir* and the *Vanir*. The first group are the principal gods and the second group are the lesser-known gods.

Odin

Odin is probably one of the best known gods in Viking mythology and is the name many think of when they hear the term "Viking god." He was considered to be the king of all the gods and the ruler over them. He is noted for wearing an eyepatch, as a reminder of the sacrifice he made at the well of *Mímisbrunnr,* one of the wells which stands near the tree Yggdrasill.

The other two wells are *Hvergelmir*, the home of a giant serpent and *Urdarbrunnr*, the well of fate which is guarded by three Norns. Their names are Urd, Verdandi, and Skuld. What happened at the well of wisdom was that Odin desired the water from it so that he could continue to grow in wisdom and knowledge. So determined was he to gain this knowledge that he offered to give his right eye in order to take one drink from it. And so it came to be that in Viking culture, Odin became the symbol of all-seeing wisdom in the form of self-sacrifice.

Frigg

Frigg was the wife of Odin and was considered a lesser being than him. However, she was still considered to be the queen of the goddesses. She is thought to be the second most powerful of all the gods and goddesses because of her rank and status as Odin's wife. She was also the goddess of marriage, and her name means 'love' in the ancient Viking tongue.

Tyr

Tyr was the god of war and battle. He was known for his bravery and courage in combat. A truly fearless leader, he lost his arm to the great and terrible wolf Fenrir. He was also the god of treaties and justice. Being as they were, a warlike people, the Vikings honored *Tyr*, as he was seen as an embodiment of all that they stood for: Expansion, conquest, bloodlust, and battle.

Loki

Loki is commonly known as the trickster god in the many books that are written about Norse and Viking mythology. But he is a vastly more complicated character in mythology than is commonly shown on screen and in TV series. In Viking literature, he is also known as the god of fire.

Loki is commonly depicted as having arcane magical abilities but in reality, his tricks stem from the fact that he is able to shape-shift at will, becoming anything he wants to be. His rank in the Viking god hierarchy is uncertain, and his power level amongst the gods seems inconsistent due to his portrayal differently in different kinds of Viking literature.

What is known, though, is that he is the uncle of Thor and son of Fárbauti. He has a few strange myths and legends attached to his name, one of which is the fact that he gave birth to Odin's mighty eight-legged horse known as Sleipnir. Loki is also depicted in much of literature as a troublemaker, who often involves himself in schemes that not only embarrass others, but also himself. He is without a doubt, one of the most misunderstood, but fascinating gods in Norse literature.

Thor

Thor is the hot-tempered relative of Loki, and the son of Odin himself. He is a symbol of strength in Viking mythology, and he is also the god of thunder—capable of feats of incredible power. He is considered one of the strongest of the Æsir gods. His name means 'thunder' in the ancient Teutonic languages. However strong Thor may be, he does have a tendency to make rash and impulsive decisions, and this is shown within Viking literature.

Frey and Freya

Frey and Freya begin the list of the lesser pantheon of gods in the Viking belief system. They were brother and sister and were considered to be the symbols of fertility within Viking mythology.

They were about equal in terms of their power level. Their role in the pantheon is not always clear, but they were made honorary members of the *Æsir* pantheon due to their special role in being a symbol of battle, fertility, and sex. Their presence seemed to create some form of tension between the two pantheons, which is told of in the Viking sagas themselves.

Aegir and Njord

Aegir and Njord are considered to be gods of the sea and oceans. Aegir, the god of the deep sea, is negatively portrayed in Viking literature, and seems to be hated and feared by the other gods and by people because of his tremendous powers. One of his brothers is in fact, the legendary Loki himself. Aegir was depicted in literature as having white hair and wave-like paws, as befitting his 'sea-like' form. He was universally despised because of his actions at sea. When a ship would overturn, he would gather the treasure for himself. His house, thought to be to the west of Midgard, was full of treasures, and he lived in great luxury. As with all the gods, there are many stories told about him in these Viking sagas. Njord was considered to be the guardian of people who travelled via the waterways. He was also considered to be the god of summer, fishing, wealth, and the more positive aspects of the sea.

Bragi

As the son of Odin, Bragi was considered to be one of the wisest gods in the pantheon. His gift was being creative with words and making artistic constructions out of them. As well as being the god of poetry and stories, he is also the god of song and lyrics.

Ull

Ull was the god of archery and weaponry. He was skilled in individual combat and proficient with the bow and also with skis. He was a great warrior, as well.

Hel

The final goddess in this list is the goddess Hel. She is also known as the goddess of death. There is a distinction between the place in Viking mythology called 'Hel' and the goddess herself, who inhabited and ruled over this realm. She is tasked with receiving the dead as they arrive in the underworld—a similar role to Hades in Greek mythology.

Paganism in Viking Culture

Paganism in Viking culture involved the worship of the natural world and everything that could be perceived with the eyes. The Vikings saw the mystical in everything around them. Supernatural origins were given to phenomena that they couldn't easily explain by natural means. It's helpful, in this case, to look at examples of where the Vikings saw strange occurrences in the world around them, such as the changing of seasons.

Lacking a scientific understanding of why seasons changed, the Vikings might have believed that good and pleasant weather was a blessing from the gods. When it was inclement, the adverse was true, and someone must have done something to anger the gods.

While little is known about the practices of the Vikings as far as their beliefs are concerned, there is some material which discusses the mythological side of this belief system. What material we have comes from Viking literature and the sagas. The reason for this is because the Christian church and medieval writers suppressed much of the original material about these beliefs, seeing them as being evil in origin. A key factor to remember about Viking religion is that it was not an institutionalized set of practices. Rather, it was a set of beliefs practiced by people in their homes, in the way that they saw fit.

According to *Pagan Religious Practices of the Viking Age* (2009), an example of this personalization in religion was when traders in Sweden once made sacrifices to their gods on an island in the Black Sea under a large oak tree in order to give thanks for a safe and fruitful voyage on the river Dnieper. This ritual was not done with any other group of people at that time.

The sagas do, however, tell of large and ancient temples in Iceland. They are described in great detail, however, the measurements seem improbable going by real-life standards. It seems more common that Vikings, if they wanted to worship their gods, set up their own personal backyard shrines and made use of those. Religion, it seemed, was an intensely personal thing. Everyone had his or her own way of doing things. They might keep any number of important and sacred objects within the shrine such as small bowls, armrings, and other items of worship.

Although it has been noted that Viking religious customs were a personal issue, there did seem to be a handbook that gave certain regulations for how to practice the various belief systems. This text is known as the *Landnámabók*. It was meant to give guidelines on what to keep in the public shrines, and directives on what to do when swearing an oath on a sacred ring. It seems that these rings played a large role in Viking pagan practices. Failure to adhere to the rules could anger the gods and incur their wrath and punishment. Chieftains themselves were required to wear the rings at sacred ceremonies and during sacrifices. There are also records requiring a tax to be paid to temples, the same as would have been paid to churches in other European countries.

Trees were a common symbol in Viking pagan belief systems, and temples were often set up next to them or under them. This might have had to do with the fact that the great tree Yggdrasill was at the center of the universe.

The word *vé* appears on many different Viking place names throughout the ancient Viking world. It is a shortened form of the Norse word *vígja,* which means to consecrate. Where the word appeared, it meant that the place was in fact holy and therefore could not be desecrated. Special rules governed the spilling of blood here. If a person spilled blood in this place, their place in the society of Vikings would be forfeit, and they would become an outcast. How this form of consecration took place or what these places were for is unknown.

In the 10th century, Olaf Tryggvason became the king of Norway. He imposed Christianity on the Viking people by destroying their idols, burning their temples, and taking the sacred rings. With the advent of Christianity in Scandinavia, these practices no longer had a place in Viking society and within a hundred years or so, they all but ceased to have been practiced.

Christian Beliefs in Viking Culture

The advent of Christianity changed Viking society forever. Religion became an institutionalized normality, and there were expectations placed on the people of Viking towns. Many were forced to accept Christianity or face some kind of sanction. Viking sagas tell of a group of farmers living under the rule of King Olaf in the 11th century. They lived in the Fjord region of Norway, and kept a small idol filled with bread and meat, which they offered to the gods each day.

The king found out and was very angry, confronting the farmers one night and causing their ships to be damaged and their horses to run away. At dawn, the farmers approached him carrying their idol. As they walked towards him, the king stated that the sun would rise with a great light, and it did so. One of the king's men then struck the idol with a heavy club, causing it to break and the contents to spill out. The king pointed out that the idol had no power because it had been broken. The terrified farmers, looking at their ships filled with water and their horses running away, had no choice but to accept Christianity there and then.

It seems that in spite of the advent of Christianity in Viking culture, there were some who still tried to practice the two belief systems concurrently. Records of these incidents are included in the Viking sagas.

The Sagas and What They Tell Us

It is worth investigating these sagas and seeing what they reveal to us about the Viking mindset. They are probably the best and most complete resource that we have, and they give us great insight into life during the Viking age. The following accounts give some brief examples of Viking practices, from their construction of pagan shrines and temples to their practices. Also included in these sagas is the way in which Christianity impacted the Viking system of pagan worship.

Accounts of Pagan Practices in Viking Sagas

In chapter 15 of the *Vatnsdæla* saga, there is evidence of Viking temple construction and use. Although the Vikings valued individuality within the context of their religious beliefs, this did not stop the building of these often impressive structures. One well-known settler by the name of Ingimundur Gamli constructed a temple in the picturesque Vatnsdalur valley. As he was busily digging the holes for which the pillars that held up the structure would be placed, he discovered the amulet of Freyr, which had been prophesied would happen by a seer before he left the shores of Norway.

Another example of the Viking dedication towards building temples for their gods is seen in the *Kjalnesinga* saga. A man by the name of Þorgrímur built a temple at Hof and placed an image of Thor inside it. Also in the building was a fire that never went out, a copper bowl for collecting blood for sacrifice, along with a number of oath rings. Outside the door was a pool into which the bodies of people who had been sacrificed were hurled.

The Viking belief in human and animal sacrifice was steadfast, as grim as it may seem. Accounts of people and animals being sacrificed to the gods exist in the Viking sagas. It was important for Vikings to be on favorable terms with the gods, and for this to be the case, a steady supply of blood had to be provided to them. Accounts of animal sacrifice are found in Haakon the Good's sagas, which were written by the well-known documenter of Viking experiences, Snorri Sturluson, much later in the 13th century.

To begin with, a story is told about animal sacrifice. A man named Sigurd Håkonsson regularly made sacrifices to the gods. It was a common practice amongst farmers to gather at the temple and to give their grain and animal offerings. Animals were butchered, and their blood was collected in small bowls and with twigs. It was then sprinkled on the altars, walls, and over the people themselves. The meat was then boiled in large pots or cauldrons and eaten in celebration. Glasses of beer were carried around the fire in the room, which were then blessed by the chief worshipper, also called a 'magnate.' These cups were passed from person to person. Toasts were made to Odin and to the Viking king. At the end of the feast, Sigurd Håkonsson covered the costs of the feast himself.

But what of the idea of human sacrifice? Could the Vikings sanction something so bloodthirsty by our standards? The answer is to be found in the idea that the Vikings valued human life very highly. To them, to give a life to the gods was no small matter. It was one of the most costly gifts that they could provide. Written sources do tell that Odin demanded human sacrifices. How did these sacrifices take place and what was the context surrounding them?

A German monk from Bremen wrote an account in 1072 of a meeting at Gammel Uppsala, where a sacrificial ritual was carried out in order to dedicate the temple to the gods. According to his writings, nine male animals (of different kinds) and nine male humans were sacrificed. The number nine was seen as mystical to the Vikings. At the end of the ritual, the bodies of the victims were hung from trees. Speculation abounds as to whether this account (and many others like it) are true. This is due to the fact that the monk never witnessed the killings himself, and it is likely linked to Christian propaganda after the turn of the millenium, due to the fear that they had of Viking practices. However, it is a fact that there are accounts of Viking human sacrifice littered throughout the sagas and Viking literature. Much still has to be learned about the way in which the Vikings approached these practices and the value that they placed on human life.

Viking Mythology and Folklore

Much can be found within the stories that are written in Viking literature, both fictional and non-fictional. These stories not only tell of the Viking gods and their exploits, but also of the people they watched over. These stories entertain, amuse, and make us question aspects of our lives. Viking mythology is some of the most diverse and interesting in the world due to the multitude of perspectives it appeals to. It is still popular to read these stories even to this day. Apart from the gods we have already encountered, it is also important to note some other significant characters in the Viking stories.

Heimdall

Heimdall was the gatekeeper of the 'bifrost', in the great and glorious realm of Asgard. The bifrost was the rainbow bridge that connected Asgard to the other nine realms, including Midgard or Earth. His role was to ensure that no evil thing entered the realm, and to keep a watch on all that went on in the other realms. He was the all-seeing eye that looked for danger and raised the alarm if there was any.

Thiassi

Thiassi was king of the frost giants in Jotunheim, their realm.

Iduna

Iduna was a goddess who is said to have possession of some apples, which if eaten, would cause eternal youth. They were regularly consumed by the gods in order to keep themselves young.

Skrymnir

Skrymnir was a noted frost giant from Jotunheim.

Fenrir

Fenrir was the name of a ferocious wolf sent by Loki at the end of all things in the time called Ragnarok.

The following stories give some accounts of the gods and their exploits. These stories only form a fraction of the many tales handed down from Viking times.

Freya and the Goblins

Freya, the Viking goddess of fertility, was exceedingly beautiful. Odin had given her a special place amongst the gods because of this beauty. One day, Odin invited her to go to a magnificent feast with her husband, Odur. Unfortunately, she discovered to her horror that she had nothing to wear. In spite of her husband's protests, she insisted that she must have a rare and expensive piece of jewelry. So, she set out across Asgard to find something interesting to wear to the party.

She hadn't gotten very far before it started raining. Worried that she might mess up her hair, she sheltered in a cave that happened to be conveniently placed. Once inside the cave, she started to hear hammering sounds. Who could it be? Further down the tunnel, she could see a light shimmering. As she went closer, she saw that it was a massive cavern! And encrusted on the walls of the cavern were precious stones of every shape and sort—gold, silver, diamonds, emeralds, rubies, and sapphires. What she also saw were hundreds of tiny little men beating hard at the walls with their picks and shovels, trying to extract the precious stones. They were the goblins—evil, mean, and cruel little creatures—and greedy to boot.

However, as cruel as they were, they were very skilled at making stunning jewelry. Some of them were clustered around a table, looking at something. It flashed as bright as the sun and shimmered against the cave walls. As she approached, drawn nearer by the stunning light, they all turned to look at her. She saw that they were holding a necklace of great beauty. With evil grins on their wicked little faces, they said, "Welcome Goddess Freya!" They offered to give her the necklace, at a price. "What was the price?" she asked. "A kiss for all of us!" they answered. At first, she hesitated, repulsed by the thought of kissing all those grimy little faces. But she wanted that necklace so very badly she was willing to do anything. So, she kissed each one of the hideous little faces and then grabbed the necklace and ran out of the cave, all the way back to her home where she met her husband Odur.

Feeling rather pleased with herself, she showed the necklace to her husband. "How did you get it?" he asked sternly. When she replied and told him all she had done, he grew pale with rage and shame. He ran from the house over the rainbow bridge and was gone.

Freya was heartbroken and told her tale to Odin, asking him if she could return the necklace to the goblins. But he refused, saying that she was to wear it for eternity as a curse. As she was nursing her grief, an unexpected helper came to her — the trickster god Loki. He noticed that she had been crying and that she wanted to get rid of the necklace. He, too, was fond of jewelry. He waited until she was asleep in her room, took the form of a fly, and flew in and landed on her pillow while she was sleeping. Turning himself into a bird, he grasped the necklace in his beak and flew out of the window with it.

However, he forgot that Heimdall could see everything that went on in the city of Asgard, and didn't realize that he had been spotted by him. Heimdall rode after Loki shouting, "Stop thief!" But Loki refused to stop. "You'll have to catch me first!" he called. And with that, he said the magic words and turned himself into a fireball. But Heimdall was unimpressed. "Do you think you are the only one with magic powers?" he responded, and turned himself into a rain cloud, drenching Loki and putting out the fire. Grabbing the thief, Heimdall took the necklace from him and went before Odin. "Shall I return it to Freya?" he asked Odin. "No," Odin replied. "She has learned her lesson. Return it to the goblin cave and tell her husband it is time for him to return."

Thor Against the Frost Giants

Thor was noted as the mighty god of thunder, and there were few who dared cross his will. However, one day, he had an encounter with some titanic creatures and learned a valuable lesson from the experience. One day, Thor, the god of thunder, went to Odin and announced that he was going to the land of frost and ice to pick a fight with some frost giants. Loki was with Odin at the time, who thought the matter a merry affair. Nonetheless, he consented to let Thor go on the adventure, and Loki went with him. Setting off in Thor's chariot which was pulled by two goats, they crossed the rainbow bridge all the way to the land of Midgard, where they halted before a rickety, broken down cottage. They knocked on the door and asked if they might stay the night. What little food the villagers had was set before the gods, and it wasn't very nice, but then Thor had an idea. Raising his hammer above his head, he brought it down on the head of one of the goats, killing them. So, with meat now provided, they all sat around and had a merry meal of goat stew.

Now Thor had expressly forbidden anyone at the table to crack open the bones, but Loki ignored him and told the villagers that they could do what they liked. So, the unwitting villager cracked open the bone he was eating and sucked out the marrow that was inside. When it came to the end of the meal, they all lay down to sleep.

The next morning, Thor once again raised his hammer over his head, said the magic words, and all at once, the goats were back to their normal selves. Except, a part of one leg of one of the goats appeared to be missing, and that goat was now limping around. "Loki!" roared Thor, knowing at once who was responsible.

So, they continued their journey to the frost giants' country, all the way to the mystical land of Jotunheim. All at once, they found themselves there and a huge mansion stood before them with a peculiar round opening in it but no door. Thor entered through the doorway, confidently followed by the others. They found themselves in a room with a large open hallway and five small narrow rooms at the end of it. As they settled down to rest for the night, they felt a massive shaking beneath them, like the sounds of an earthquake. An eye appeared in the round doorway they had entered through. A large voice called out, "What are you doing in my glove?"

They realized that they were in a giant's glove and the narrow 'rooms' at the end were where the fingers went. With a roar, Thor flung himself at the giant and struck him on the head with his hammer. But it had no effect on the giant. He simply yawned and said, "Someone's throwing acorns at me again." Even angrier, Thor threw the hammer at the giant's eye, with the same result. "Oh dear, there seem to be a lot of flies around today. One just flew into my eye," the giant said in a bored voice. Now absolutely enraged, Thor struck the giant on the skull with all his force, the hardest blow he could muster. "Oh dear, it seems like some bird has done his droppings on my head," the giant lamented, not at all bothered. He let out a hearty laugh and strode away. The giant, whose name was Skrymnir, said as he was leaving: "Farewell my friends! Tell your king how you tickled Skrymnir today." But Thor was determined to go after him and defeat him.

Following the giant's footsteps, which were very large, Thor and Loki arrived at a large and stony cavern, and found there a number of giants feasting, sitting in a circle. "It is I, Thor, god of thunder!" Thor announced. They all looked at him, including Skrymnir. "Oh, it's you again?" he looked at Thor quizzically. "Well, what do you want?" he asked. "To feast with you before I do battle with you," Thor answered. "Do you think you're fit to feast with us?" they asked him. "I can drink like no other god in Asgard," Thor answered. "Very well," they answered.

"Drink this cup empty and we will believe you're stronger than us." It was a cup shaped like a horn with a wide mouth and a point at one end. But try as he might, Thor could not finish the liquid in the horn. He drank and drank and still the horn was filled to the brim. Eventually, he had to give up. He had failed the first challenge. "No matter," said Thor. "I'll beat you in a feat of strength." "Very well," the giants replied. If you can lift our cat off the ground, we'll believe you're stronger than us." The cat was very large, belonging, as it were, to a giant. Try as he might, Thor could not lift the cat off the ground, only managing to lift a single paw. He had failed the second challenge. Finally, he said, "Enough! This time I will beat the strongest of you in hand-to-hand combat." The giants agreed to this and sent for the goddess Hel to wrestle with Thor.

When she arrived, Thor was insulted. She was a tiny, shriveled old woman. So they wrestled. Before Thor could even cry out, she had him on the ground and pinned, and he could not move a muscle. Three times he had failed, and he now accepted his defeat. Before he left, Skrymnir said that it had all been by magic. You see, the reason why Thor could not finish the liquid in the horn was because one end is dipped into the sea and the sea can never be overcome. The reason he failed the second challenge was because the cat was not a cat at all, but a serpent who's tail wrapped around the whole earth and could never be dislodged.

The reason he failed the third challenge was because, being death itself, Hel could never be beaten by anyone. No one can win against death.

Enraged, Thor aimed a mighty blow at the head of Skrymnir, but the giant only laughed mockingly and disappeared into thin air before they could move, leaving the two gods speechless and ashamed.

The Apples of Iduna

One of the most well-known stories in Viking lore is the story of how Iduna was abducted, and the gods had to go and rescue her. It was a well-known fact that Iduna was the goddess who kept the apples that were the secret to eternal youth. Every day, the gods and goddesses of Asgard would eat the apples and grow a little younger. In this way, they were effectively immortal and immune to aging. One day, Odin decided to go on a trip and he took Loki with him. While they were waiting for the daily meal which was being cooked by Loki, Odin looked up and saw a bird sitting in a tree outside. It said, "Give me some of your stew and it will cook faster!" The two gods were surprised, but the bird kept repeating the same words over and over. Loki attempted to strike the bird with a big stick, but it grabbed the stick and started to carry Loki away. The bird's name was Thiassi, but he was really a frost giant.

Eventually Loki cried so hard that the bird said, "Give me something and I will put you down in return." Loki agreed to this and then asked the bird what he wanted. "Revenge on the gods," it answered. "Why?" Loki asked. "I don't know yet," answered the bird. "Help me find out." Loki took the bird to Iduna's garden. He called Iduna and told her that he had seen some apples that were better than the ones in her garden. He asked her to come with him, but she refused, saying that the gods might be in need of the apples. Eventually, though, he persuaded her and she came out carrying her basket. But as they were leaving, a voice from the treetops called out, "Don't go, Iduna!" Thiassi swooped out of the sky and grabbed Iduna, carrying her into the sky. Loki watched her go from the ground. She was gone for two weeks. However, with Iduna gone, there were no more apples of youth. The gods started to age, including Loki. So, they had to make a plan to get her back.

At this time, the all-seeing Heimdall went to Odin and told him that he'd seen Loki, Thiassi, and Iduna together. From this it was easy for them to discover what had happened. Odin was very angry and promised to punish Loki when he returned from rescuing Iduna. Loki turned into a falcon and sped towards the frost giant's castle. He sat on a window sill and listened to Iduna and the frost giant talking. He wanted the magic apples.

He took all of them that were in Iduna's basket, but as soon as he touched them, they shrivelled up like little peas. Frustrated, he threw the basket back at her and said that she would be locked up forever. Loki flew into the room and turned into his normal shape. She was not pleased to see him, but eventually he convinced her that they needed to go back together. He turned her into a sparrow and her basket into an apple pip. Turning back into a falcon, he flew with her all the way back to Asgard.

However, the angry Thiassi had followed them and turned himself into an eagle. He followed them all the way back to Asgard. "What are we going to do? cried the little sparrow. Odin saw them coming and commanded that every twig and branch be gathered. Loki and Iduna saw that Heimdall was on the ground building a big fire. As the flames from the fire started to leap higher and higher, they heated the wings of Thiassi. He crashed to the ground while Loki and Iduna changed back to their original forms and were unharmed. The basket of apples also turned back to its original form. The gods could finally taste the fruit again, and return to their younger selves. Thus ended the story of Loki and his flight with Iduna.

These are some of the tales of Viking lore. They give insight into a truly unique and interesting culture.

Chapter 5: The Viking Army and Famous Battles

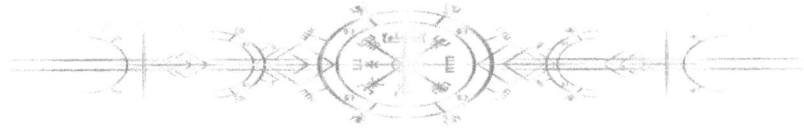

How Did the Vikings Fight?

If there was one thing that the Vikings were known for, it is the fact that they were great warriors. In fact, their military prowess is considered to be the stuff of legend. Viking warriors were not noted for their tactical acumen, and it was not on par with some of the best armies in the world at that time, but they were unparalleled in individual combat. Their awe-inspiring troops operated on the principle of fear, and this gave them the mental edge in battle. So magnificent were Viking warriors in battle that they were often thought to have mystical powers with the way they fought.

Viking troops did not fight in formation usually, although they did make use of some rudimentary formations. This may have been because they were not educated enough in this style of warfare to make it effective. Their movement was described as being like bees swarming all over the enemy and overwhelming them before they could recover or realize what was happening to them. These tactics were especially effective against the small, unarmed towns they often came into contact with.

One of the most well-known types of Viking troops was called a 'berserker.' This was a kind of warrior which was said to have been imbued with the power of the gods. They seemed to be almost immune to physical injury on the battlefield, and were known for entering sudden rages that would render the enemy helpless against their onslaught. Hence, the name 'berserker.'

One of the reasons that the Vikings were so successful on the battlefield is that they ignored much of what was thought to be conventional military discipline and tactics. Instead, they relied on their emotions to guide them in battle. Vikings were not above using any and every tactic to win a fight, including using deceit and subversion. Their mentality was a win-at-all-costs one. This is evident in literature detailing the history of the battles that they fought.

Vikings on the Ocean

One of the areas where the Vikings thrived most of all, of course, was the ocean. They were unparalleled in naval battles and their longships did not seem to be troubled much by the navies they encountered—even some of the most powerful navies in the world. Viking naval combat was swift and deadly, often known for its ambush-style tactics. The Vikings could be the aggressors and attack directly, but they could also be subversive and wait for the enemy to come to them if they needed to. A common tactic seemed to be that they would beach their ships and attack the beach and the forces on it en-masse, almost like a resisted landing in modern warfare. Vikings would attack the beachhead, or other area, using a wedge-like formation with the best troops stationed at the front.

The Great Heathen Army

After around 865 AD, the Vikings formed into a more organized army unit, composed of men from different regions of Scandinavia and Denmark primarily. The aim of this coalition was a targeted assault on the Northern English territories. Before this coalition was formed, the Vikings had only been making sporadic assaults on various monasteries around the coastlines of various European countries. This force, however, was much larger and aimed to seize and capture territory with a long-term focus.

The name "Great Heathen Army" was taken from a set of chronicles written in 865. The expedition was led by the four out of the five sons of a chieftain named Ragnar Lodbrok. Their names were Halfdan Ragnarsson, Ivar the Boneless, Bjorn Ironside, and Ubba. The timeframe for the existence of this coalition and its activities lasted for about 14 years. The large invading force first landed at East Anglia, where they were given horses and promised to spare the inhabitants of that region. After dwelling at Thetford for a number of months, they marched north to capture York. York had belonged to both the Romans and, much later, the Anglo Saxons.

During 867, the group marched into Mercia. After agreeing terms with the Mercian army, the group moved back to York in 869 but returned to East Anglia much later on and killed the king there. In 871, they invaded Wessex, where they were given money to leave by Alfred the Great. The next seasons were spent reinforcing their already formidable ranks in preparation for an attack on Mercia. In the years that followed, Mercia was overrun. After the king of Mercia fled across the ocean, it seems that the group divided itself into two groups: One went to Wessex, and the other went to Northumbria.

In May 878, the Vikings were finally overcome and agreed to peace terms with Alfred the Great. They would be allowed to settle in Northern England and establish a more permanent presence there.

The size and composition of the group is a matter of debate. Sources claim that a raiding party would be around 35 men. This was the smaller 'unit', as it were, of the Viking army. The Viking king issued a proclamation that any party smaller than this number would be considered a raiding band, and not part of the main army. This was to differentiate between the larger and smaller Viking forces.

As for the Viking ships themselves, they were of the smaller variety and could carry around 35 men. These smaller ships had their advantages and disadvantages. They could slip into enemy waters unnoticed and were far quicker than anything the European forces could muster, which gave them a huge advantage in battle. By this, historians have concluded that the average Viking fleet could consist of about 1,000 men, far smaller than anything they could face. But they had the advantage of morale and training. During the Viking raids on various European countries, they augmented their forces by forced conscription and by paying off men to join their army.

The invasion started in 865 in East Anglia. The Vikings were offered money by the people of Kent in return for peace, but they raided and pillaged the area anyway. Further invasion of British regions followed, and the Vikings installed puppet rulers in these places, such as in Northumbria in 867.

In 871, a large force called the "Great Summer Army" arrived in Wessex and engaged the forces of Alfred the Great, where they were defeated. It was one of the first major military reverses of the Viking age, and it brought with it a new understanding of how their forces could be tamed. In the wake of these battles, the Viking group split into two and settled in two distinct parts of England. They became farmers and started to establish themselves as a presence there. Further victories over the Vikings by Alfred the Great in 878 meant that these newer groups of warriors had to sign peace treaties and accords with the people living on the land. It was agreed that the Vikings should take portions of English territory for their own, and boundaries were clearly demarcated between these territories.

In the aftermath of repeated conflicts in the late 9th century, King Alfred realized the value of having a strong navy and set about the creation of it. It is possible that this realization and the beginnings of the British navy would set the scene for their naval dominance over the next thousand years. The English navy would always be known as one of the strongest in Europe, if not the world. Their proximity to the water made this a necessity, and the Viking raids only served to underline the importance of this fact.

King Alfred also fortified the coastal cities and generally strengthened English defences, cleverly making use of old Roman cities that were already strong. Because of the speed of Viking raids, Alfred the Great needed a force that could be quickly mobilized—and so a standing army was created. By the 10th century, it seemed that the Viking raids had all but ceased, and the strength of their army shattered. They were still a latent threat, but the fortitude of yesteryear was gone. Broke and without leadership, many migrated to Europe and settled there while others spread out from their cities of Northumbria and East Anglia. They did still, however, control much of Northern England. The Vikings, on the whole, saw no real reason to keep expanding into the British and European territories.

So, how did the Viking army fight and what were their weapons like? The nature of Viking warfare was to attack quickly and to get out as soon as possible. Viking terror started with the very nature of their attacks. The way they attacked was unexpected, and they used the cover of darkness to hide their movements. Their ships were specifically designed to cut through the water as smoothly and with as little friction as possible. The lightness of their ships made it so they could traverse shallower waters, and therefore they were able to access areas with their ships that were difficult. The mobility of the Vikings was not a new trait in warfare. It had been used by many civilizations before them, such as the Huns way back in the 5th century. The idea of raiding and then getting away was still a new phenomenon to many conventional armies.

Viking hardware or weaponry was dependent on the sword, shield, and axe. These were their main tools, and they had the strength to use them well. Attacks were not a free-for- all as are commonly depicted in the media. Instead, they were carefully planned and executed. Viking attacks could be planned for months in advance and were meticulous in nature.

The Viking steel was of an exceptionally good quality and stood up well during the rigors of battle. During the siege of Paris in 885 onwards, the Vikings made use of siege weapons such as catapults, battering rams, and other projectile-based weapons. This showed that far from being just a raiding force, they also had understanding of how to plan and prepare for longer battles.

But far from just the physical side of combat, the Vikings also held the edge mentally. They lived in a violent warrior culture that glorified battle and victory. So, they were always ready to go to war. Let us look at the way in which the Vikings were trained militarily, as this will show why they were able to accomplish great feats in battle.

As in any army, there are different classes of military professionals in the Viking regiments. Although they were unconventional in their style of warfare, they still kept organized in different groups of soldiers, from the most experienced and dangerous to the least professional. Training was everything to Viking warriors and they pushed themselves hard in battle.

Training could include running, swimming, jumping, various physical activities such as lifting heavy weights like rocks and logs, and many other kinds of disciplines. For specific kinds of Viking warriors, different kinds of exercises were required. They learned how to move and attack as a group, how to defend in a shield wall (a noted tactic of Viking warriors), and many other defensive and offensive disciplines.

More wealthy Viking warriors could have men under their command. These groups of men were known as *hird*. The bigger a man's *hird* was, the more wealthy he was seen to be, and the more influential he was. He could be seen to be someone who was capable of protecting himself and everything he owned. These groups of men practiced in the pig's snout formation, which was a wedge-shaped arrangement used by the Vikings. It was meant to crack open enemy lines with the narrower point of the wedge. The shield wall was also widely practiced, but this was more of a defensive maneuver.

Vikings would train by actively pushing against opposition shield walls (amongst themselves). By doing so, they strengthened their forces, and gained a sense of the resistance needed in order to hold back the enemy during the battle.

From a young age, Vikings were trained to be battle-hardened and ready for war. It was necessary to instill the proper techniques that they would need in later years. Young boys and children got used to using their weapons before they became men. By the time they were grown, they were proficient in using many different kinds of weapons due to their long years of training. They became experts in using swords, spears, shields, bows and arrows, and axes. All of these weapons required their own special kind of training and innate skill to be able to master them, and it was considered essential for a Viking to master both offensive and defensive techniques.

Due to the Viking way of life and the savage nature of their culture, many did also die young. Life expectancy during this time must have been much lower for the Vikings, as opposed to other cultures where war was not glorified in such a way. But to the Vikings, death was just another adventure in their journey.

Famous Viking Warriors

In a culture such as the Vikings, military figures and warriors feature highly amongst some of their most famous people ever. This does not mean that there were not other people of high status in Viking culture (i.e. kings, nobles, royals, artists and writers). However, being an expansionist culture, men who went to war held a special status. What follows is a list of some of the most notable people in these wars and what their accomplishments were.

Ragnar Lothbrok

Ragnar Lothbrok is considered to be one of the most influential figures in Viking history. He was a great warrior and military commander during his time. He frequently led men on raiding missions of the English and European coastlines. At some point, he attempted to invade France and was offered 7000 lbs of silver to turn around and leave by the Frankish King Charles. He met his demise while on a raiding mission off the English coast in around 852, although there is a debate about the date of his death. He attempted to assault English forces with just two Viking ships and was captured, being subsequently killed by being thrown into a pit filled with vipers.

Rollo of Normandy

King Rollo was one of the first Norman kings in France, and left an indelible mark on French, Viking, and European culture. In 911, he signed treaties with the king in France, which allowed the Vikings to settle there. Included in the deal was the provision that he would protect France from any further Viking raids. He died in 928, and his son William Longsword took his place. His descendents, the mighty Normans, were responsible for invading English in 1066, leading to significant changes in English culture for centuries to come.

Egil Skallgrimsson

Egil Skallgrimsson was a complicated figure in Viking lore due to his complex personality and volatile nature. He was a true artist and was responsible for creating some of the most beautiful poems in all of Viking literature. From a young age, he was a violent and brutal individual, killing another boy at the age of just seven. His tumultuous nature carried on into later life, and he was part of prolific raiding teams. For a period of time, he had a blood-feud with another great warrior king named Erik Bloodaxe, who sent men to kill him and his son.

However, Skallgrimsson killed every man who was sent to assassinate him. When he was eventually taken captive, he appeared before Erik Bloodaxe and constructed a poem of great beauty and emotion. So impressed was the king by his poetry that he decided to spare Skallgrimsson's life.

Cnut the Great

Cnut the Great was one of the greatest warriors in Viking history. He was responsible for conquering most of England in 1013. After his father's death, Cnut made treaties with King Edmund of England and was allowed to remain there. After King Edmund's death, he assumed leadership of the whole of England. During and after his rule, Scandinavia experienced a period of stability and flourished greatly. He died in 1035 and his son Harthacnut took over until his own death in 1042.

Harald Hadrada

Harald Hadrada led possibly the last major Viking incursion into Europe, namely England. He is most noted for conducting the Viking forces at the battle of Stamford Bridge. He could be considered to be the last of the truly great Viking chieftains.

His name means "hard ruler" in the Viking language. As a young man, he spent time in Eastern Europe and worked as a mercenary there. Later, he joined the prestigious Varangian Guard in the Middle East. After gaining wealth and power, he returned to Scandinavia and ruled Norway with the help of Magnus the Good. He then became embroiled in a battle with Svein Estrithsson, which ended with Hadrada giving up his right to the throne, and instead focusing on defeating the English instead.

He invaded England in 1066 and won a great victory at the battle of Fulford Gate. Encouraged by these early successes, he decided to push the assault even further. He faced the English forces under the leadership of Harold Godwinson, and was overwhelmingly defeated by him, leading to his death during the battle. Harold Godwinson himself would be killed a short time later at the Battle of Hastings against William the Conqueror. These battles marked the end of the Viking raids on England and Europe.

Bjorn Ironside

The son of Ragnar Lothbrok, Bjorn Ironside inherited his father's ruthless nature and desire for conquest. He is noted for his triumphs in Southern Europe and the surrounding regions. According to *12 Famous Viking Warriors You Should Know* (2020), one of his most notable victories came when he infiltrated the town of Luna, pretending to be dead. When his men took his apparently lifeless body inside the city, he jumped out of the coffin and fought his way through towards the gates, where he let his men inside, leading to a glorious rout of the enemy. He continued to raid, pillage, and plunder for many years after this. But one day, during a battle, things went wrong, and he lost 40 or more ships during a single skirmish. After this incident, he retired to Sweden where he saw out the last of his days in ease and comfort as the king of that region.

Erik the Red

Erik the Red is most noted for being one of the first Europeans (if not the first) to land on the shores of Greenland. He was ruthless, violent, and had a dangerous temper. After his father was expelled from Norway for killing a man, he went to Iceland where he lived out his formative years. However, after killing several men himself, he was expelled from Iceland, and decided to take on the life of a nomad.

Returning to Iceland several years later, he recruited several hundred men and set sail for Greenland where he established a colony there. His son, Leif Erikson, was the first man to reach the shores of the New World, or as we call it today, America.

Ivar the Boneless

Ivar the Boneless was the father of the noted Ragnar Lothbrok, one of the most influential figures in Viking military history. He led the Great Heathen Army to York, where they overcame the forces of King Edmund and settled there. His unusual name came from the fact that he was born with a condition that rendered his bones more liable to break than that of other men. Hence, his reputation as a great warrior was well-earned.

Famous Viking Battles

Vikings took part in many battles over the course of their history. Some they won, and some they lost. But they always fought bravely and to the last man. Examining these battles gives an insight into the Viking way of fighting and the tactics they used. It helps us to understand their mindset in battle. The following list gives an account of the most famous Viking battles in history, and also highlights how each battle shaped and was shaped by the historical context it was fought in. No battle is ever fought in a vacuum. There is always a political and historical context to every conflict. Let us look at Viking battles that shaped history.

York

The Battle of York was fought in around 866, when a massive force known as the Great Heathen Army attacked the kingdom of Northumbria and took it over. One year prior, the people of East Anglia had sued for peace, but it was not to last long as the Vikings came back in even greater numbers.

The Vikings took advantage of the element of surprise they had over their hapless victims and massacred them in the freezing English winter, when they were least prepared for it.

This battle marked the last rites of the Northumbrian kingdom, and the Vikings effectively established a presence in the North of England.

Englefield

The Battle of Englefield was fought in 870 between the Vikings and the inhabitants of the town of Reading in Berkshire. These men were West Saxons. Before this, the Vikings had been inhabiting Wessex. The Vikings marched towards Englefield, led by the Viking leader Sidrac. Aethelwulf of Berkshire was the leader of the West Saxon forces, and led his men to a hard fought victory over the Vikings, who retreated with heavy losses.

Ashdown

The town of Reading was once again in the spotlight in 871 when Viking raiders sailed down the Thames and took over the town of Reading. At this time, feast days were being celebrated by British soldiers. It was, in fact, Christmas, and everyone on the English side was in a merry mood. The English army mobilized but were pushed back as far as Englefield where the Vikings followed them. Unfortunately for the Vikings, the British forces fought back and routed them. They attacked them again and were again defeated by the great leader Alfred, who was only 22 years old at the time.

Edington

Edington was an early battle in the Viking age between the Viking and English forces. It represented one of the major English reverses over the Vikings, at that time when they seemed so dominant. The Great Heathen Army attacked the forces of Alfred the Great at Wessex. The Vikings encountered an unexpected defeat, and the Viking leader Guthrum agreed to be baptized and converted to Christianity at that time.

Maldon

The Battle of Maldon was fought between the Vikings and the West Saxons around the year 991. The commander of the Saxons was called Ealdorman Byrhtnoth, and the Viking commander was called Swein Forkbeard. The West Saxon commander approached the battle with far fewer forces than the Vikings and was soundly defeated, having to pay the victorious commander 10,000 Roman pounds of silver in tribute.

Stamford Bridge

The Battle of Stamford Bridge represented the end of the Viking age and the end of their military might. It was fought between the English forces of King Harold II, and the Viking forces of Harald Hadrada from Norway. In 1066, the Viking king was killed along with most of his army. The English cavalry won this battle in overwhelming fashion, and crushed the idea of Viking invulnerability forever. There would be other battles, but it was clear that the Vikings were not the force they once were. Their reign of terror was over.

Chapter 6: Viking Language

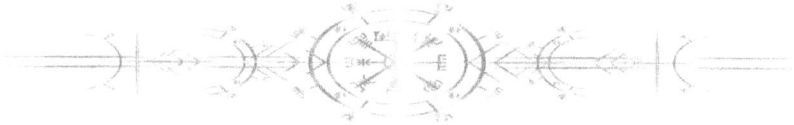

Out of all the evidence of the Viking age that is left behind, there is one crucial element that many people miss, that is the most important piece of history we have about the Vikings. It stays with us in our speech and it impacts the way we communicate with others. It is the Viking language itself, passed down from generation to generation in many forms.

We still make use of the Viking language today, in modern times, especially in English. There are little traces of the Vikings in the way we speak to each other.

What Was the Viking Language Like?

What did the Viking language look like? It surely looked nothing like what we have today in our own modern languages. It was written in a completely different script and would be impossible for us to decipher nowadays.

Nonetheless, there are similarities in some instances. Certain words sound alike and sounds have been passed down through the centuries. But what did the Vikings used to write with? What was their alphabet like? We have the answer: They used runes. These runes were symbols that the Vikings used to communicate with each other through the written word. Let's look briefly at how these runes work. Each symbol represented a specific sound in the Viking language, just as our own alphabet represents different sounds in English. However, runes went beyond just the written sound, to being symbolic of mystical elements in Viking culture. Vikings made use of runes as a way of warding off evil and in spells and rituals. By using runes, they believed they could heal people, imbue objects with magic properties, predict the future, protect themselves or other people, and conjure curses or blessings. Their literature, including the sagas and famous poems known as 'Eddas', were all written using runes. Runes were used all across Scandinavia and in Iceland as well. It is worth noting that the Vikings spoke many languages using different scripts, but the one that most people talk about is Old Norse. Let us look a little more closely at Old Norse and what it looked like.

Old Norse

Old Norse was a Northern Germanic language. It had its roots predominantly in Northern European countries—and in Western Europe as well—just after the time of the Roman Empire. Old Norse was used in Scandinavia from about the ninth to the thirteenth century amongst the Vikings. The name of the language that came before Old Norse was known as 'Proto-Norse', and this was spoken before the eighth century. There were different types of Old Norse, or different dialects. Let us look at some of these dialects. There were three main ones: Old West Norse, Old East Norse, and Old Gutnish ("What language did the Vikings speak?" 2019).

Old West Norse came out of Old Icelandic and Old Norweigan. It was spoken in the British Isles, Normandy, France, and areas of Scotland. Old East Norse was spoken in Denmark and Sweden, as well as further East in what would eventually become Russia and Ukraine. Old Gutnish was an obscure language that was heard on the Swedish island of Gotland. It has its roots in Old Gothic, which is a language now extinct in Germany.

The written form of Old Norse is called the 'Runic' language. Following on from Old Norse, we have the more modern Icelandic, which came to prominence after the ninth century, and which still continues to be used to this day. More forms of Icelandic are influenced by Danish and Gaelic. Old Icelandic is the language which formed much of the writings by famed Scandinavian historian Snorri Sturluson. Anglo-Saxon is another language that has its origins in Old Scandinavian languages. It came before Old English, and has its roots in Celtic and Latin, as well as other Germanic languages. One of the best known Anglo-Saxon works is the famed text *Beowulf*, which many still read today. Another work which is closely associated with Finnish, Old Norse, Anglo-Saxon, and Old English is the work of J.R.R. Tolkien, more specifically his critically acclaimed series of books called *The Lord of the Rings*. The languages used in these books closely mirror the patterns of old Scandinavian and Germanic languages from the Viking period. These patterns can be seen in the way the Elvish (Quenya, Sindarin) and Dwarvish (Khuzdul) languages are constructed in the novels.

Below is a verse from the Poetic Edda, *Völuspá*, stanza 19 (The Poetic Edda, 2019). The language is Old Norse.
Ask veit ek standa,
heitir Yggdrasill,
hár baðmr, ausinn
hvíta auri;
þaðan koma döggvar,

þærs í dala falla,
stendr æ yfir grænn
Urðarbrunni.

One immediately recognizes a few things about the language in this poem. What immediately jumps out is the name Yggdrasill, or the name of the great tree that stands at the center of the mythical Viking universe. The translation of the poem is as follows (The Poetic Edda, 2019):

There stands an ash
called Yggdrasill,
A mighty tree showered
in white hail.
From there come the dews
that fall in the valleys.
It stands evergreen above
Urd's Well.

From what this poem tells us, we can deduce that it is introducing one of the Viking stories in the sagas and is setting the scene for what follows. One can also note the naturalistic imagery that is used in the poem.

The only names that one might not understand if one was an outsider are the hints to specific items or places within Viking mythology, such as *Urd's Well*. This text shows the Viking propensity for using trees in their poems, songs, and stories. It also showed that they believed that nature and the elements had mystical powers. It gives us a lot of insight into how they viewed the world and the environment.

The most interesting thing about the Viking languages is that they have had a clear influence on our own English usage today. Many of the words that we don't even take notice of have their roots in Old Norse. If one looks at the way in which English is structured, you can quite clearly see the influence of these ancient languages on the spelling of specific words.
Let us look at the history and development of one specific and very common word in the English language. This word is 'wrong.' Many people wouldn't suspect that it actually originated from Old Norse, and the word *rangr*. Over time, it changed to 'vrang' in the Danish language, which eventually became our modern 'wrong.'

One can see that words can evolve into different forms as time passes. The example of 'wrong' can be applied to many other words in the English language today. And language is always changing. One day, people might look back on English as we do on the ancient Viking languages and think and say the same things we do now.

Several other words that came from Old Norse are also common in the English language today. Examples of these words include: Guest (*gestr*), egg (*egg*), gift (*gipt*), want (*vant*), anger (*angra*), trust (*traust*), and score (*skor*). The names of the days of the week are unmistakably taken from Old Norse, such as the words 'Friday' (Frigg's day) and 'Thursday' (Thor's day).

The amazing thing about Old Norse and Viking languages is that there is a ton of material available for us today to learn and understand this language better.

The Viking Language Throughout History

The earliest Viking language evidence that we have is found in Denmark, in an inscription called the Vimose Comb. The Vikings were not called Vikings at this point as it was the year 160 AD. The inscription is in a runic language called "Elder Futhark."

Let us look more closely at the runic alphabet itself. It was divided into distinctive periods in which it underwent significant changes. Sometimes these periods overlapped with each other. These periods were Elder Futhark, Younger Futhark, Anglo-Saxon Futhorc, and Medieval Futhorc, the last of which appeared in around the 13th century.

Elder Futhark contained about 24 runic letters. The name of the language comes from the sounds of the first 6 letters of the alphabet. There are only a few surviving examples of this language because the inscriptions were usually carved on wood, which unfortunately does not survive over time. Thus, much has been lost to the elements. However, from what we do have, we're left with a good understanding of what this runic system was like. Some of these inscriptions are also inscribed into items such as jewelry and coins, which has survived much better. However, why these items were inscribed with the language is unknown at this point. Younger Futhark was the written language of the Vikings, and it is a very much more refined version of the language with a reduced number of runes.

The problem with Viking writings is that because we as modern historians lack context about the inscriptions and etchings on various objects, the overall meaning of these phrases and ideas is lost. There is much that is still not understood about the Viking language and the way that they thought and acted.

Runestones

Runes are the best evidence of Viking language that we have, because they do not disintegrate, and the etchings are clearly visible to modern historians. These are very large stones with many different writings on them, found in various places throughout the Viking world. Let us look at specific examples of these runestones: One particular group was discovered in English, with a number of runic writings on them describing the Viking raids in England and their purpose there. Many tales and stories of Viking accomplishments and their victories are recorded within these inscriptions. As the influence of paganism in Viking culture faded, so did the frequency of these inscriptions. They also started to show more of a Latin influence with the advent of Christianity in Viking culture.

Poetic Edda

Another one of the best examples of Viking language that we have is called the "Poetic Edda." These poems are some of the most important resources that we have about Viking writing.

These writings are a recorded account of stories and oral recollections, passed down from generation to generation of Viking families and writers. They tell of the historical sagas and adventures of Viking warriors, and other similar stories. The influences of these Eddas are widespread, and many other writers, authors, poets, and artists have made use of them in their own work, many centuries later. Let us look at some of the examples of people who have been impacted by these works. They generally tend to focus on pagan themes in

Norse mythology, and so are sought after by writers and authors who are interested in these topics for their own benefit. The works of Wagner are heavily impacted by the Eddas, and J.R.R. Tolkien raided the works and used their material to influence the creation of his own fantasy world.

The Uses of Viking Language

Different forms of the Viking language had different uses in society, much like how we do in English today. They used more formal or less formal versions of particular languages depending on the social situation they found themselves in. The language that was most commonly used amongst common folk in their daily life and in informal situations would have been Old Norse.

In pagan rituals and in religious ceremonies, they might have used a more formal version of the language. Much still remains to be discovered. However, one thing that is clear is that post-pagan Viking culture relied much more on the Latin influences in their language. This is clearly evident within their religious texts from the time. One way in which we can see how the language changes is to look at the way in which the references to specific pagan images changed. Allusions to items, objects, beasts, and other items not associated with Christianity naturally decreased as the mindset changed.

Chapter 7: What Happened to the Vikings?

The final question we should ask ourselves is what exactly happened to the Vikings? Where did their culture go, and what did they do once they started to settle in Europe? Much remains unanswered, but by examining the literature and historical evidence we have, we can learn a lot about where they went and what their eventual fate was. There are several schools of thought about what happened to the Vikings and the factors that led up to the inevitable end of the Viking age. Let us start by examining the factors that led to the weakening and fading away of their power.

Factors Leading to Viking Decline

Strengthened Opposition

During the arbitrarily defined period from 793 to 1066, the people of Northern Europe had the greatest impact on Europe through their activities—either through their raids or through trade and industry. This is why this time is called the period of Viking dominance or Viking age. When the Vikings first launched their raids on the English and European coastlines, their presence caused great fear amongst people living in those lands. But over time, as the people of those countries grew stronger and more technologically advanced, they became more adept at dealing with the Viking raids. By the time the turn of the millennium came, the British forces in particular had strengthened greatly both militarily and on the ocean, which had traditionally been the Viking's greatest strength. Faced with more significant opposition on the sea, the Vikings could not always break through, even to make their famed raids, and thus one of their chief weapons was no longer as effective.

Weakened Viking Army

The Great Heathen Army of the 9th century could be said to be the high point of Viking dominance on the continent. It contained probably the largest force of Nordic warriors that there would ever be in a single standing army. After it split apart, it grew significantly weaker. Other smaller forces followed, but those would never be able to replicate the original army in terms of its size, organization, leadership, and strength. Periodically, the Vikings would send armies over into Britain and other countries, but they were often defeated by British and Germanic army leaders. This was because they had gotten to know how they worked and were able to counter their tactics. As they faced a shortage of funding and supplies, the Vikings were forced to adopt other tactics besides using military might.

Changing Viking Mindset

It can be said that by the time the Viking army was on the wane and no longer raiding Europe as frequently as it did in the past, Viking attitudes towards conquest had changed. To put it simply they did not seem all that concerned with expanding beyond the territories they had conquered. It is fair to say that Vikings, although weakened militarily, still controlled vast swathes of North England.

They had established settlements all over Europe where they could live peacefully without needing to go to war with everyone around them. In short: They had no need to go to war, and it showed both in their actions, and in the fact that they pursued peaceful rather than aggressive means.

The Impact of Christianity

Christianity arrived in Viking culture during the time of the turn of the millennium, and it had a great impact on how they saw the world and how they felt about war and military conquest. It is also fair to say that pagan Viking culture tended to view the people they came into contact differently. Christian Viking culture sought to pursue constructive ends, and the formation of friendly trade routes and connections with other countries, regions, and cultures. This seemed to be the new Viking way, established after the battle of 1066, which is heralded as the official end of the Viking age in Europe. There would still be other battles, but Europe had turned its focus away from its Scandinavian invaders in lieu of other more serious conflicts. Christianity could be said to have 'tamed' the Viking invaders, and they held no serious ideas of making any more large scale invasions of Europe.

Changes in Social Structure

When the Vikings started raiding, they were a different society in comparison to that which they ended up as. They were largely independent communities governed by what they called 'kings' but were actually just local rulers or magnates. For the most part, every man was responsible for his own land. This meant that they could build up their resources, and they had the time to go on these raids. By the end of the age, there were no longer any of these men available. Those that remained were wealthy and privileged, preferring instead to adopt an isolationist view. Supporting a family was seen as the most important thing, not conquest. So, one could say that the Viking era died out because they simply did not have the time to be able to engage in these activities anymore.

At the beginning of the Viking age, the kings of Europe were divided, scattered and leaderless. They did not have the strong leadership needed in order to counteract these determined raids. As a result, they were decimated. But as time passed and newer and more effective leaders rose to power, they began to think of new ways to deal with the threat of these raiders, and their attacks diminished ineffectiveness.

Monasteries were initially built on the coastlines, which made them easy targets for the Vikings. Over the years, they were moved inland and fortified against attack, making them less desirable for conquest by the Vikings.

The Final Years of Viking Dominance

Absorption Into European Culture

The events of 1066 had marked the official end of the Viking reign of terror over Europe, but they had been a declining force long before this. This was due to the mass Christianization of Europe and the conversion of the Vikings who were a part of it. In the previous century, the Vikings had lost much of the territory they had won.

The final nail in the coffin was when King Erik Bloodaxe was killed during battle. This meant that the English kingdoms could finally unite under one rule, which made them a much more difficult proposition for the Vikings to take on. But more than just Vikings converting to Christianity and the increased opposition they faced on their raids and conquests, the Vikings were beginning to mix into the people of Europe.

This meant that they no longer had the sense of nationalism that drove them centuries earlier. They were becoming more and more like the people they had set out to conquer. They would still retain a sense of their own heritage, but they no longer had the desire to overcome and kill as they once did. A newer and more peaceable generation was being born that was simultaneously Viking and European—jointly multicultural.

These final years of the Viking age experienced battles, but they also experienced something else: The formation of a different kind of Viking age. This age was one that was built on trust, friendship, trade, and partnership with others rather than all out warfare.

The Aftermath of Viking Expansion

One must also ask the question: What exactly happened after the battles of 1066 and the official end of the Viking age? Did they just stop fighting or did they carry on in their own ways? There are various schools of thought about what they did, and we also have access to historical records that help us understand this post-Viking period.

The first misconception that many people have is that after the Viking empire waned, the people themselves ceased to act like Vikings, and thus disappeared from the European landscape altogether. This is not entirely true. The reality is that they still existed. Did they disappear? Not at all. They went about living their lives as they had done for hundreds of years before that. The only thing that was different was that they, collectively, no longer had the lust for conquest that they once experienced. That was gone, never to return. It can be considered that the Vikings stopped raiding the European countries because it was no longer profitable for them to do so. The Vikings were never conquered. They simply ceased their activities and went about their daily lives as they did before. They became Scandinavians as they always were before. But the memories of past glories would always be with them.

Where Are the Vikings Today?

Asking the question, "Where are the Vikings today" is really the same as asking, "What happened to Viking culture?" We can see that remnants of Viking customs still exist in many countries around the world today. There are even movements set up to mimic what the Vikings were like, in a non-threatening and friendly way. But there are people who have taken this lifestyle upon themselves. These are people who not only dress up in the garb of the Vikings and take their customs upon themselves, but are true Vikings in their attitudes, ways of thinking, and beliefs.

These men and women have dedicated themselves to the preservation of Viking customs and traditions so that the ways of these people never die out. So, who are these people and what are the values that they adhere to? What does it mean to be a true Viking in today's world? Lunde (n.d), states that many Norweigans are working to figure out what their true history was about, and in the process of making these discoveries, they are finding out what it really meant to be a Viking during the Viking age.

Popular places to meet fellow Viking enthusiasts and those who have adopted this type of lifestyle for themselves are what is known as "Viking markets." These markets are not only a great place to buy various kinds of goods and services, but also a great way for fellow modern Vikings to meet with each other and build community. Many of these markets are famous in their own right, as they historically housed Viking kings of the past. Authentic village recreations are also present, faithful to the style of original Viking constructions.

There are many Viking reenactment camps around Scandinavia these days. There are also many thousands of participants who take part in these camps each year as well, and many more fans of the Viking lifestyle abroad. Children are also welcome to learn about the Viking culture and replicate the battles that the Vikings fought for themselves. With the advent of virtual reality, it is possible to feel like you're going back in time with none of the pitfalls of being a Viking. Children can immerse themselves in Viking culture to their heart's content. As one of the modern-day Vikings said, it was like combining the ancient culture with the new. People are drawn to the Viking culture because of the blood and gore and because of the battles and excitement it seems to elicit. But when we look beyond the obvious, we see that they were complex and sensitive people.

Conclusion

Viking culture fascinates many because it speaks to something within us that we can relate to: The fight to succeed and to grow stronger. Vikings only did what they did because they wanted to better themselves, fight for their people, and to expand their territory. Like them, we also desire things for ourselves. But if we don't go out and take what we want, we will never experience the satisfaction of knowing that we did something to improve and further our lives.

We learned that they started off with a vision and a plan, and that they were not afraid to get out of their comfort zone to go and take what they wanted. Their methods may have been questionable, but the heart and attitude of their community can never be questioned. When they achieved what they wanted, they stopped fighting for it, and things changed in their mentality and culture. What this shows is that sometimes in order to survive, you have to keep fighting for what you want. If you stop fighting, things change. And so it is with the cultures of the world.

On the opposite side of the spectrum, what their history demonstrates is that people often thought of as barbaric can undergo a shift in perception, and a change in mentality. Nothing stays the same forever. And when we realize that nothing stays the same, we will stop holding on to memories of the past. We have to allow the past to change us, but we also have to learn when to let it go.

The Vikings themselves showed incredible fight and spirit in adverse circumstances. When they were faced with challenges, they didn't simply carry on as if they believed they were invincible. They withdrew and thought about how to deal with situations they had to overcome. This is the essence of being a true Viking warrior—having the right attitude in every circumstance, having a sense of purpose and of destiny, and having the determination to fight for the things you hold dear.

The reason why the Vikings were successful was not only because they fought well. It was because they knew what they wanted, and they were not afraid to go after it. They had the utmost faith in what they were doing. Throughout their entire history, from the time they first arrived on the shores of the countries they were attacking, they had a sense of pride and certainty in what they wanted to do. In other words, they had clear vision, foresight, and understanding of their enemies. It might have had to do with the fact that they had no choice, a lot of the time.

When they elected to leave their home it was a bold step, and the choices they made after that also needed to reflect this boldness.

So, overall, what we've learned from our journey on the Viking ship, as it were, is that we need to have the right attitude to succeed in life. Without the right attitude, we'll never have the strength and correct mentality to achieve what we want. Remaining where we are might be more comfortable in the long run, but this doesn't necessarily mean we will be safer. What the Vikings have proven throughout their years is that confidence breeds further confidence. If we have the right mentality, we'll never be afraid to take risks. This doesn't mean that we should make uninformed decisions, but that we should allow ourselves to be guided by the right parts of our feelings, as the Vikings did. They were successful because they used the emotion and rage bottled up inside of them to drive them to ever greater heights. The result is the fact that they will be forever remembered as a great and powerful society. The Viking era may have ended, but there is a little of their legacy in all of us. We have to take what they have taught us and apply it to our own lives. By doing so, we can tap into a little of what made them successful: Their tenacity, will to win, fighting spirit, and never-say-die attitude.

References

Ager, B. (2001). *Viking Weapons and Warfare*. BBC. http://www.bbc.co.uk/history/ancient/vikings/weapons_01.shtml

Bartley, J.-A. (2018, May 20). *The Ultimate Guide to a Viking Wedding*. OddFeed. https://oddfeed.net/viking-wedding-ultimate-guide/

BBC. (2016, July 28). *Viking Sagas (Age 7 - 11)*. https://www.bbc.co.uk/programmes/articles/20stJyBvh9mv7kpSVgDfKPw/viking-sagas-age-7-11

BBC Bitesize. (2019, September 16). *Who were the Vikings?* https://www.bbc.co.uk/bitesize/topics/ztyr9j6/articles/zjcxwty

Beer and Mead. (n.d.). National Museum of Denmark. https://en.natmus.dk/historical-knowledge/denmark/prehistoric-period-until-1050-ad/the-viking-age/food/beer-and-mead/

Bread and Porridge in the Viking Age. (n.d.). National Museum of Denmark. https://en.natmus.dk/historical-knowledge/denmark/prehistoric-period-until-1050-ad/the-viking-age/food/bread-and-porridge/

Butler, S. (2019, May 23). *The Surprisingly Sufficient Viking Diet*. HISTORY. https://www.history.com/news/the-surprisingly-sufficient-viking-diet

Campbell, H. (2020, January 27). *12 Famous Viking Warriors You Should Know*. Viking Style. https://viking-styles.com/blogs/history/12-famous-viking-warriors-you-should-know

Christensen, C. (n.d.). *Did the Vikings Have a Written Language? Get the Facts*. Scandinavia Facts. https://scandinaviafacts.com/did-the-vikings-have-a-written-language/

Clothing in the Viking Age. (2019). Hurstwic. http://www.hurstwic.org/history/articles/daily_living/text/clothing.htm

Death in Norse Paganism. (2019a, May 6). In *Wikipedia*. https://en.wikipedia.org/wiki/Death_in_Norse_paganism

Famous Viking Battles. (n.d.). Medieval Chronicles. https://www.medievalchronicles.com/medieval-history/medieval-history-periods/vikings/famous-viking-battles/

Fruit and berries in the Viking Age. (n.d.). National Museum of Denmark. https://en.natmus.dk/historical-knowledge/denmark/prehistoric-period-until-1050-ad/the-viking-age/food/fruit-and-berries/

Great Heathen Army. (2021, May 25). In *Wikipedia.* https://en.wikipedia.org/wiki/Great_Heathen_Army

Great Viking Food - What Did The Vikings Eat For Over 300 Years? (2019). Medieval Chronicles. https://www.medievalchronicles.com/medieval-history/medieval-history-periods/vikings/viking-foods/

History. (2019, June 7). *Vikings.* https://www.history.com/topics/exploration/vikings-history

Horte, R. M. J. (n.d.). *The Viking Age Geography.* Vikingeskibsmuseet I Roskilde. https://www.vikingeskibsmuseet.dk/en/professions/education/viking-knowledge/the-viking-age-geography

Human Sacrifices? (2019). National Museum of Denmark. https://en.natmus.dk/historical-knowledge/denmark/prehistoric-period-until-1050-ad/the-viking-age/religion-magic-death-and-rituals/human-sacrifices/

Kjølberg, T. (2019, April 9). *Language of the Vikings*. Daily Scandinavian. https://www.dailyscandinavian.com/language-of-the-vikings/

Knattleikr. (2020, January 20). In *Wikipedia*. https://en.wikipedia.org/wiki/Knattleikr

Lunde, M. (n.d.). *The Modern Vikings*. Visit Norway. https://www.visitnorway.com/things-to-do/art-culture/vikings/the-modern-vikings/

Parker, P. (2018, November 26). *A Brief History of the Vikings*. History Extra. https://www.historyextra.com/period/viking/vikings-history-facts/

Mark, J. (2018, January 29). Vikings. World History Encyclopedia. https://www.worldhistory.org/Vikings/

McCoy, D. (2014). *Daily Life in the Viking Age.* Norse Mythology for Smart People. https://norse-mythology.org/daily-life-viking-age/

Meat and Fish in the Viking Age. (n.d.). National Museum of Denmark. https://en.natmus.dk/historical-knowledge/denmark/prehistoric-period-until-1050-ad/the-viking-age/food/meat-and-fish/

Nicki. (2016, January 26). *Barley honey flat-breads.* Roots & Wren. http://rootsandwren.com/barley-honey-flat-breads/

Norse Mythology: Norse Afterlife. (2019, June 3). Norse and Viking Mythology. https://blog.vkngjewelry.com/en/norse-afterlife/

Norse Mythology: Viking Religion. (2020, March 30). Norse and Viking Mythology. https://blog.vkngjewelry.com/en/viking-religion/

Norwegian Vikings. (2015). Visit Norway. https://www.visitnorway.com/things-to-do/art-culture/vikings/

Old Norse (Dǫnsk tunga / Norrœnt mál). (2021, April 23). Omniglot. https://omniglot.com/writing/oldnorse.htm

Old Norse The Language of The Vikings. (2016, December 9). Verbling. https://www.verbling.com/articles/post/old-norse-the-language-of-the-vikings-5781d9e65c69247b005203ed

Pagan Religious Practices of the Viking Age. (2009). Hurstwic. http://www.hurstwic.org/history/articles/mythology/religion/text/practices.htm

The Poetic Edda (H.A. Bellows, Trans.). (2019). Sacred Texts. https://www.sacred-texts.com/neu/poe/index.htm

Ray, D. (2018, August 21). *7 Misconceptions About The Vikings That Might Surprise You.* The Franklin Institute. https://www.fi.edu/blog/viking-misconceptions

Rouă, V. (2016, April 25). *Discover Denmark's Viking Age Ring-Shaped Fortresses.* The Dockyards. http://www.thedockyards.com/discover-denmarks-viking-ring-fortresses/

Rouă, V. (2016, October 22). *Architecture In The Viking Age: Urban Planning, Emporia, And Strongholds.* The Dockyards. https://www.thedockyards.com/architecture-viking-age-urban-planning-emporia-strongholds/

Sjøgren, K. (2017, December 20). *What made the Vikings so superior in warfare?* Science Nordic. https://sciencenordic.com/denmark-history-society--culture/what-made-the-vikings-so-superior-in-warfare/1452248

Snow, A. (2020, October 1). *Art of the Viking Age*. Smart History. https://smarthistory.org/viking-art/

Útgarða-Loki. (2021, June 12). In *Wikipedia*. https://en.wikipedia.org/wiki/%C3%9Atgar%C3%B0a-Loki

The Viking Blót Sacrifices. (2019). National Museum of Denmark. https://en.natmus.dk/historical-knowledge/denmark/prehistoric-period-until-1050-ad/the-viking-age/religion-magic-death-and-rituals/the-viking-blot-sacrifices/

Viking Clothing: Warm and Durable. (2018, May 29). History On The Net. https://www.historyonthenet.com/viking-clothing-warm-and-durable

Viking Food. (2019). National Museum of Denmark. https://en.natmus.dk/historical-knowledge/denmark/prehistoric-period-until-1050-ad/the-viking-age/food/

Viking Games and Entertainment: Life Wasn't all Work. (2018, May 29). History On The Net. https://www.historyonthenet.com/viking-games-and-entertainment-life-wasnt-all-work

Viking raid warfare and tactics. (2019b, May 6). In *Wikipedia*. https://en.wikipedia.org/wiki/Viking_raid_warfare_and_tactics

The Viking Social Structure. (n.d.). Norse Mythology for Smart People. https://norse-mythology.org/viking-social-structure/

Vikings Customs. (n.d.). Medieval Chronicles. https://www.medievalchronicles.com/medieval-history/medieval-history-periods/vikings/vikings-customs/

The Vikings in the West. (n.d.). Vikingeskibsmuseet I Roskilde. https://www.vikingeskibsmuseet.dk/en/professions/education/viking-knowledge/the-viking-age-geography/the-vikings-in-the-west

What Happened to the Vikings? (2019). Hurstwic. http://www.hurstwic.org/history/articles/society/text/what_happened.htm

What Language Did the Vikings Speak? (2019, July 2). AleHorn. https://www.alehorn.com/blogs/blog/what-language-did-the-vikings-speak

Williams, G. (2011, February 17). *Viking Religion.* BBC. http://www.bbc.co.uk/history/ancient/vikings/religion_01.shtml

Norse Magic & Runes:

A Guide To The Magic, Rituals, Spells & Meanings of Norse Magick, Mythology & Reading The Elder Futhark Runes

History Brought Alive

Table of Contents

Introduction 324

Chapter 1: The Time & People 330

    More Than Just Norsemen 331

    Slavery 334

More Than Just Vikings 336

    Different Ventures 337

    Icelandic Settlements 340

Conflicts and Raids 341

    Their Influence 341

    The Celts 342

    The Norse-Gaels 343

Chapter 2: The Gods & Realms 345

The Pantheon 346

    Odin 347

    Loki 350

    Baldr 351

    Heimdallr 352

    The Vanir 353

    Freyr 354

    Njorðr 355

    The Valkyries 356

Cosmology 357
Nine Realms 358
Ragnarök 360
Trolls, Dwarves, Elves, and Giants 361
Trolls 361
Dwarves 361
Elves 362
Giants 363
Chapter 3: The Myth & Folklore 364
-Völuspá in Poetic Edda 366
The Eddas 367
The Helgi Lays consisting of six stories: 368
The Icelandic Sagas 370
Some Stories and Themes 371
Skirnismál: The Lay of Skírnir (Poetic Edda) 372
Grímnismál: The Lay of Grímnir (Poetic Edda) 378
Skáldskaparmál: The Kidnapping of Idun (Prose Edda) 382
Scandinavian Folklore 385
The Huldra 386
The Nisse 386
Pesta 387
Nokken 388
The Draugr 389
Chapter 4: Seiðr, Spà, & Galdr 390
Seiðr 392
Performing 393
Derivation 395

Spá 397
Connection to the Norns 398
Performing 399
Derivation 400
Connection to the Songs 401
Performing 401
Derivation 403
Chapter 5: Runes & Runestones 405
Odin's Gift 408
Elder Futhark 410
Younger Futhark 412
Rune Poems 414
Icelandic Rune Staves 419
Runestones 421
Tools Used 422
Reading the Stones 426
Runemasters 427
Chapter 6: Runic Divination 428
The Three Ættir 430
The Mother 431
The Warrior 434
Casting 435
Rune Spreads 438
One, Two, and Three-Rune Layouts 439
Four-Rune Layout 440
Five-Rune Layout 440
The Blank Rune 444
Chapter 7: Religion 445

Public and Private Faith 446
　Public 446
　Private 447
Death & Reincarnation 449
Chapter 8: Connection to Nature & the Unseen 455
　Cyclical View of Time 456
Herbs and Potions 458
Sacred Numbers 459
Spirit Worlds 460
　Wights 460
　Útiseta 462
　Totemism 463
　The Fylgjur 463
　Militaristic Totemism 464
Chapter 9: Norse Morality & Ethics 466
Law 466
Virtues and Values 467
　After Conversion 469
Conclusion 471
References 476
Free Bonus from HBA: Ebook Bundle 489

Introduction

The night is cold and silent. No wind stirs the snow-covered Rowan trees; the only sound is the soft snow footsteps of Bo and his son Arne as they climb slowly up the ridge to the viewpoint above their village, this being a tradition spanning back many moons of old. Bo remembers the times when his father would take him up the same journey to witness the magnificence of the northern lights.

"This was a moment for clarity and presence," he always said. His father enjoyed telling stories while they stood there and watched with awe, in a way to honor and remember their gods and their influence over the men in the world.

Now Arne places his last step before they finally arrive at the leveled area between two Ash trees. He takes his place beside his father as the lights above them stir like ribbons of color dancing and mingling with one another in ridges and sways.

The stories Bo tells his son are the same stories his father told him as a young boy—stories of legendary warriors and mischievous trolls, old mysterious seiðmenn, and beautiful, fair queens. But none spoke more to his heart than the story behind the northern lights.

Odin is the chief god of Asgard, and the Valkyries, his faithful embodiments of strength and wisdom, were the women of war who would ride by his side to battle or would collect the souls of fallen men and return them to Valhalla, the hall of the slain. As they rode in the skies, the reflection of light off their mighty shields would illuminate the night sky above their heads, creating the northern lights.

The myths and tales told were not fictional but an honest guideline to every aspect of their lives. Arne knew it to be true, and that was all that mattered. When they returned home, the house was warm and inviting. The smell of dinner and the loving embrace from Bo's wife, Frida, was the usual evening greeting and always appreciated.

Frida was a woman of magic, you see. Arne always understood the need to sit quietly with his mother in the morning and at night to make offerings to the gods for blessings and chant to the spirits for answers—some for Father's health and protection, some for Mother's fertility and strength, and some for Arne's own courage and virility. Daily rituals of worship were led by both his mother and father, and they encompassed the honoring of many gods and goddesses alike.

They were always assured that the gods were with them, even when they closed their eyes.

Welcome

Hello there friend! Welcome to the world of *Norse Magic & Runes*!

Here at History Brought Alive, we like to tell history through the mind of the reader. Meaning that when you come back to this book each day you will bring your mind into the life of a Norseman—breathing, feeling, and smelling their environment around you.

The worldview of these ancient Nordic people was so incredibly different from ours that it can be hard to imagine yourself in their shoes. That is why we take the time and care to transport you to the cold, green hills, plains, and mountains of Scandinavia between the 8th and 12th century.

Your interest in learning about the magic of the ancient people of Scandinavia is saluted! The experience of finding a piece of work that tells a story you can understand, relate to, and be intrigued by all at once is what you desire and deserve; therefore, look no further. *Norse Magic & Runes* will take you right into the heart of their magic and ritual practices.
The varied and complex history of Norse people can become a rather confusing ordeal to get through, considering the large language variants and influences of Christian beliefs in the historical evidence. Many manuscripts find themselves falling quite short of the hope and expectation given by readers interested in the truth behind the mythology and magic of the Nordic people. Often enough they are long-winded and honestly rather boring in their retelling. Instead of having text that just talks at the reader, we want to create a text that allows the reader to immerse themselves in the writing.

We know you cannot wait to learn the ins and outs of the different practices and the language used, but like any journey, we will have to start at the beginning.

We will first look at the people who lived during this time and the lengths to which they went to achieve greatness, because without the creation of a context, the meat of this manuscript would come across empty and lacking in meaning.

Then, we will guide you into the pantheon of the gods and goddesses and the various realms they ruled over. Once we pass over the deities, we can begin with the stunningly elaborate descriptions of the mythologies and folktales filled with heroes, gods, and common people striving to find their truth. These stories hold so much weight that they still reflect in our modern lives today.

And then onto the magic! That's what you have been waiting for, right? The magic arts we delve into are the three main acknowledged and studied forms of magic: seiðr, spá and galdr. Magic is where silence and peace were each an equal tool to the gods' ears as rage and chaos. We will discover more about the practices used and the principle reasons behind calling the spirit realm.

From there we take a step into the world of runes and runestones and the power they wield. We will go over the characteristics of each rune language and its evolution over the 500 or so years, from the early Germanic migrations into the Medieval Period.

Rune magic cannot be explained without understanding the influence the gods had on each rune and the practice of casting them for divination, while also learning the methods and patterns applied to rune spreads and which rune to cast. The way in which you read the runes and the type of energy you put into the art is a practice that requires time and patience, allowing you to come back to this manuscript many times over.

Once we have finished that chapter, we can seep into the next section and enlighten you on the concept of Norse religion from birth to death—their enchanted connection to nature and wilderness along with the animals who roam it.
Lastly we will uncover the morals and ethics that upheld a civilization so strong, yet so malleable, allowing them to rule and be ruled.

On the arrival of the concluding chapter, we are sure that you will have a brighter and more integrated knowledge of Norse magic and the people who practiced it.

History Brought Alive is the leading author of historically significant books, this particular piece being no exception. So, without any further ado, enjoy!

Chapter 1: The Time & People

Norse culture is famously shrouded in mystery, where loose ends lay everywhere and the archeological world is beyond curious in finding the truth behind their daily and religious practices. There must be a distinct understanding of what it meant to be a Norseman and what other civilizations influenced and molded their culture. They existed as a group of people settling from their migrations as Germanic tribes up into the creeks and mountains of Scandinavia.

Let us take you back in time for a minute. The era is roughly between 500 and 800 C.E., called the Scandinavian Iron Age, and Roman influences are leaving a mark on these Scandinavian tribes that had migrated north from Germanic regions. The trading, warring, and interaction with these Romans passed on the beliefs and myths of their Roman pantheon onto the Northmen, thus evolving over the centuries into the Norse gods we know today.

Then, between 800 and 1100 C.E., the Viking Age was in full throttle. Ships were built, warriors were made, trades were finalized, and slaves were sold. The seas were the roads to new worlds, to riches, to new languages, and to a new god. Christian influence started taking hold both within Scandinavian kingdoms, introducing politics and economy, and within the many Viking settlements it also affected social and religious life.

The truth is that Norse history is a Sudoku puzzle. Bits and pieces try to fit into place in historians' minds, but it's almost impossible due to our obvious lack of context. That makes the incredible mystery even more intriguing as there is so much more to learn and discover each time!

More Than Just Norsemen

Norsemen is a term used for the Nordic people who lived in the North Atlantic region of what we know today as Scandinavia (Norway, Denmark, Sweden, and later, Iceland). An Old Norse language was established based on Germanic and Indo-European origins before the Viking Age. Although basic agriculture collapsed by 550 C.E. and only restored towards the 8th century, historical evidence begins to show us a more detailed picture of set practices and beliefs coinciding with foreign influences. A more controlled paganism, if you will.

Their early society was not technically a literary one, and looking into their lives requires an understanding of their oral tradition, seen in early rune inscriptions and later in the sagas and poems. The stories were told, but the reasons and methods were left for interpretation.

The Norse were predominantly farmers, fishermen, and traders. It is often overlooked that their lifestyles were more than just pillaging and conquering. Their connection with their mythologies and their rituals of magic is rooted heavily in their actual day to day lives, rather than it being, for instance, a civilization polarized by different beliefs. They were unified and complex.

Daily Life

The Norsemen, as we call them today, were not connected to the name or function of Viking when at home in their Nordic countries. If you had to be in that time, Norse or Viking would not be a word you understood or conceptualized the way we do in the modern world. You were a part of a people who lived simply in the Scandinavian wilderness and who hunted, farmed, fished, cultivated livestock, spoke to the gods, and, at times, partook in civil war among neighboring villages and clans.

Positions of hierarchy were established and overthrown many times, and slaves were commonplace. Kings and magnates (chieftains) were quite literally the men who owned the biggest farm or the most ships. Each clan or merchant town stood independent from the other and later, with social evolution, regions and kingdoms were formed.

A simple subsistence level of farm work and living in rural farmsteads was a picture of normal Norse life. Villages usually consisted of between 15 and 60 people depending on their location for trade and agriculture.

Throughout the Viking Age, social structures began to evolve and encompass three main tiers:

- The elite, who were the wealthiest families like kings or chieftains.
- The free men and women. Here we see the majority of the population who might have owned their own land, worked the farm, or traded goods and slaves.
- Slaves were known as thralls. Before slavery ended towards the late Middle Ages, the purchase and sale of human lives was considered standard practice.

Mortality rates were also very high and it is said that around 30–40% of children died before adulthood due to famine and diseases. We could see why the Vikings decided to venture to new lands, as theirs was hostile and unforgiving, especially in winter.

The trade routes of spices, silk, pottery, and silver were established and became a vital source of income as well as the trade of knowledge and information.

Curious by nature and strong by breeding, these people were tenacious and courageous, capable of feats that later civilizations would never reach. A mixture of magic and hard reality was what they lived and abided by—basic rules of engagement both with their peers and with the spirit world.

Slavery

Many historians turn to the belief that Viking raids were assembled first and foremost to enslave the local people and take them back to their country to make use of or trade with. Mainly women were captured, but men and children were also taken. The slave trade focused on the continent of Britain but also extended across the Mediterranean from Spain to Egypt.

The evidence seen besides oral accounts is in the finding of collars and shackles around the ancient urban centers. Slaves were used for many activities such as textile manufacturing, ship building, farming, and most of the unpleasant jobs done around the homestead. Sexual slavery as well as intermarriage was another reason the Vikings traded so loosely with the slave women and children of England and France.
Women

As the Norse had a very patriotic culture, most women stayed in the villages while the men went on their raids or fishing trips. Some women did join in sailing to other lands to settle with their families and some did really train as shield maidens and joined the men in battle. We speak of the free women who were wives, sisters, and daughters. Slave women were nowhere near treated the same.

The women had a strong standing when it came to matters of healing, magic and rituals. This book is centered on magic and ritualism, and women played a central part in that field. Within the threshold of the home, women were in charge of preparing food, cleaning the house, purchasing and repairing clothing items, baking, cooking, preparing alcoholic drinks, and making dairy products. The men hunted and maintained their agriculture and livestock farming, though both women and men took the role of shepherd. In summer months, when the work was plenty, usually the whole household pulled their weight and assisted in the sowing and reaping.
Women did have a voice in gatherings and meetings, and were able to divorce their men if they chose. Such an oddity if you think how other civilizations operating at the time still held a very backwards view of marriage and fidelity. This is not to say that men were faithful in the way we know fidelity today.

Normally unions and weddings were arranged by the patriarch of the family, both for social uplifting and monetary gain, but seen too were relationships based on love and companionship.

More Than Just Vikings

Vikings were those who sailed the northern Atlantic seas to run raids or settle in new lands. The word Viking is technically the verb for "making a sea voyage" in the Old Norse language, so the Norsemen would "go Viking."
The period is now 800 C.E. and the Norsemen have mastered shipbuilding in a way that allowed them to navigate rough seas as well as narrow rivers with dexterity. The people are eager and strong, ready to venture to new lands. Many warriors were sailing across the Atlantic or traveling the Mediterranean, some strategizing river access to major cities across Europe, and others accessing the far regions of the East through the Baltic channels of trade. Other Norse-Icelandic people even attempted to settle in the Americas. The headgear they wore never consisted of horned helmets, as is usually portrayed in media, but rather simple iron helmets. This misrepresentation was established through Christian-influenced literature.

The pièce de résistance was their ability to sail. Building ships that were both agile and strong, they designed them with planks that followed the tree's grain, making them naturally stronger. The clinker method, which was a pattern for building the hull with overlapping planks riveted together, was ingenious in allowing flexibility with a comparatively lightweight and shallow depth structure. This allowed smooth navigation during raids where speed and maneuverability were crucial. With the addition of sun stones and sun charts that would track the sun's path over the sky during adverse weather, the Vikings were unstoppable.

Making use initially of water advantage, stealth, speed, and brute strength, the Vikings later evolved into a more sophisticated and political force and what some widely considered the reason the Viking Era ended.

Different Ventures

Historical resources from the first Viking raids in the late 7th century are terribly limited. What we do know is that the Norse were not strictly divided into separate states or regions as we may see now. The *Anar-Ulstar Chronicles* from Ireland and the *Anglo-Saxon Chronicles* mention that the Norwegians, Swedes, and Danish all considered themselves as different people and different groups.

"The difference between these groups would have been small, if not imperceptible to our modern lens, but to the Vikings, they would have been paramount," (Adrien, 2021).

So it's safe to say that they were broadly separated into three main groups:

- The **Danish Vikings** were seen as the strongest of the factions, with a more militaristic people and a stronger political mind. They dominated over their initial raids and settlements and conquered with more ease. Due to their affinity for political agendas, they grew faster and stronger by ensuring their confirmation to Christianity would be conducive to gaining more title and protection over land and people.

Much more is known about the Danish Vikings than their cousins, and it is believed to mainly be due to the fact that they dominated regions that had people who were better at chronologizing and depicting the battles and events of history at the time.

They were able to both outwit and outmaneuver the enemy, which consisted mainly of Britain, Normandy (a region of France), and certain parts of the Mediterranean. The Danish settled well in Normandy where native women were taken as wives which brought about more social coercion.

- The **Swedish Vikings** were also known as Varangians or the Rus due to their founding the regions in what is known as Russia today. They were tradesmen and explorers, rather than pillagers and murderers like their counterparts. They excelled and focused their trade on the Middle Eastern areas of the Baltic. If you look at the map of Scandinavia, you will see that Sweden's waters face more eastwards than north or west, giving them more availability and access to those lands and regions. Being merchants and mercenaries too, the Swedes took to more honest work than raiding and pillaging. Being especially proud of their heritage, they were the last of the three groups to convert to Christianity.
- With the **Norwegian Vikings**, we see the most brave, crazed, and barbaric warriors of their time and standing. Berserkers (Vikings who wore the pelts of wolves and bears to bring strength in battle) were found among these warriors and were the only Vikings to be known to use the axe as a weapon in battle. The Norwegians were the best shipbuilders and sailors who reached the farthest coasts of Iceland, Greenland, and the Americas.

Icelandic Settlements

During the 9th century, Iceland was covered in forests and woodlands, and was quite a bit warmer than the Scandinavian lands to the east. Both unsettled and rich in resources, it was perfect for the taking, allowing them to settle there for around 56 years.

The Norwegians were the first to sail to Iceland, with the settlement of Ingólfr Arnarson broadly being considered the first settler in 874 C.E. Thanks to the ample details given in the *Landnámabók* writings of the 13th century, we can find more historical information about Norse life in the Icelandic sagas and stories than anywhere else.

The genetic makeup of human remains in these lands suggests that many of the settlers were of Irish and Scottish descent, with a smaller portion hailing from Scandinavia. This meant that there must have been a great intermingling of cultures during the settlement age. We know that the settlement failed and many of the initial settlers either died due to harsh conditions or returned home.

Conflicts and Raids

Along with the constant civil conflicts between Scandinavian kingdoms, which were led by kings and earls to gain land and power, the conflicts occurring overseas and in Europe were far more organized and strategic. Even though many of the raids were on English monasteries, this was not due to their hatred of the religion, but for the easy access and weakly defended wealth in these locations.

The raiding of monasteries was already in play by late 700 C.E. in England, and now it was time to take advantage of the resources available and begin a prosperous trade, both in goods and in slaves. In the Viking's eyes, this is no terrible thing. It is a concept of the strong taking from the weak, not the wicked taking from the good.

Their Influence

The one thing that still allows us to study and evaluate their ancient lives is what they left behind for us—all those relics that have survived so long. But one influence that remains close to many hearts is their social influence on various other cultures at the time, like the Celts and the Gaels.

The Celts

During the Bronze Age, the Celts and Vikings were the largest groups to inhabit the northern world, and the fusion between the two was inevitable. The Celts inhabited northern England, Scotland, and Ireland but also spread to Northern Italy and Spain. Some think that due to similarity in language and culture there is a genetic connection between Vikings and Celts. The truth of the matter is that they were equally influenced by each other but had no genetic correlation. Celtic people were not seafarers and were more oriented in growing their own lands than pillaging others.

The Celts and ancient Germanic people were neighbors before they decided to migrate and settle in separate lands during the Dark Ages. The Celts took to Ireland and Scotland from their Indo-European and Anatolian migration while the Germanic people mostly settled in Scandinavia.

During the Viking Age, the Celts had more influence on the Vikings in culture and language as they were already Christianized by the 5th century, whereas the Vikings contributed riches and the contact with foreign goods from trades.

The Vikings landed in Ireland around the 7th century after having had some practice raiding and pillaging in East England and Scotland. They were incredibly important in the foundation of some major Irish towns known today, like Dublin and Cork. This clearly tells us that there was not solely violence, but some diplomacy and shared trade too.

Ancient Celtic tribes did not invent their own runic language; it was adopted from the Norse influence before and during the migrations, where both feuds and social interactions took place.

The Norse-Gaels

These people were a mix of Norsemen and people from Ireland, called the Gaelic. When the Viking Age was in full bloom around the 9th century, the settlers that arrived in Ireland and Scotland interbred with the local people, adopting language and customs. Leaving behind the Norse gods and converting to Christianity was termed Gaelicization. This meant that their culture was altered to such a degree in influence over a few generations that they considered themselves more Gaelic than Norse.

Even after the conversion and after the Norse-Gaels disappeared entirely as a people, they still left a long lasting history in Ireland and Scotland. For instance, many Irish towns bear Norse-Gaelic names and the Scottish gallowglass warmongers were descendants of these people.

Chapter 2: The Gods & Realms

The Norse had a concept of deities that expressed more than just omnipotence and fear, but also knowledge and kindness. These gods inspire countless myths and folktales around creation and destruction. Each having a specific character reference and theme, they were more than ethereal powers in another reality, but real flesh and blood beings that directly affected their everyday lives.

As we take you further into the book and touch more on the subjects of influence from Christian ideas, you will notice that the inscriptions of historical myths change depending on the time written. The various gods were depicted differently depending on who wrote it, sometimes adding or removing certain characteristics of their theme and influence. The alteration is best seen in the aspects and powers of the female deities' beings transferring into that of male deities, centralizing the worship in patriarchal figures. Even more, the various names given to the gods and realms are sometimes changed or altered with a literature largely more descriptive and narrative than its earlier works.

The information between pre-Christian influences and post-Christian influences on historical events has a major impact on accuracy and truth. What we mainly know of their stories comes through late 19th century poems and sagas from Icelandic mythographer Snorri Sturluson, who was already a Christian at the time and wrote with that mentality, thus changing the themes accordingly to his views.

The Pantheon

The most powerful magic known to the gods was that of seiðr, the power to see fates, and it was first and foremost practiced by the goddess Freyja of the Vanir. Due to equal jealousy, disapproval, and fear of this power, another group of gods called the Æsir, who were more prone to the use of weapons and brute strength rather than magic, waged wars on the Vanir. As was customary, wagers were eventually met to stop the fighting, and hostages from each group were given to the other as a peace treaty. Therefore as seen below, the pantheon certainly does contain more Æsir gods than their Vanir counterparts, but their intermingling in mythology helps create more intricate stories and themes.

The Æsir became the more prominently known gods associated with war and strength, while the Vanir were more associated with fertility, magic, and agriculture. The Æsir reside in the realm of Asgard and the Vanir in lands of Vanaheim.

The Æsir

Odin

Known as the All-father, god of war, king of Asgard, bearer of wisdom and searcher of truth, Odin forms the head in the Triad of the mightiest gods, next to Thor and Freyja. Considered the first *sieðmann* (or male seer), he is known for his fervent pursuit of knowledge and is both revered for his standing in the pantheon as war leader and also shamed for his practice of seiðr magic, which was seen as a weakness in the use of it by men. Both Odin and the goddess Freyja are heavily associated with shamanism and the use of seiðr magic. Odin is mainly worshiped in the pursuit of nobility, wealth, and prestige. He is acknowledged in helping mankind but also instigating and creating war for his own fickle purposes of gaining the most valuable warriors in his hall of Valhalla. It is said that he also has a general disregard for fairness and the law, making him more of a ruler by chaos rather than by peace. His use of magic and cunning to control is what makes him both deviant and inspiring.

He is the son of Borr and Bestla, along with his brothers Vili and Vé, arriving upon the creation of the universe. He is associated with his eight-legged horse Sleipnir, with whom he rides into battle and visits the underworld within countless stories. The two wolves, Geri and Freki, are usually by his side; and most noticeably, the two black ravens, Huginn and Muninn, are the projections of Odin and bring him information from Midgard, the realm of men. In his possession is always the spear Gungnir, which is often used in self-injury to sacrifice himself for the knowledge of all things, and the gold ring, Draupnir.

He is married to Freyja, the goddess of motherhood and love, often interchanged with the goddess Frigg in some tales. They have three sons: Baldr, Hermod, and Hodor. He is also famously the father or Thor, whose mother is the earth goddess, Jörð. The day of the week associated with Odin is Wednesday due to his other Old English name Woden.

Thor

The god of thunder, often seen as the hero of the common man, was the most worshiped god during the pre-Christian Scandinavian Era. He is associated with strength, the protection of mankind, and storms. The characteristics most valuable to the Norse people often surrounded Thor, like honor, loyalty, and the unshakable sense of duty. It was also his place to bless and consecrate holy places with his hammer Mjölnir, but in the same light it could also be used for destruction. A dual purpose of the mighty hammer reflects the dual properties of human existence. During the Christianization of Scandinavia, the image of Mjölnir was a tool for private revolt against the new God. Wearing pendants in the shape of the hammer was a deliberate contrast to the symbol of the cross.

Thor seems to fall onto the second tier in the deity scheme, which is the function of warrior and military power. Being the god of both tempestuous storms and sunny, fair weather, he is married to Sif, a golden-haired goddess linked to the earth and crops. Their marriage is often considered the divine marriage of sky and land.

His familiars are the two goats, Tanngrisnir and Tanngnjóstr, who pull his chariot, and of course his famous hammer Mjölnir. The day of the week dedicated to him is Thursday, from the Old Norse term *thorsdagr* meaning "Thor's day."

Loki

The sometimes malicious and sometimes helpful god of mischief is known to be part jötun (giant) and part deity. He holds a very unique position within the pantheon and contradicts the many notions Odin and Thor stand for. He "is portrayed as a scheming coward who cares only for the shallow pleasures of self-preservation" (McCoy, 2009), often using his shapeshifting abilities for that very purpose.
Loki is son to the giant, Fárbauti, and the goddess, Laufey. With his wife Sigyn, he sired the god Nif, and with the giantess Angreboða he sired the wolf, Fenrir, the giant serpent, Jörmungandr, and the goddess of the underworld, Hel.

His name is often thought to derive from the most direct translation of 'knot' or 'tangle,' which may very well be his main influence on the events in the mythologies. He holds a theme of contradicting the nature of things by shapeshifting and disguising himself often in female forms to deceive or to trick. He's not necessarily seen as a god like his counterparts, as no trace of worship for this deity has been found.

Baldr

This particular god has a central, positive role in mythology due to his overall good nature and cheerful demeanor. Scholars disputed what function he might hold in the mythology, but he is often associated with love, peace, and forgiveness.

His benevolent, handsome, and gracious themes were more heavily constructed at the end of the Viking Age, when poets and skalds (poets who write skaldic poetry) were creating literature through a Christian lens. This can be seen in the idea of him shining like the sun, and having died and been resurrected, thus removing the original warlike disposition of the god from original pagan sources.

Baldr is the son of Odin and Frigg and is married to Nanna. He is the father of the god Foresti. Nanna and Foresti are obscure and are rarely mentioned in earlier works.

Heimdallr

Known as the god of foresight, guardian of the Bifröst Bridge, and watcher over Asgard, he resides in his high fortress called Himinbjörd and is depicted to have brilliant eyesight and hearing so he may watch with diligence over the worlds. He possesses the horn of Gjallarhorn to alert Asgardians of intruders. Some agree that he is the son of nine mothers, who are the nine daughters of the giant Aegir.

The other gods who are part of the Æsir are:
- Odin's two brothers, Vili and Vé, who together form the Triad of Spirit, Will, and Holiness.
- Hœnir, who assisted Odin in the creation of man.
- Týr, the one-handed god associated with the rules of law and heroic glory.
- Máni and Sól, the representation of the moon and sun.
- Bragi, the bard of Valhalla, responsible for welcoming the fallen warriors into the hall, and his wife Idun who cares for the fruit tree in Asgard that gives everlasting life.

The Vanir

Freyja

This is the most powerful goddess in Asgard. She is associated with love, sexuality, fertility, seiðr, beauty, and death. She is an honorary member of the Æsir like her father and brother. Norse women worshiped her for their feminine needs and practices, especially in family protection and health.
She is most commonly portrayed as the goddess personification of the völva who practices seiðr magic.

Sometimes depicted as promiscuous and unfaithful to her husband, the goddess often manipulates those around her according to her will. Ruling over her field of Fólkvangr, she receives half the warriors who die in battle for her hall, thus she is strongly connected to both war practices and the ideal of shamanism and magic.

Important to note is that in many accounts she and the goddess Frigg are often one and the same, as Frigg is married to Oðr, which translates to Odin. The post-Christian Germanic split went underway around the 10th century. Meaning we can easily assume the assimilation of the two goddesses becoming one at some point in history. Freyja derives from the Old Norse word 'lady' which can be perceived more as a title than a name.

Freyja is the daughter of god Njorðr and sister to the god Freyr. She is married to Odin and has two daughters, Hnoss and Gersemi, along with her three sons. Her familiars consist of her chariot pulled by two male cats, which were gifts from Odin. She also owns the boar Hildisvíni and wears a cloak of falcon feathers that allows her to shapeshift into the bird. The day of the week mentioned to Freyja/Frigg is Friday, attested as *frigdæag* meaning "Frigg's day."

Freyr

This god is connected to fair weather, sunshine, virility, and sacral kingship. He is known as the god that bestows peace and pleasure to the mortals. He is often worshiped at weddings and harvest festivals for his themes of both sexual and ecological fertility. Boars were sacrificed to Freyr at weddings, especially the boar Gullinbursti as his familiar, and this was the main symbolism of his virility.

He is the son of the god Njorðr and brother to the goddess Freyja. He presides over the realm of Alfheim, which was given to him as a teething present, and later marries the giantess Gerðr. His familiars are his boar Gullinbursti and his magical sword Sumarbrander, which could fight on its own. He also sails the ship Skiðblanðir, which always sees good weather and which could be magically folded away into a carry bag.

The god is known to be a lover to many goddesses, giantesses, and even his own sister Freyja, as incest was not frowned upon by the Vanir. His name, like that of his sister Freyja (lady), means 'lord.'

Njorðr

Like his children, Freyja and Freyr, Njorðr is a representative of fertility. He also encompasses the ideologies of wealth and, most noticeably, he is considered the god of seas and seafaring where he resides in his beach kingdom, Nóatún.
He is the principle god of the Vanir and, unfortunately, very little is known about him as he was mostly worshiped during the initial stages of the Viking Era, therefore giving us few resources to work with.

The Valkyries

What we know of the Valkyries today, being graceful shield maidens who fly to battle with their lord Odin and retrieve the souls of fallen warriors to take to Odin's hall, might be another Christianization and softening of their actual roles from original pagan times. It is found that their original traits were far more insidious—they personify the carnage of war and at some points are depicted as wearing intestines as belts and using heads as weights.

It was thought that the goddess Freyja was the leader of the Valkyries, as she would retrieve for herself half of the fallen warriors for her fields in Fólkvangr, while the other souls would either be taken to Valhalla by the Valkyries or go to the realm of the Underworld, Hel (which is where most common folk were thought to go).

There is knowledge of many Valkyries, but six in particular are mentioned in the Eddas:
- Skuld (debt)
- Skogul (shaker)
- Gunnr (war)
- Hildr (battle)
- Gondul (wand-wielder)
- Geirskogul (spear-bearer)

Cosmology

There are nine realms existing in Norse cosmology. The center of their universe and what connects all the realms together is situated in Asgard, and it is known as Yggdrasil, the World Tree.

The story from the *Völuspá* poem describes the events that took place during the creation of all things.
Two great realms once existed: one of ice and one of fire. They were separated by a terrible void called the Ginnungagap. These realms were to be known as Niflheim and Muspelheim, in turn. From the eventual collision of these realms, the ice on Niflheim melted and revealed Ymir, the proto-giant, and a cow called Audhumla.

Now, Audhumla licked away at the ice and uncovered Búri, forefather of the gods. Audhumla and Búri sired son Borr and daughter Bestla, who in turn sired the brother gods known as Odin, Vili, and Vé. The three brothers take it upon themselves to kill Ymir so that they may create the world of men from his remains. Flesh for earth, skull for sky, bones for mountains, and blood for sea. The World Tree emerged soon after the world's creation along with all the many beings and realms. Once it was all done, with the help of god Baldr, from the deep woods emerged the first two humans, named Ask and Embla, and they began populating the new realm.

The early Norse works of Eddic and Skaldic poetry assumes the reader has knowledge of the cosmology, and thus, not much explanation is given on location and specific characteristics. Although Snorri's work of the nine realms changed it slightly adding and removing realms to include Helheim, or Hel (the Underworld), there is an importance of understanding that in Scandinavia at the time these descriptions would probably not be recognized and be quite different. Theirs was a living dynamic faith, and our knowledge is but just the surface of a much larger iceberg.

Nine Realms

Their mythology had various details about the worlds created and some written sources are less clear than the others. What were known to be the original nine realms are

- Godheim - Realm of Æsir (Asgard)
- Alfheim - Realm of Bright Elves
- Svartalfheim - Realm of Black Elves
- Niflheim - Realm of Ice and Mist
- Muspelheim - Realm of Fire and Chaos
- Mannheim - Realm of Men and Trolls (Midgard)
- Jötunheim - Realm of Giants (Utgard)
- Nidavelir - Realm of the Dwarves
- Vanaheim - Realm of the Vanir

Yggdrasil and the Norns

An ash I know there stands, Yggdrasil is its name, a tall tree, showered with shining loam. From there come the dews that drop on the valleys, it stands forever green over Uror's well.
–Völuspá in the Poetic Edda.
Yggdrasil, the World Tree, is thought to be the center of the Norse universe. The origins of the name have various sources, but it is generally understood as 'gallows' in Old Norse. Situated in the realm of Asgard, upon its roots live multiple creatures and beings: the dragon of death, Níðhöggr, the four stags Dáinn, Duneyrr, Dvalinn, and Duraþrór who eat at the branches and roots, and the great unnamed eagle. Below the roots lies the Serpent of the World that chokes the roots surrounding Midgard. The tree has three roots that feed on three different wells: the Well of Urd in Asgard, the Well of Mímir by the frost giants, and the Hvergelmir Well in Niflheim.

But most importantly we see the connection to the three Norns: Uror, Verðandi, and Skuld. Their purpose is to nourish the World Tree with water from the sacred Well of Urd to prevent it from dying, and to twine the threads of fates of all things, often thought to be the roots of the tree themselves. They are secretive and unseen, rarely revealing their fateful secrets to men. They could be malevolent or benevolent, often determining the future of newborn children.

Ragnarök

Ragnarök was known to all. It was the inevitable end of all things both divine and mortal. The concept that war and destruction would take hold of the realms through fire was what every commoner, slave, and king believed. Therefore, one could say that their fate was set in stone.

Initially attested in the Poetic Edda in the 13th century by Snorri Sturlersun, it was written as the *Twilight of the Gods*. What we see is a long and interesting poem told by the völva, who visits a village and prophesies the end of all things. She tells us of the clash between the gods and giants, the deceit of some, and the loss of loved ones due to others. The fire giants burn the worlds and all that is left is a few gods and a few humans who step out of the destruction to begin the world anew. It is important to the Norse that a theme of renewal comes through the final chapter, as nothing is ever the end.

Trolls, Dwarves, Elves, and Giants

Trolls

Some tales from Sweden describe trolls as monstrous beings with many heads who can either live in the forest and mountains or in caves. The first kind of trolls that live in the mountains are known to be large, aggressive, stupid, and slow beings, always getting outwitted by the hero in the story. Those that live in caves are shy and seen as shorter than humans with stumpy arms and legs but with a fair amount of intelligence. They use the environment around them to influence their power or protect themselves and hide. These creatures emerged into mythology from the idea of the giants (jötun) in their cosmology and realms, as the word troll in Old Norse is *jätte*.

Dwarves

The dwarves were known to be crafty beings that live in the realm of Midgard, hidden from humans in subterranean realms. The tales of dwarves go far back into mythology and creation, as they were known to be born of the flesh of the giant Ymir, along with the rest of their cosmos. They were molded by the Æsir into figures that resemble humans, but much shorter and gifted with intelligence and skill.

These beings are artists in creating all sorts of things from jewelry to weapons and other intricate pieces. We see their skill in the creation of Thor's hammer Mjölnir crafted by the dwarves Brokkr and Eitri, as well as many other weapons in the gods' possession.

Elves

The elves, as from the many references we have in popular culture today, are known to be fair, beautiful, and tall beings that are swift in battle and powerful with magic. Initially, in pre-Christian myths, these demi-gods were one class of being who lived in one realm. Later, their mythology developed and they were divided into Light Elves (Ljösáfar) that lived in the realm of Alfheim reigned by the god Freyr, and the Dark Elves (Dökkálfar) that lived deep within the earth and had a darker complexion. Elves were known to cause illness to the humans and, when offered something in return, they could heal them too. Humans were known to also become elves after they died due to the connection of the worship of ancestors to the worship of elves.

Giants

These supernatural beings of the natural world have, from the beginning of time, been the arch rivals of the Æsir and Vanir. They often warred, fought, cheated, and married each other. The *jötun* live in the icy realm of Jötunheim, which is closely connected to Midgard by mountain ranges and dense forests, while the fire giants live in Múspellsheimr, their realm of fire. They are the catalyst of the great ending in Ragnarök, setting fire to the tree Yggdrasil and ending everything in flame. What one would think of giants in physique is their immense stature, but in fact they were no bigger than an average human and resembled the humanoid beings of other realms. They represented the original nature of chaos and destruction in comparison to the gods representing life and order.

Chapter 3: The Myth & Folklore

During the Viking Age, the Norsemen started developing an extensive poetic literature about their gods and heroes. These stories would be committed to writing by their Christian descendants many centuries later.

The characters within these poems often act in a way that is incompatible with the social norms that we are accustomed to in our present day. The warlike and aggressive attitude in men and in the gods they worshiped has been associated with their lack of resources and harsh climate in Medieval Scandinavia. Fighting for these resources and the aggression against their neighbors was not necessarily considered wrong or unjust. If it advanced their wealth and honor, then it was only fair for them to take what is deserved. The honor gained and maintained by confronting enemies with strength and valor was a moral in itself. A readiness to use violence in return for violence done to one's friends and relatives was commonplace and reflected in the characters of many of the gods that, in our society today, would probably be considered barbaric and cruel.

It must be stated that a person's word was considered absolutely binding and stood stronger than the family unit or even the self. Many of the stories shadow the choice the hero has to make to either keep his word by then having to hurt or kill the people closest to him or lose his honor by choosing the loved ones life over the oath made.

The stories and poems are attuned to the strict class structure present at the time, most noticeably in the Poetic Edda. The characters are tightly bound to these social structures and don't deviate from them. If one was of noble birth, then they would not consider the life of the common free man any more than they would a dog roaming the village. Large differences in activities, dress, and diet expected of people at different social levels were the stepping stone to the rest of the story. "Heed my words all classes of men, you greater and lesser children of Heimdall."

–Völuspá in Poetic Edda

Another noteworthy characteristic of Norse poems is the idea that all people had predetermined and fixed dates of death determined by the Norns who sit at their pool and weave their fates. "A man would not live one day longer than the Norns had decided. The characters in these myths are marching towards their doom, unable to change course or step off their predetermined path even if they fight it the entire way" (Crawford, 2021).

The boldness and defiance of their fates must have galvanized something in the Norse audience surrounded by their cold rural farmsteads. Many of the stories end in tragedy, but that need not mean they left the audience in despair; it was simply the light and dark realities of life.

Mythologies and legends living within Norse culture are either minimal in their true pre-Christian pagan times, or are post-Christian and influenced by Latin poets and writers. Scandinavian cultures were an overwhelmingly oral society in the retelling of history. Many holes and loose threads are present in the current knowledge of their customs. "Although some of these tell complete myths, most of them assume - unfortunately for us - that their audience was familiar with the mythical context" (Groenavelde, 2017).

The Eddas

The Eddas are a collection of two Medieval Icelandic manuscripts of mythology that use prose (stories) and poems in different stanzas to describe, depict, and detail the religion, cosmology, and history of ancient Scandinavian culture. The composition of the poems can either use the Eddaic or Skaldic genre of poetry and mainly uses alliterative versing and symbolism.

It is still unsure where the term 'Edda' derives from exactly, and there are quite a few hypotheses, but the easiest etymology to point towards is the Old Norse word *óðr* meaning 'poetry.'
The two collections of work are known as the Poetic Edda and the Prose Edda.

Poetic Edda

Poetic Edda, or Elder Edda, is a compilation of Icelandic and Norwegian tales that first appeared in the 13th century and is contained in the *Codex Regius* or "Royal Book." Many other poems were added to the Poetic Edda over the years and they were composed with visionary force and dramatic quality. The Poetic Edda was more often written in an Eddic genre of poetry and follows these four rules:
- The author is anonymous.

- It uses a certain meterage (*fornyröislag, ljóðaháttr,* and *málaháttr*).
- It has a direct approach to word order.
- Kennings (ancient figures of speech) are used less.

By far the most extensive source of Norse mythology, the Poetic Edda consists of two separate parts: the Mythological Poems and the Heroic Lays.

The Mythological Poems tell us about the adventures of the gods from their own perspectives and carries eleven poems: Völuspá, Hávamál, Vafþrúðnismál, Grimnismál, Skirnismál, Hábarðsljóð, Hymiskviða, Lokasenna, Þrymskviða, Völundarkviða, and Alvíssmál.

The Heroic Lays, in three parts, depicts the challenges and journeys of heroes and heroines and carries nineteen songs:

The Helgi Lays consisting of six stories:

Helgakviða Hundingsbana I, Helgakviða Hjörvarðssonar, Helgakviða Hundingsbana II, Helgakviða Hundingsbana I, Helgakviða Hjörvarðssonar, and Helgakviða Hundingsbana II.

The Niflung Cycle consisting of fifteen stories:

Frá dauða Sinfjötla, Grípisspá, Reginsmál, Fáfnismál, Sigrdrífumál, Brot af Sigurðarkviðu, Guðrúnarkviða I, Sigurðarkviða hin skamma, Heimreið Brynhildar, Dráp Niflunga, Guðrúnarkviða II, Guðrúnarkviða III, Oddrúnargrátr, Atlakviða, and Atlamál hin grenienzku.

The Jörmunrekkr Lays consisting of two stories:

Guðrúnarhvöt, Hamðismál.
Prose Edda
Prose Edda, or Younger Edda, is an Icelandic textbook written in the 13th century. Scholars assume that a large part of the text was written by law speaker and poet Snorri Sturluson. He was known for a verse use that was reflective of court poetry, putting him in higher esteem with peers.
Snorri Sturluson has long proven a paradoxical figure for those who think and write about medieval Norse culture. Many scholars believe that a satisfactory understanding of Snorri and his work will only be possible once the contradictions that surround this most famous medieval Icelander have been resolved. (Wanner, 2008)
The recomposing of stories altered the characteristics and influences of the gods in some writings but made them easier to comprehend.
The Prose Edda was typically written in the skaldic genre of poetry following these rules:

- The author is known.
- Ornate meterage is used (*dróttkvætt* or a variation).
- Sentences are commonly interwoven and contain ornate syntax.
- Kennings are often used.

The Prose Edda consists of four sections:
- Prologue
- Gylfaginning
- Skáldskaparmál
- Háttatal

The Icelandic Sagas

Staying around the 12th to 13th century, we see a composition written in Old Icelandic of accounts in prose format, meaning that the story is written in a narrative progression rather than the more poetically composed Elder Eddas. They depicted the events that occurred in the 9th and 10th century settlement stage. The term 'saga' derives from Old Norse and translates as 'utterance' or "oral account."

During the settlement of Iceland, also known as the Saga Age, most accounts were pre-Christian and their authentic and detailed retellings of their pagan world are what make them so precious and valuable. These family sagas are especially complete in their family connections and detailed genealogy. There are stories of struggle and conflict, and they give us a broader picture of their culture and practices.

These sagas can then further be separated into the King's sagas (sagas of legendary Nordic kings), Legendary sagas (Norse sagas accounting pre-Icelandic settlement), and the Contemporary sagas (mainly the accounts of the Sturlunga family).

The un-surety of authorship from these pieces of work allow for more study and discussion, but many like to attribute some to Snorri Sturluson, in the case of Egil's Saga.

Some Stories and Themes

The relation to love and lust and the surrounding principle of marriage are central to many stories in Norse mythology. The hero either has to win his affection or cheat for such affection, always simplifying the exception of the female characters in some way by giving in or being the weaker sex that should not fight back.

Another is the relation to destiny and fate. The Norns are seen as some of the most important and strong beings in the Norse universe. They control all the fates woven through Yggdrasil and weave them according to divine plans. Even though Odin does receive the knowledge of the runes, they were still only given to him and never really his. Therefore, one can say that the mythological stories centered on the pursuit and inevitable connections to one's own fate are highly regarded.

Another strong theme in the tales and myths is revenge. It was a common idea that one could take the hurt they felt for either being deceived or angered by another and return that pain tenfold. The vengeful characters and gods who were too proud or vain to be deceived would plan and strategize this theme, even if it meant their mutual destruction.

Skirnismál: The Lay of Skírnir (Poetic Edda)

The god Freyr sits on Odin's throne, *Hliðskjálf,* and looks out over the many worlds. As his eyes pass over the realm of giants, Jötunheimr, he sees a beautiful giantess named Gerðr and is taken by desire to pursue her.

Freyr cannot bring himself to speak with her directly, fearing doom and rejection, but the goddess Skaði, wife of Njördr, sees his gloom and asks if Freyr's servant Skírnir could inquire about the sulking god.

Skírnir is told by Freyr that he is afraid and unable to speak to her, and he asks if maybe Skírnir could go talk to her in his stead. Of course Skírnir agrees and is given Freyr's faithful steed and his magical sword to go forth and woo this giantess on his behalf.

Once he arrives in Jötunheimr and steps into the hall of giants, the beautiful Gerðr sees him and greets him kindly. Skírnir, not one to waste time, jumps straight into the songs to express the desire his master, Freyr, has for the giantess. His many attempts to get her to accept a meeting with Freyr are shut down, even after bribing with gifts and chanting melodies of lust. Frustrated and most likely tired, Skírnir resorts to some forceful and violent threats towards her and her father if she doesn't agree to the rendezvous:

"Seest thou, maiden, this keen bright sword
That I hold here in my hand?
Before its blade the old giant bends, —
Thy father is doomed to die.
I strike thee, maid, with my gambantein
To tame thee to work my will;
There shalt thou go where never again
The sons of men shall see thee" (p. 115).

So now Skírnir has threatened enough and Gerðr accepts the request for a meeting with this god. Content with having done his duty, Skírnir returns to Freyr in Asgard and before he can get off the horse and hand back the sword, Freyr is there to quickly know how it went:

Tell me, Skírnir, before unsaddling
Or stepping forth another pace
Is the news you bring from Jötunheim
For better or for worse? (p. 119)

Skírnir replies:

In the woods of Barri, which know we both so well,
A quiet still and tranquil place
In nine night time to Njörd's son
Will Gerðr give herself. (p. 120)

How delightful and excited Freyr is! He responds:

One night is long enough, yet longer still are two;
How then shall I contend with three?
For months have passed more quickly
Than half a bridal eve. (p. 120)

The idea of the curses laid out gives significance to what power and masculinity the Æsir hold over the females of other worlds. The concept of romanticism and lust hold strong meaning in many tales.

This could have possibly translated to the patriarchic and forceful nature of men at the time towards unclaimed women, meaning that the choice was there, but if chosen incorrectly, then either death or shame would come your way.

Frithiof's Saga (Legendary Saga by Esaias Tegnér)

King Beli of Sogn had two sons, Helgi and Halfdan, and a beautiful prized daughter named Ingeborg. Now King Beli had many friends, but his closest friend was his neighbor Thorstein, who lived across the fjord. Thorstein's own son, Frithiof, was a strong and bold man, known for his bravery and physical height.

Ingeborg's mother unfortunately passed away when they were young, and one of King Beli's goodmen, Hilding, took Ingeborg and her brothers, as well as young, strapping Frithiof under his wing as foster-father, so all the children had grown up together and become fast friends. Over the years, Frithiof found a deep and maddening love for Ingeborg that bloomed from childhood into their adult lives.

During a civil war, both King Beli and Frithiof's father, Thorstein, were killed on the battlefield, leaving the two brothers, Helgi and Halfdan, as brother-kings to rule over the kingdom. The brothers were particularly jealous of Frithiof and his incredible qualities of bravery and strength and were aware of his desire for their sister. In a petty and sly maneuver, the brothers transferred Ingeborg to a sacred dwelling far away called Baldrshagi, where intercourse and love relations were forbidden. This never deterred Frithiof's devotion to Ingeborg and still he visited her and they continued to share their love.

This angered the brother-kings terribly, so they took action and sent Frithiof off to the Orkney Islands in Scotland in an excuse to put distance between him and their fair sister. While away to pay tribute as requested, the brothers decide to burn down Frithiof's house and marry Ingeborg off to the Norwegian King Ring of Ringerike. Surely Ingeborg is mortified and obeys nonetheless, but her beloved Frithiof has no idea what has transpired.

Upon his return to Norway and finding the remains of his homestead and the absence of his love Ingeborg, he inquired with the brother-kings and discovered their treachery. In a rage, he burned down the sacred temple of Baldrshagi where Ingeborg once stayed, and took up his weapon and shield to sail to far lands as a Viking.

For three years he ventured, raided, and traded, gaining many riches and a grand reputation. When he returns home he decides to take up winter residence with King Ring so he may be closer to Ingeborg once more. Frithiof is a noble and kind man, so naturally he becomes strong friends with the old king. Just before the king's death, Frithiof is named earl of King Ring's domain and care-taker of Ingeborg's first child. He then marries Ingeborg almost immediately, finally getting the love he craved all his life.

After the death of the old king, Frithiof takes up his revenge against the petty and untrustworthy brothers who he grew up with. He kills the eldest brother and makes the youngest a liege of his kingdom, bound to his service. And so the patient and valiant Frithiof now can rest and love in peace.
This inspiring and immortal Scandinavian tale of love, conquest, and revenge has many variations, but the moral is always the same. Ture love does not need to be rushed. Patience, courage, and honor will guide the true hearted on their path to happiness.

Grímnismál: The Lay of Grímnir (Poetic Edda)

King Hraudung had two sons: Agnar, the oldest, was ten winters old, and his younger brother Geirröd was eight. They both enjoyed fishing together and decided to row the boat out so they may catch some small fish. Being preoccupied by the task at hand, they had not noticed how far the wind had driven them out into the open sea. Stranded till dark, they were eventually wrecked onto shore out in the country. Cold, hungry, and tired, they walked up to the nearest cottage they could find, where a peasant and his wife lived. They welcomed the boys into their home and kept them for the winter, where they taught the two boys many things and gave them sound advice. The wife took charge of the younger Agnar, and the husband mentored Geirröd.

Once spring had come along, the husband and wife assisted the brothers in returning to their kingdom with a ship they procured. Accompanying them along the journey back home, they had good weather and spoke about many things. Once the ship arrived at shore, Geirröd jumped off the ship with speed and pushed the ship back out to sea with force while insulting the two peasants as they drifted away. Geirröd managed to return home and the people were rejoiced, but his father, the king, had died, therefore it was Geirröd's time to be king. He and his kingdom prospered. On the other hand, his younger brother Agnar went to live in a cave with a giantess.

Now Odin is sitting on his throne, Hlidskjalf, with his wife Frigg beside him, watching over the worlds in quiet contemplation. As they gaze over Midgard, the realm of men, Odin notices how his foster-son Geirröd was going for himself as king, while Agnar, Frigg's foster-son, was simply living in a cave with his giantess.

Odin and Frigg often enjoyed disguising themselves as humans, and they were the two peasants who had helped the stranded brothers that winter many moons ago.
Frigg, offended, responded by saying that King Geirröd was very frugal and inhospitable if he knew that too many guests would consume his food stores and other resources.
The two gods argued over this until they decided to settle it with wager. Frigg would send her maid Fulla to the king, where Fulla would inform him that soon one night an evil magician would come calling at his court and that this magician could be recognized by the fact that the hounds would not show aggression towards him. So, Fulla does her goddesses bidding and King Geirröd heeds the advice given. Not long after, Odin, in disguise, does appear in a dark blue cloak at the king's home, and just like the maiden had advised, the hounds were tame towards the man. This man was immediately imprisoned and would only say that he was named Grímnir, and no more.

King Geirröd tortured Grímnir for more information by placing him between two fires for eight nights. In pity, Agnar, the king's young son named after his uncle, decides to help the man and offers him a drink, complaining that his father did not have to be so cruel. Grímnir tells Agnar that no one else had bothered to assist him during these horrendous eight days and nights of torture, and upon burning his cloak in the fire he reveals himself as the All-father. Odin had prophesied that Agnar would become Lord of the Goths and promised him great reward for his kindness.

Fire! thou art hot,
and much too great;
flame! let us separate.
My garment is singed,
although I left it up,
my cloak is scorched before it.
...
Eight night have I sat
between fires here,
food has offered,
save only Agnar,
the son of Geirröd,
who alone shall rule
over the land of the Goths.
...
Be thou blessed, Agnar!

as blessed as the god of men

bids thee to be.

For one draught

thou never shalt

get better recompense. (p. 20)

Odin then teaches Agnar about the expanse of the known cosmology and many realms that exist and all the beings that live there, and tells him the names of his many other disguises.

Odin reveals himself to the king as well and promises him misfortune for the treatment he has received. King Geirröd, understanding the severity of the mistake made, attempts to retrieve the man from the fires but in doing so his sword, which was lying on his lap, slips and falls hilt down. In a rush, the king stumbles and falls upon the open blade where he immediately dies. Odin disappears in that moment, and Agnar becomes the new king who rules from that day forth with more generosity and kindness.

Please note that only the first three of the 54 stanzas of Odin's monologue were inserted into the above depiction of the tale, as maybe the full 54 would be too heavy an insert for the book.

The concept of hospitality, kindness, and the threads of fate being inevitable are the main morals of this story.

Skáldskaparmál: The Kidnapping of Idun (Prose Edda)

Three great gods were on a journey through the mountains of Asgard. These gods were Odin, Hœnir, and the trickster, Loki. Through the long passes and days of not eating, they were famished and tired. They came across a herd of Ox and decided to take one for their dinner.

This meat was on the fire for quite some time and no matter how many times they looked to see if it had been cooked, they found it to be just as raw as it had the moment they pulled it off the carcass.

A large eagle was flying up ahead and as Loki looked up to observe it, the eagle spoke. It said that it was using its magic to prevent the meat from cooking, and unless they gave it a portion of the meat, it would not release the spell that bound it. Reluctantly, they agreed. The eagle swooped down and took the best portion of meat available, which angered Loki, as he thought he had been deceived.

Loki proceeded to lunge with a stick at the eagle, but unbeknownst to Loki, this eagle was the giant Thjazi in disguise, and he snatched the stick still being held by Loki and soared high into the sky.

Loki begged the eagle to release him on solid ground, but Thjazi once again required a bargain to be met. The eagle would release Loki only once he swore an oath to kidnap the goddess Idun from her sacred tree in Asgard and bring her, along with her fruits of eternal youth, back to him. Loki agrees once more with reluctance and fear.

Upon the three gods returning home, Loki, honoring his oath in evil deeds, goes to Idun who is always in the vicinity of her precious tree. He tells her of another marvelous tree beyond the wall of Asgard that has fruits even more wondrous than those in Asgard. He tells her to take some of her own fruits and follow him into the forest so she may compare the quality. A trickster indeed! Once they arrive in the false location of the false tree, Idun is surprised by the arrival of the large eagle, being the giant Thjazi, and is kidnapped and taken to his home in the icy mountain realm Thrymheim.

Now, the gods, without their fruits of eternal youth being cared for by the sweet Idun, were beginning to feel the heavy burden of age and frailty. They query with all on the location of Idun, and it is found that Loki was the last to be seen in her presence. The gods, knowing very well that this was not a good thing, cornered the trickster with all means of threats and pain. When he eventually spoke the truth and told of what had transpired that day in the forest, the gods gave him an ultimatum, to die now or to save poor Idun from her fate. Generously, the goddess Freyja gave him her cloak of falcon feathers in assistance on his journey, which allowed him to change into a falcon and fly to the far away land. Once he arrived at Jötunheim to retrieve Idun, he saw with delight that Thjazi was out fishing, therefore Loki took the advantage and turned Idun into a nut and flew away with her in his talons back to Asgard.

Thjazi was furious when he found his prize missing. He transformed back into his eagle form and pursued day and night to catch Loki before he could get back into the realm of Asgard. The other gods saw Loki approaching the borders and the eagle close behind, so they got together and built a fire around the fortress. As Loki was just able to avoid the eagle and enter the border, the fire exploded and killed Thjazi instantly.

Here we see the themes of honoring vows and avenging that which was taken.

Scandinavian Folklore

Also called Nordic folklore, these are tales about mythological creatures living in nature, and it encompasses both their Norse mythology and the Christian worldview at the time. These tales are influenced by the folklore of Germany, England, Finland, and the Baltic lands.

These stories were either light and filled with kind creatures who taught the hero a lesson, or dark and scary where an evil being needed to be defeated. Many were told to the children at night or when they were misbehaving to keep them from trouble.

Fairytales from Peter Christen Asbjørnsen and Jørgen Moe have become very popular in our modern era and have been adapted and changed, including some tales by Hans Christian Anderson. The original collection is of around 60 tales called *Popular Tales from the Norse* and was written in the 18th century.

From their lore, we can get a better idea of what the ancient Norse people truly feared or what kind of health and morality issues hung over their heads by interpreting some of these with historical eyes. Let us take a look at some of the interesting creatures behind Scandinavian folklore.

The Huldra

The Huldra, or known in Swedish as the Tallemja, was known to be a beautiful female troll who lived in the woods. Its origins derive from the Norse variation of the story of Adam and Eve, where Eve has to wash and clean all her children when God comes to visit, but those who were unclean before God's arrival would be hidden in the earth from his view forever. Tallemja was the dirty girl who refused to be bathed and escaped her mother's clutch to roam the land instead of being hidden under the ground due to her filthy appearance. These tales were told to scare children so if they were dirty and lied to God about where they had been, their souls would join the other hidden children under the earth forever. We suppose it is a good way to get the children to clean themselves and be truthful.

The Nisse

This was a creature that originally was known to live in the outskirts of every house, in their barns or vicinity, also known as the "household spirit." The Nisse was associated with their winter solstice, and what we would call a Christmas folklore. These creatures look like little garden gnomes but with immense strength, and they guard homes from evil. Often disapproving of bad manners or unkempt farms and animals, it is said that if one spills a drink in their house they must shout a warning to the Nisse who lived under them.

A bowl of porridge was given as a sacrificial offering to please the Nisse every Christmas Eve. If the porridge was not there, the Nisse could cause trouble to the house and the animals; therefore, this tradition was practiced to make sure the farm was kept safe and healthy by the Nisse who looked over it. The most treasured of the farm animals by this creature was the horse, and it was said that whichever horse was the healthiest and most beautiful was most likely the favorite of the Nisse, as it would take better care of that animal than the rest.

Pesta

The Pesta was a personification of the Black Death that killed many Scandinavian adults and children during the Medieval Period. Disease was something that took many lives in rural communities in Norway and Denmark.

This figure was portrayed as an old woman wearing a black cloak and red skirt, roaming the country and causing illness and death. It was said that if she was seen carrying a rake near a house, then not all would die and some would pass through the teeth of the rake, thus being spared.

But if she was carrying a broom, then it was doom for the whole family. This personification is an attempt at explaining a horrible experience of death due to disease. The path she traveled was a map of where the disease spread, through the countryside, over mountains, and even traveling on boats—this being particularly interesting as the Black Plague was thought to have arrived to the shores of Norway via infected ship rats.

Nokken

Also called a Nixie, this is a monster that takes the humanoid shape of a water creature in Germanic and Scandinavian folktales. The characteristics of the Nokken change depending on the geographical location of the story's origin. For instance, in Norway this monster resides in lakes, rivers, and ponds lurking at the surface and looking out with dark evil eyes. In Sweden, the creature is actually seen as a beautiful man who entices women to jump into the water and then drowning them. Many consider this creature to be related to the mermaid or siren who sings to sailors but with deadly consequences. One of the central attributes of this monster is its capability to shapeshift and therefore take on any form it wishes.

The Draugr

The Draugr is known as a horrendous undead sea monster covered in seaweed and sometimes seen sitting in a rowing boat in the form of an old man. Scandinavian sailors were known to be afraid of the Draugr, who would drown them at sea during storms. If the man appeared in his boat screaming to the sailors, someone was going to drown that night. The term *draugr* in Old Norse means "a ghost or spirit."

Chapter 4: Seiðr, Spà, & Galdr

The magic that was possible in ancient times has probably been diluted to such a degree that we no longer feel a fluid connection to the spiritual world as deeply as they did. The Norse were highly entwined with what was not seen. Magic was a connection not just to a consciousness but to the entirety of the living world. Spirits resided in everything and influenced everyone.

Norse magic revolved around the understanding of things and having a deep knowledge of the methods and techniques needed to perform the art. It most likely took many years to learn how to hear and read the signs around them, remembering the songs and asking the right questions. The Norse people were almost obsessed with the concept of fate, destiny, and the changes of course in one's future. Prophecies and enlightenment on the "way things will be" is what guided everyone from common folk to the elite and the kings. Magic was used in almost everything they did and the one person with the most knowledge on the subject was the most regarded.

These women were known as seers, sorceresses, or *völva*. Depending on the magic used, they are also referred to as *sieðrkona, spákona,* or *seiðrfolk*. This art was highly regarded as a women's task, that is, the practice of divination and the speaking to spirits. It was frowned upon if men used magic, as it was seen as unmanly and shameful. Strangely enough, as you might remember from above, Odin himself learned the magic of the runes and is known to practice seiðr, along with his wife Freyja, which is what gives him that shamed, unmanly facet of his theme.

Dreams and their meanings were evaluated and studied too, and they were given great importance. Some dreams were foretelling of doom and death, and some were messages from spirits in other worlds or from ancestors long gone.
The seers would travel the regions and counsel men and their families. They would travel to large events or gatherings and assist in the rituals of sacrifice and worship, prophesy new births, and bless for new unifications. They were brewers of healing potions and casters of curses. They could change the weather or make people fall in love by chanting the Galdr chants and songs.

There are three main branches of the craft: Seiðr-craft, Spá-craft, and Galdr-craft.

Seiðr

A common mistake is to assume that seiðr is the general term for all Norse witchcraft, whereas each magic has a specific branch, form, and use. Seiðr in particular was used as a base for the idea of weaving the threads of fate and destiny, allowing the seer to hear the secrets of the spirits that they called to them and prophesy their benefit or loss.
Seiðr translates from the Old Norse to "string, cord, or snare" and was practiced in Norse society in the later Scandinavian Iron Age. Depending on the need, it was used in blessing the family or cursing the enemy, increasing fertility or crop growth, as well as influencing animals and the weather.

Connection to Shamanism

These women mostly traveled their regions and that of their neighbors, keeping a nomadic lifestyle so they may search for new truths and gain as much knowledge about the world around them. Going from village to village, they performed their magic in return for money or housing for the night.

The act of shamanism comes into play when we see how they induced intricate trance states by meditating and chanting to the spirit realm. The magic was that of illusion and manipulation as well as soul-healing.

Partial nudity in these states was common and some connect this type of shamanism to the origins of the pagan witch on a broomstick, flying naked, and chanting around a fire in a group. Women who performed seiðr were usually marginalized in their communities, as this was sometimes seen as dirty or sexually shameful chaos magic, even as it was respected and revered.

Initially connected to the goddess Freyja, it was later also associated with the god Odin (who received the magic of seiðr from Freyja). The influence of Christianity pushed more association of 'good' magic onto male gods and outlawed the use of female worship. The men who performed this magic (and there were even those who took it on professionally too) were called *seiðrmenn*.

Performing

We know that these women always performed on a platform (*hjälle* or "high seat") that was usually covered in fur pillows and placed in the middle of the room. Surrounding the platform would be gifts and food. She would be carrying a distaff, a type of ritualistic stick that symbolized her power, along with pouches or bags filled with various magical items (pieces of bone, stone, or wood) used in the ritual.

The völva would sometimes drink a mead or beer that contained some herbs or intoxicating plants to assist in the ecstatic trance work or burn these as incense. At bigger events or for more critical needs, sometimes the magic was performed with other practitioners to increase the magnetic draw of the spirits.

The point was to seek what was hidden from their base of reality and existence and listen for the answers and actions that needed to be made from the spirits that are drawn in. When one goes into meditation, the brain waves decrease and reach an alpha wavelength state that brings you into a deep calm. Now the völva must have been able to get to that level while at the same time keeping the physical body connected and energetic by moving, spinning, humming deeply, or even just doing breath work. The use of either the excited trance work or the more calm and still meditation probably depended on her personal mood that day or on the type of medium connection she was trying to make.

It is often believed that the witchcraft performed by the völva was surrounded by the invoking of inanimate objects. Often river stones were used in conjunction with steel nails or plates to cause a spark that would tell what the weather was going to be like. The distaff used by the völva in rituals would be adorned with crystals and stones to increase the spiritual connection. Or stones were set into the hilts of swords so warriors could heal wounds that were given when using the weapon. Warriors also used to suck on river stones during battle to ward off thirst and hunger.

Apart from being used to grasp the fates, the seer would use her magic to protect men in battle and ensure their enemies death. Women would perform this war magic to the warriors before they left for war to give them hope, courage, rage, and energy while assuring that the spirits and gods were on their side. Sometimes these women would join the men on their battles and raids to keep the magic 'flowing' and to heal the wounded.

Derivation

Here we read a section from the *Saga of Erik the Red* describing *Þórbjörg,* the völva who traveled across Greenland revealing her knowledge:

A high seat was set for her, complete with a cushion. This was to be stuffed with chicken feathers. When she arrived one evening, along with the man who had been sent to fetch her, she was wearing a black mantle with a strap, which was adorned with precious stones right down to the hem. About her neck she wore a string of glass beads on her head and a hood of black lambskin lined with white catskin. She bore a staff with a knob at the top, adorned with brass set with stones on top. About her waist she had a linked charm belt with a large purse. In it she kept the charms which she needed for her predictions. She wore calfskin boots lined with fur, with long, sturdy laces and large pewter knobs on the ends. On her hands she wore gloves of catskin, white and lines with fur. When she entered, everyone was supposed to offer her respectful greetings, and she responded according to how the person appealed to her.

Farmer Thorkel took this wise woman by the hand and led her to the seat which had been prepared for her. He then asked her to survey his flock, servants and buildings. She had little to say about all of it. That evening tables were set up and food prepared for the seeress. A porridge of kid's milk was made for her and as meat she was given the hearts of all the animals available there. She had a spoon of brass and a knife of ivory shaft, its two halves clasped with brass hands, and the point of which was broken off. (p. 3)

It is important to note that in these accounts we only get an idea of what she wears, what she eats, and where she sits. What is not explained is the actual act—that is how she moved, what she said during the trance, or what she revealed, which is what keeps historians on edge.

Spá

The chief function of a spá-wife or *spákona* was as prophetess. The relationship between the spá magic and that of seiðr are often seen in a similar sense. The main difference between the two could be that the *spákona* derives her power from within (something she already possessed), unlike the *seiðkona* who used the spirit's influence as a middle-man of sorts. Even the word *völva* can be classified under the two magics, as it was found to be used loosely for a woman with the gift of foresight.

Considered the fairest of soul-crafts, the worship of forebears was a respected role in the community and the women who practiced it were too. They were also known to be more accepted by the Christian *seiðmann* during the conversion period.

Connection to the Norns

This type of magic leans more towards welfare-working and psychic sensing. The *spákona* would prophesy the *örlögs* (luck or fate) of men and women in their village or community. The origins of the *örlög* can be directly pulled from the telling of the three Norns, the women who sat at the Urd Well under the World Tree and decided the path of everyone's life. Therefore, in some way these women were able to bypass the usual roots of divination and go right to the source. The *spá-wife* was often also associated with the lesser Norns or *dísir* who would come down from their tree and read the *örlögs* of a newborn's fate.

Practiced with more dignity and favor than what we see of the *seiðrkona* women, this form of magic was inspired by positive connections towards the fates and ancestors. Although there was a reference to the spá-wife performing some kind of trance work, it was more likely to be in the use of *útiseta*, going under the cloak for two days meditating, rather than the ecstatic trance work of the seiðr.

The Wyrd (personal destiny) with which they work was seen as an interconnected mesh of choices and actions. All actions, no matter how small, affect the Wyrd like a pond rippling out in concentric circles. Therefore, it was crucial that the dísir would foretell the child or adult's general direction in life so they were able to get a "general feeling" of what they should strive for and accomplish.

This magic was a part of many of the goddesses' themes in the pantheon and even Odin was said to often need their assistance on matters of foresight. Goddess Frigg/Freyja and the goddess Sif, who is Thor's wife, were noticeable characters who stepped into the shoes of völva.

Performing

The performance of spà magic occurred mainly around times of deaths, births, and the counsel of kings and lords on battle plans connecting to the past, present, and future.

Men of spá magic, known as *þule* (thule), were more accepted in their practice of this divine telling. The term refers to the Old Norse word "to speak" and is sometimes used as a religious title. Both men and women were known to receive an honorary seat and the offerings of food and drink for their efforts.

A special characteristic to the thule's seat is that it may often have been set upon a burial mound. As kings had religious seats of power, so did the thule or *spá-wife* when they spoke, most often seated in a holy place of power like the burial mounds of great ancestors.

The mounds were flattened at the top so one could stand or place a chair for the speaker. This was both practical in the sense that the community could hear and see them clearly, as well as symbolic, showing their divine power over the common people and over the hallowed dead who dwelt below. And surely the art was easier to practice when you were in the vicinity of the religious spaces and spirits who live there.

Derivation

From the *Hávamál* verse in the Poetic Edda, we can decipher the use of the known term thule when *Fimbul-þulr* (The Great Thule) tells:
It is time to speak as a thule, on the thule's seat,
at the Well of Wyrd;
I saw and was silent, I saw and thought,
I listened to the speech of folk;
I heard deeming of runes, and they were not silent of redes,
at the halls of the High One, in the halls of the High One,
thus I heard tell (p. 79)
Galdr
The practice of galdr was by far the most common idea of magic during the medieval time. The origins can be found way back before the Viking Era, and the term *galdr* can be associated with the Germanic word for magic itself!
The term *galdr* in Old Norse means 'spell' or 'incantation,' and it was commonly associated with both men and women.

Connection to the Songs

It was said that to connect to the deep power of the gods and spirits one would chant these songs as spells to assist and empower Viking warriors in battle or deter enemies from harming them. Many of the magic spells chanted in galdr were connected to symbols or staves to heighten their magic and power. Some would also apply these power signs in graphic detail in the air in front of them, on a piece of wood, or on their skins as tattoos.

Certain "words of power" were sung, creating vibrational power in song and used in poetry done alone or in a group, which could have been extremely healing. Sunforms and certain breathing techniques were used to create more intention and focus. Some masters of the songs were known to use the art as a weapon against enemies to blunt swords, soften armor, and even raise giant storms from the sea.

Performing

The spells and incantations, or rather the saying of magic, were chanted for all sorts of occasions and were usually added as an extra element to the practice ritual of seiðr. This is quite a specific type of sorcery, focusing mainly on the characteristic of a high-pitched singing.

It is said that the falsetto in which they sang these songs was rather pleasing to the ear as they used a specific meterage called the *galdralag*. Some poems ascribe the use of galdr as more cursing, using the tongue as a tool for destruction.

They could make people sick or even kill them. How they sang and what they sang depended on the situation; whether in celebration or war, the song was performed by both men and women, and was either recited on its own for personal purposes or done in conjunction with reading runes or making herbal potions.

The song did not necessarily have to be vocal; it could indeed also be interpreted as an internal voice. Galdr was also used for practical reasons like in the process of childbirth, where women would sing the songs to assist in the delivery of the child, which gave courage to the mother and helped control her breath. The same can be applied to when chanting with the rune divination where one would either do it internally, as imagining the sound, or externally, therefore vocalizing each sound—breathing into the nostrils and holding the breath in your naval center, which is the source of life-force energy, as you chant out the first rune in a drawn out syllable for syllable. Fehu, for instance, would be sung as "Feeeeeeeeh-huuuuuu," each syllable being the exhale from the naval center in a deep tone.

Often understood to be performed in an informal and impromptu setting that would better activate the magic and incantation, the vocalizing of the spells is what was thought to make it more potent. Unfortunately, there are not many surviving artifacts from the Medieval Period of actual spells performed, but there is a vast amount of mentions of these incantations being performed and sung.

Derivation

Various galdr songs can be found in the *Grógaldr* or the Spells of Gróa.

There was the use of galdr in the necromantic practice of Svipdag's attempt to bring his mother Groá, a völva, back from the grave. Groá had requested this of her son if he may ever need her assistance or guidance.

Here we see a reference to galdr in the poem *Skirnismál* in the Poetic Edda where Skirnir, the messenger of Frey, goes to the giantess Gerðor and sings this galdr so that she may fall in love with Frey.

Heyri jötnar, rulers,	Give heed, frost- hear it, giants.
heyri hrímÞursar,	
sybir Suttungs,	Sons of Suttung,
sjakfir ásliðar,	And gods, ye too,
hvé ek fyrbýð,	How I forbid
hvé ek fyrirbanna	and how I ban

manna glaum mani,   The meeting of men with the maid,
manna nyt mani.   (The joy of men with the maid). (stanza 34)

Chapter 5: Runes & Runestones

Runes were first thought to appear around the 1st century and uncertainty still surrounds their place of origin. '*Rún*' in Old Norse means 'symbol,' 'letter,' or 'character.' In some cases, the translation points towards the word *runo*, being a 'mystery' or a secret of sorts. Like many of the other characteristics of Norse culture, absorption of external influences was most likely the creation of the language in the first place.

The shape that developed for each rune was a pragmatic one. Firstly, parchment and inks were expensive and hard to come by, which meant carving onto already available materials from nature was more practical. Straight vertical lines, rather than the curved letters, were easier to carve with tools into tough surfaces.

The resemblance to the Egyptian hieroglyphs gives the language a very perplexing image to those accustomed to the Latin alphabet. One character can represent various sounds and at the same time also represent whole words or phrases. Characters could be read left to right, right to left, and top to bottom without the use of spacing, making a runologist's job quite tough. We suppose the fact that it's a lot less straightforward to decipher is probably what makes the job so interesting to begin with!

The original runic inscriptions in Elder Futhark were carved onto materials that held significance, therefore elevating the status of the object itself. Their use varied depending on the need, and the materials on which they were carved varied just the same. Wood, iron, stone, and bone each held an inert power and influence over the runes themselves.

The Norse were not technically illiterate, as is the misconception, and most people could read and carve runes, or at least knew the basic inscriptions. They were simply more interested in using the runes to tell stories, give personal messages, and express love rather than record their daily practices and rituals with more detail. The passing on of their detailed knowledge to the next generation was mostly oral.

Archaeologists have found these ancient inscriptions most famously on the large runestones, but also in cliff walls and around sacred groves and waterfalls where offerings and worship took place. Runes were used as trade markers for merchants detailing their goods or were carved near grave mounds and on other religious objects. Runes were carved on pieces of wood to send messages to family and people in neighboring villages or even as graffiti when people just passed through the village. Riddles and various jokes are also found on runestones, with a plentiful number of love letters to women and dead relatives as well.

Runes were often carved into and around the house walls, into various house items and accessories such as combs, around mirrors, on the sole of shoes, on plate ware, and carved onto pendants and pieces of clothing. Protection in battle was a straightforward need; therefore, finding protective runes on weapons, helmets, and shields was commonplace.

Some of these inscriptions also bore the interaction they had with other cultures. For instance, the runic inscription, "love conquers all," which was originally a Latin phrase from the poet Virgil, had somehow passed into their society and took form through runic inscriptions.

The use of runes before the Christianization of the Scandinavian kingdoms was more practical than divine. Even though some small accounts do attest to the use of runes for divination in the sagas of the Poetic Edda, most were largely for protection and practical use.

Odin's Gift

Throughout the many sagas and poems surrounding the gods and heroes of Norse mythology, it is comprehensible that the idea of sacrificing something important to the main character in return for knowledge and power is a key element. The ultimate sacrifice was the one of self-sacrifice. We see the original theme in the poem *Hávamál* from the Poetic Edda, in which we experience Odin's challenge and strife from his own perspective.

The great Odin, sitting on his throne, is hungry for the wisdom of all things. He decides to venture in search of this mighty wisdom at Mímir's Well, where he sacrifices his eye and throws himself onto his own spear, Gungnir, all in the name of the quest. Here he only receives half of the knowledge he requires, therefore, he still ventures forth in search of more.

From his throne in Asgard, he looks out at the Norns by their well below Yggdrasil and sees their power in weaving and threading the fates of all beings. So, Odin takes it upon himself to learn their magic, but in order for him to receive the knowledge of the magic of the fates he again has to sacrifice something. So, self-wounded by a spear, he hangs in the tree for nine days and nights, looking into the pool and denying any assistance from the other gods.

I know that I hung on a wind rocked tree,
nine whole nights, with spear wounded,
and to Odin offered myself to myself;
on that tree of which no one knows from what root it springs.
Bread no one gave me, no horn of drink,
downward I peered, to runes applied myself,
wailing learnt them, then fell down thence. (*Hávamál*, stanza 138)

Finally! The runes had revealed themselves to him through visions and secrets. But he is not the same as he was; he has changed and been reborn. The symbolism that half of Odin's self had died in that tree and that he came out of the ordeal a stronger being is the idea of passing the physical limits of the mortal self to arrive at the divine and immortal.

Then I fertilized and became wise;
I truly grew and thrived.
From a word to a word I was led to a word,
From a work to a work I was led to a work. (stanza 163)

History Brought Alive

From there he uses his gained knowledge to pass on the runes to the men of the world so they may be able to learn and grow like he did.

Myth aside, what the evidence tells us is that historically, Germanic tribes often warred and traded with Roman people in the south and eventually brought back with them to Scandinavian kingdoms their own take on the Old Italic language, molding it and altering it to their own worldview, thus creating the Elder Futhark.

Elder Futhark

This is the original and oldest used language of the Scandinavian region, which appeared in the 1st century during the Dark Ages, also called the Germanic Futhark. The name Futhark actually derives from the first six letters of their alphabet (ᚠᚢᚦᚨᚱ‹).

ᚠ - fehu

    ᛖ - ehwaz

ᚢ - uruz

    ᛗ - mannaz

ᚦ - burisaz

- laguz

ᚨ - ansuz

    ◊ - inguz

ᚱ - raido

    ᛞ - dagaz

ᛏ - naubiz

ᛁ - isa

᛬ - jera   ᛚ

ᛃ - eihwaz

ᛣ - perb

ᚲ - kaunaz
ᛟ - opala
ᚷ - gebo
ᚹ - wunjo
ᚺ - hagalaz

ᛉ - algiz
ᛋ - sowilo
ᛏ - tiwaz
ᛒ - berkana

Since the names in these runes are not preserved anywhere in Elder Futhark, historians have had to try and reconstruct them from the names preserved in the later runic alphabets, almost like retracing steps of language. The Gothic alphabet is the earliest available Germanic language in large cohesive texts from 300 C.E. when the names of the letters in the alphabet were based on runes.

Another adaptation of the writing system came from the Anglo-Saxon (Old English) texts in the 5th century, creating the Anglo-Frisian Futhorc. Consisting of between 24 and 33 characters, this version was used by Frisian (Germanic group of Netherlands and Denmark) cultures and brought to England as seen in the use of manuscripts. This lasted until the late 11th century before being supplanted by the Latin alphabet.

Although very rare in the Viking Age, and mostly seen in the proto-Norse migration period, bind-runes were used as a ligature of two or more runes. They were either a simple two rune (rarely three) combination to make a single conjoined glyph. Then the same-stave rune, which is a larger conglomeration of runes, stemmed together and was usually found on runestones.

There are two choices one needs to make when transcribing from modern English to Runic: either you write it as a direct letter for rune translation, which might not come out as it would be pronounced (but how it is spelt), or you write it phonetically (as it's pronounced) which removes or changes the placement of runic letters accordingly. There are no runic alphabet letters that are equivalent to all the 26 letters or to all the sounds used in English today.

Younger Futhark

The Elder Futhark slowly underwent a reform in the late 7th century and 8 out of the 24 characters were eventually removed. This established the 16-character Younger Futhark of the Viking Age, also called the Scandinavian Futhark.

Some serious changes occurred to the language as vowels were added and characters removed. Therefore, one could see a trend towards a more minimalistic and useful form of the language where diplomatic and trade orientated subjects could be expressed. These changes included some distinct sounds that were written the same.

ᚠ - Fé

ᚼ - Hagall

ᛒᚠ - Bjarkan

ᚢ - Úr

ᚾ - Nauðr

ᛦ - Maðr

ᚦ - Thurs

ᛁ - Is

ᛚ - Logr

ᚨ - As/Oss

ᚼ - Ar

ᛧ - Yr

ᚱ - Reið

ᛋ - Sol

ᚴ - Kaun

ᛏ - Tyr

A further division went under way in the Younger Futhark, splitting into the long-branch Danish runes, which were better used for documenting information on stone, and the short-twig (Rök) runes, which were thought to be a shorthand for personal messages on wood. They originated in the Swedish and Norwegian cultures.

Some runes were adapted even further and lacked the normal strokes and lines used in the Younger Futhark. These runes were called Hälsinge Runes or staveless runes, meaning they lack the 'stave' or stroke—something like a "budget rune."

Rune Poems

Rune poems are the top source of relevance to the Younger Futhark's 16-letter alphabet. They provide for their user an explanation of each runic letter in a poetic stanza to help remember pronunciation and relevance for each rune. Each of these rune poems has a couple of lines giving memorable images to help remember the name of the rune.
They are divided into three parts: Norwegian Rune Poems, Icelandic Rune Poems, and Anglo-Saxon Rune Poems. Norwegian and Icelandic poems were based on the Younger Futhark, while the Anglo-Saxon used the relevant Anglo-Saxon Runic alphabet.

Due to the sheer amount of information on each region's version of the poems, we will provide the most well systematized of the three: the Icelandic Rune Poems of the 15th century.

- ᚠ - Fé (Wealth)

Fé er frænda róg	Source of discord among kinsmen
ok flæðar viti	and fire of the sea
ok grafseiðs gata	and path of the serpent
aurum fylkir.	

- ᚢ - Úr (Shower)

Úr we skýja grátr	Lamentation of the clouds
ok skára þverrir	and ruin of the hay-harvest
ok hirðis hatr.	and abomination of the shepherd.
umbre visi	

- ᚦ - Thurs (Giant)

Þurs er kvenna kvöl	The torturer of women
ok kletta búi	and cliff-dweller
ok varðúðar verr.	and husband of a giantess.
Saturnus þengill.	

- ᚨ - As/Óss (God)

Óss er algingautr	Aged Gautr
ok ásgarðs jöfurr,	and prince of Asgard
ok valhallar vídi.	and lord of Valhalla.

- ᚱ - Reið (Riding)

Reið er sitjandi sæla	Joy of the horsemen
ok snúðig ferð	and speedy journey
ok jórs erfiði.	and toil of the steed.
iter ræsir.	

- ᚴ - Kaun (Ulcer)

Kaun er barna böl	Disease fatal to children
ok bardaga för	and painful spot
ok holffúa hús.	and abode of mortification.
flagella konungr.	

- ᚼ - Hagall (Hail)

Hagall er kaldakorn	Cold grain
ok krapadrífa	and shower of sleet
ok snáka sótt.	and sickness of serpents.
grando hildingr.	

- ᚾ - Nauðr (Constraint)

Nauð er þýjar þrá	Grief of the bone-maid

ok þungr kostur   and state of oppression
ok vássamlig verk.   and toilsome work.
opera niflungr.

- ᛁ - Ís (Ice)

Íss er árbörkr   Bark of rivers
ok unnar þak   and roof of the wave
ok feigra manna fár.   and destruction of the doomed.
glacies jöfurr.

- ᛌ - Ár (Plenty)

Ár er gumna góði   Boon to men
ok gott sumar   and good summer
algróinn akr.   and thriving crops.
annus allvaldr

- ᛋ - Sól (Sun)

Sól er skýja skjöldur   Shield of the clouds
ok ísa aldrtregi.   and shining ray
rota siklingr.   and destroyer of ice.

- ᛏ - Týr

Týr er einhendr áss   God with one hand
ok ulfs leifar   and leaving of the wolf

ok hofa hilmir. | and prince of
temples. |
Mars tiggi. |

- ᛒ - Bjarkan (Birch)

Bjarkan er laufgat lim | Leafy twig
ok lítit tré | and little tree
ok ingsamligr viðr. | and fresh
young shrub. |
abies buðlungr. |

- ᛘ - Maðr (Man)

Maðr er manns gaman | Delight of man
ok moldar auki | and augmentation of
the earth |
ok skipa skreytir. | and adorner of
ships. |
homo mildingr. |

- ᛚ - Lögr (Water)

Lögr er vallanda vatn | Eddying stream
*ok viðr ketil*l | and broad geysir
ok glömmungr grundi. | and land of the fish.
lacus lofðungr. |

- ᛦ - Ýr (Yew)

Ýr er bendr bogi | Bent bow
ok brotgjarnt járn | and brittle iron
ok fífu fáarbauti. | and giant of
the arrow. |
arcus ynglingr. |

What we see here is the relevance of each poem to the theme and character of each rune. Just like one would sing rhymes to children to help them learn English and word association, this too was used as a method of learning and remembrance. The stress put on the first syllable of the word is what makes it complicated to relate to modern English. Norse poetry alliterates the first letter of the word whereas English normally uses rhyming of the last letter of the word.

Icelandic Rune Staves

With the settlement of Norse people in Iceland around 870 C.E., the Younger Futhark alphabet was taken with them and further adapted for magical purposes. This can be seen as a conglomeration of different characters to wield more powers. You would find three or more runes combined into an intricate character that possessed combined magic and meaning.

The use of this white magic was known as Galdrasafur, meaning "magical stick" or 'stave,' and it was practiced more by men in Iceland. They were carved, like other Nordic runes, on specific materials and influenced a certain effect or outcome.

A small drop of blood was also used as a personal sacrifice to the magic. Being very specific and relevant to what the Icelanders needed at the time, their magic was used as a tool to kill an enemy's cattle, for increased fertility, "to guide through bad weather or bring victory during competitions of wrestling, called glíma," (Iceland Rovers, 2017). Some were used to help with fishing or rowing your boat, the healing of fox bites, or even to make your sheep more docile.

We see that in the middle of the 16th century the outlaw of runes was heavily forced and many men were put to death for still having an intimate relationship with their pagan religion and use of runes around their abodes.

The most common runic staves used were:

- *Aegishjálmur*, "Helm of Awe," had the shape of a four or an eight to form an equal cross with branches at its terminals. Here we see the saga of Sigurd who slays the great serpent Fáfnir in order to win a treasure horde of the Niflungs. Part of the treasure is the symbol of *Aegishjálmur*, which surrounded him in an ethereal way with power and protection. It was named Solomons Innsigil once Christianity took hold.
- *Að unni* was a simplified version of the complex symbol of *Aegishjálmur*, with fewer branches, used mainly as a love stave. So, a man might find the love of a woman. This symbol was most often drawn with one's own spit in their right hand.

- Another to consider is the *Hraethigaldur*, a stave used to put fear on an enemy. Carved on some bark and worn as a pendant, this would keep your enemies at a distance and fearful of you. But always make sure you see your enemy before he sees you!

Runestones

Runestones had one main purpose: to be seen! They are large upright slabs of stone displaying various messages, poems, and life stories of the person or family the rune was about. The runes were often painted with bright colors and sometimes accompanied by elaborate drawings depicting scenes of battle or triumph. Both men and women commissioned runestones and were often used to elevate their social standing within the community. Most of the runestones still standing today are located in Sweden, but many more can be found across the other Scandinavian regions like Denmark and Norway, as well as the locations where Vikings traveled during their raids and trades.

The use of runic inscriptions on large stones and bedrock started in the 4th century and lasted till the 12th century when the Viking Age was at a close.

Interesting fact: Most runestones were actually carved by the converted Norse people during the Viking Era, which was right in the middle of a religious conversion, and so many of the carvings were about Christian stories, depicting crosses and invoking the name of their new God. This was probably to show their neighbors how well they had converted to the new religion and forsaken their pagan past.

Tools Used

It was quite important that the runes were carved correctly; they needed to be on the appropriate surface and location be sure that they invoked the correct deity for their chosen purpose. Bad luck and ill fortune would be your burden if you did not complete the process with care.

Carving runestones must have been a rather arduous job to complete when they worked on large stone slabs that were later erected as runestones. But for smaller objects that had personal meaning, it was a quick and manageable task done with skill and experience.

The tools used to carve the horizontal and vertical lines were:

- Chisels: Easy to make and fairly cheap, the chisel was normally a metal stick of sorts, easily held in the palm of one's hand. Blunted on one end to allow contact with the hammer and pointed on the other to create indentations on the surface of the material, the runemaster would drive the chisel into the wood or stone with a certain amount of force. It required a deft and experienced hand or the stone would chip and crack with too much pressure from the hammer, or the wood would split and splinter causing the incorrect indentations needed. Imagine having to re-do a whole piece of work because you incorrectly chiseled the last few rune inscriptions on the block!
- Hammer: Either wooden or metal, hammers were also a rather cheap and common tool. The hammer was used to smash down on the chisel and create enough force to cause an indentation on the surface. Runemasters had to be very careful to not crack the entire stone or injure themselves badly with lack of precision. Hammers could break and chisels could go blunt, therefore, the tools were often repaired and replaced to keep the quality of the work up to standard.

Where They Stand

Mainly found in large crossroads, waterways, and property boundaries, these stones were placed for easy observation by whomever passed by. The names of the runes are mostly associated with their location to the towns they are situated in. There are over 2,500 runestones found in Sweden, more than the other Nordic countries, and this is due to their earlier conversion to Christianity.

- The Ramsund carving in Sweden is found on a rocky outcrop next to a bridge and thought to have been carved in the 10th century. It is not necessarily considered a runestone per se, as it was not found elevated and standing but rather just depicted on a flat rock. It is thought to have been commissioned by a prominent Norse woman who inscribed her family's names into the rock and added mighty gods to the rune associating them with favor and good fortune. This was carved in Younger Futhark.
- Jelling runestones in Denmark show two standing stones from the 10th century memorializing two generations of a royal Danish family. One from a king called Gorm the Old, memorializing his wife, and the other from his son Harold Bluetooth after Gorems death. This too was carved in Younger Futhark.

- The Rök runestone is by far the most famously known to this day. Located in Sweden, it marks the initial stage of Swedish literature and consists of poetry of tautology (statements that tell of ideas and thoughts). Before it was moved to a new position, this stone was part of a medieval church dated to the 9th century and carved in Elder Futhark.
- The Einang runestone is found in Norway and was also initially part of a church building. This stone has been dated all the way to the 4th century and has been thought to be the earliest finding of the term 'rune' in Elder Futhark.
- The Varangian runestones are located in over 30 places in Scandinavian and Europe. They attest to the voyages of the Varangian guard from the east into Russia, to the Baltic, and into Greece and Italy.

The placement of the various runestones found in Eastern and Western Europe is almost like a dotted map, showing just how far their reach really went—in the Baltic lands near waterways or in towns in Southern Europe.

Reading the Stones

These professional carvers used a basic layout to follow: starting with a name of the commissioner of the stone, next would be the name of the person who died and what they had realized during their life, then a prayer, and the name of the carver. This demonstrates that rune carvers were quite literate and often chiseled short, to the point messages on these stones.

Most were carved in Younger Futhark and it can be challenging to pinpoint the sound used for each character, as they had so many versions.

We can also see many tender and romantic stories told about a lover's death and their memory. For instance, the runestone raised by a farmer named Holmgöt attests his love for his wife and that there was no better woman to help him on the farm than her. This runestone was placed over his wife's grave.

Runemasters

Runestones were often carved by non-professional runecarvers like merchants, farmers, and Vikings as depictions of daily life. Later in the 11th century, professional runemasters were coming to prominence who solely focused on the carving of commissions given by the family or person it related to. The runemasters would appoint apprentices to assist in the commissions, as it became a very profitable and work intensive job. The runemaster often also needed to be a proficient stonesman, as it was very difficult to select and carve correctly on the large stone blocks.

Chapter 6: Runic Divination

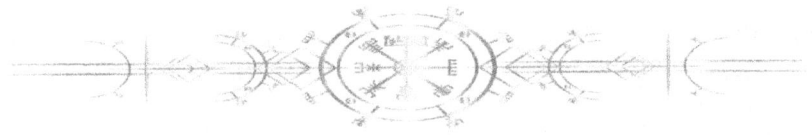

When we talk about using runes for divination, it must be specified that the magic used is that of the mind and that of the soul, not to be confused with fortune-telling. The pieces of stone or wood with symbols on them are not what contain the power to detect obstacles and great events in your future. The magic comes from the strength of human will and the intention of seeing a possible path, not an answer! "It's about looking for possible causes and effects and seeing potential outcomes," (Newcombe, 2019).

The practice of runic divination during the Viking Age has been in question for many years. Findings in Icelandic Sagas do mention the use of runes in some kind of divination, such as the *Ynglinga Saga* from the Icelandic poet Snorri Sturluson, where a king recites his visit to the temple in Uppsala: "the chips fell in a way that said that he would not live long," (stanza 40).

This could easily be interpreted as the use of runic divination, but the accounts are so small and varied that it is best to acknowledge the current idea of divination before the end of the Viking Era as negligible due to it being a late adaptation during the 13th century. Therefore, historians have not directly linked divination with rune casting prior to the Christianization of Scandinavia. Thus, could it really be considered authentic?

New ideas and patterns that are brought into the runes over the centuries should not be ostracized because they didn't apply to the ancient practices of the past, but rather be acknowledged in an esoteric way to each user. Adding or interchanging meaning with each person's personal beliefs is not a sin. We are sure that none of the Norsemen are turning in their graves just because you didn't say the word right or used the symbol in the correct way. The point is that you are using the threads of fate to guide you through the rush and rumble of the modern world so you may open your soul to the influences of past, future, and present. That is what the idea of paganism was, a very personalized variant.

The Three Ættir

Ætt, or Ættir for plural, means family, clan, or group, and Elder Futhark is the runic language used to create these Ættir's. The division of the three gods watching over each Ætt reflects the various social divisions of tribal society: the nurturer, the priest, and the warrior. What these Ættir's are to each rune is a theme using an ancient separation of writings and codes. Each Ætt is technically the narrator of the story depending on its use and meaning, and they will change the perspectives of runes to fit the theme and relate emotions specific for each Ætt. Some of these runes can be read in reverse to mean the exact opposite, most often negatively. Each Ætt is a splitting of the Elder Futhark into three equal parts of eight runes each. Natural elements are used as themes and can belong to two or three of the Æetts at the same time and thus overlap and emphasize more meaning to each character. Love for The Mother, wisdom for The King, or rage for The Warrior.

The Mother

This is known to be the Ættir of Freyr, son of god Njord and ruler of peace. Some interchange the god with the goddess Freyja, his sister, who also holds the virtues for this Ætt. The Mother symbolizes sex, intimacy, benefactor for cultivation of crops, fertility, passion, interpersonal relations, physical touch, care, and, most importantly, the function of nurturer. This Ætt often refers to the color green.

The runes falling under Freyr's Ætt are:
- ᚠ Fehu (Cattle)

This indicates material wealth, prosperity, hope, and luck. The symbol signifies cattle, which was their main source of livelihood at the time, resonating with the ideal of wealth.
- ᚢ Uruz (Ox)

This indicates strength, hard work, and motivation. The symbol signifies the ox, which is known to persevere and be a symbol of intense masculinity.
- ᚦ Thurisaz (Mallet)

This indicates challenge and conflict. The symbol signified Thor's hammer/mallet or the symbol of giant, which indicated the will of energy and power of destruction.
- ᚨ Ansuz (Message)

This indicates communication—a divine message or wisdom, truth, and inspiration. It's connected to the god Odin, his visions, and good advice.
- ᚱ Raidho (Journey)

This indicates the movement of a wheel in the cycle of life and the spiritual journey each person has to go through; the physical quest of venturing forth.

- ᚲ Kenaz (Torch)

This indicates the unknown and what needs to come to light. The symbol represents a torch for finding the secrets and the true calling of your path.

- ᚷ Gebo (Gift)

This indicates partnership and generosity. The symbol signifies the gift of understanding balance.

- ᚹ - Wunjo (Joy)

This indicates the ideal of joy, celebration, peace, and harmony. The symbol signifies the comfort and joy of others in your life.

The King

This is known to be the Ættir of Heimdall, who was the watchmen of the gods. Symbolizing shamanism, diplomacy, and guardianship, we see the function of a priest and the connection between life, death, and magic. This Ætt is often depicted in the color grey.

The runes falling under Heimdall's Ætt are:

- ᚺ Hagalaz (Hail)

This indicates a natural form of disaster. The symbol signifies hail and shows the unavoidable cost that nature brings which is out of our control. But the lesson to be learned is that we weather the storm and move forward with grace.

- ᚾ Nauthiz (Needs)

This indicates the time spent maintaining survival and recuperating from the long day. The symbol signifies restriction, disagreement, and practicing patience.

- I Isa (Ice)

This indicates the feeling of being stuck in a situation in life. It was symbolized to gather all information and patiently await the next move, avoid frustration, and keep a level head.

- ◊ Jera (Harvest)

This indicates the reaping and conclusion of hard work, symbolizing the need to show gratitude for what has come to pass and be ready for the next step.

- ʃ - Eihwaz (Yew)

This indicates the reference to Yggdrasil, the Tree of The World. It symbolizes reliability, the trustworthiness of things, and a sense of purpose.

- ɾ - Perthro (Destiny)

This indicates fortune and chance, symbolizing the ideal of making life fateful by taking what you receive with open arms and open heart; the mysteries and fates in a roll of dice.

- Y - Algiz (Elk)

This indicates the protection and defense of the family. Symbolizing guardianship and courage, one must manifest their dreams and shield their Wyrd from the evil of negative emotions.

- ƺ - Sowilo (Sun)

This indicates happiness and success, symbolizing the celebration of reaching goals and keeping the body in optimal health.

The Warrior

This is known to be the Ættir of Tyr, the sky god who stood for war and justice. Symbolizing strength and bravery, law and honor, service and loyalty, and a legacy left behind, this Æett is often depicted in the color red.

The runes falling under Tyr's Ætt are:

- ↑ - Tiwaz (Victory)

This indicates direction as symbolized by the arrowhead of Tyr. Leadership and victory while knowing your true strengths and weaknesses were the ideal of rationality.

- ᛒ - Berkana (Birch)

This indicates the ideal of regeneration, both physical and spiritual. The Birch goddess oversaw new beginnings and the creation of growth, symbolizing renewal.

- ᛖ - Ehwaz (Horse)

This indicates the need for a trusty assistant like the horse, which was the only transport at the time. It symbolized the steady progress and teamwork needed to accomplish tasks and goals.

- ᛗ - Mannaz (Man)

This indicates the social order of humanity and personal identity, symbolized by the ideals of cooperation, relationships, and eventual mortality.

- ᛚ - Laguz (Lake)

This indicates the emotion factor of intuition and fluidity. Symbolized by the element of water, it has powers of renewal but also holds mysteries and secrets.

- ◊ - Ingwaz (Fertility)

This indicates the Earth god Ing, symbolizing well-being, virtue, strength, and family.

- ⚡ - Othala (Heritage)

This indicates the ideal of inheritance, symbolizing the legacy of one's name and the values one needs to live by to live an abundant life.

- ᛗ - Dagaz (Dawn)

This indicates consciousness and clarity, symbolizing the transformative power of change and the ideals of hope and security.

Casting

Strong human intention is the key to activating the magic, and the power is in the human, not the inanimate object. Casting has been practiced for centuries and is still widely used today. Reading what was cast was not a fortune-telling magic but rather the concept of looking for answers and guidance in future outcomes. Placing energy and will power into the runes before reading is done too.

This oracular divination method requires the person to use critical thinking and basic intuition by asking certain questions to the fates and looking for the answer in the past, present, and future. Making runes was known as risting and it entailed carving onto pieces of bark from nut bearing trees or using smooth river stones and crystals. The making of runes is said to be just as important as the casting themselves therefore taking care in the magical process.

Traditionally, runes could be cast in two different ways: placing a white piece of fabric on the floor and casting the runes while looking into the skies and selecting the runes to allow the fates to fall into place, or throw the runes and only read the ones that are shown upright. Some use this base fabric or leather, but it could also be cast directly on the floor or surface. Another option is to ask a yes or no question to the universe and select blindly from the runes in the pouch, whichever you receive in your right hand will be the guidance you are looking for.
How you decide to read them is really about personal perspective, but there are some traditional methods used that could be interpreted differently depending on the personal method.

The Ætt in Casting

One can say that for each rune there is a symbol, for example the symbol of light in Freyr's Ætt, that is ken, is the torch, and for Heimdall it is sowilo. As well as the referral of wealth and achievement, you will see that it reflects in Freyr's Fehu, in Heimdall's Nauthiz, and in Tyr's Tiwaz.

It is important to see that at the end of each Ætt the rune used is always a positive and hopeful one, like Sowilo as Sun and Dagaz as Dawn. This symbolized the end of the lesson and the venture onto new challenges.

What you might also notice is how the overlapping of some themes do not reflect in the third Ætt, like death, found in Perthro in Heimdall's Ætt and Raidho in Freyr's Ætt. Tyr's Ætt does not indicate this theme, telling us that maybe the warrior had already come to learn all those lessons and moved to the next stage, where Freyr and Heimdall still need to make choices.

Casting runes is a sacred tool; therefore, it is important to remember that reading too deeply into what is shown might not reflect directly with something happening in your life. It could be subversive and miscellaneous, so keeping a positive attitude towards what is presented is vital.

Rune Spreads

There are many different ways to spread runes in reading for divination, from the two-rune layout to the more complex 24-rune layout.

It is said that before casting one should close their eyes and mix the runes carefully inside the pouch or box in which you keep them safe. This is to allow the flow of past, present, and future within the user's Wyrd. The runes will answer your question in a way that you personally can comprehend. As we said before, there is no "right way" to practice runic divination as long as the user understands that it is a light shining on your path to the answers, not on the direct answers given.

Your rune casts can also be recorded in a way for you to look back at what was shown the previous day, week, or month and see if the tides of fate are falling in your favor.

One, Two, and Three-Rune Layouts

These are the most basic options for calling the runes to your needs:

- The one-rune layout is an interpretation and general feeling of the question asked when you pick one single rune from the pouch. You would mentally or verbally ask your question, and whichever rune is chosen blindly from your pouch will give you the direction of your answer.
- The two-rune layout represents the ancient Germanic ideal of a twofold concept of time, for "that which is" and "that which is becoming." The first rune picked is the rune of "that which is," enlightening you on the path that you are already walking on. The second pick is "that which is becoming," which could reveal that unseen chance for you to change your path, so you may adhere to what is shown.
- The three-rune layout requires you to select and place three runes next to each other on the fabric in front of you. Each of the three you chose signifies a different stage or answer. The first being the general idea and overview of your question, the second in line being the challenges you face with such a question, and the third is the possible outcomes coming from that question.

Four-Rune Layout

This is a placement of the four runes in a cross formation in front of you. Each position of the rune is related to the north, west, east, and south location of the dwarves: Nordi, Vestro, Austri, and Surdi, who in mythology hold up the sky of Ymir's skull. The first rune placed in the north position in front of you is signifying the past relation to your question. The west rune signifies the present relation to your question. The east rune stands for the future obstacles that may hinder your path, and the southern position stands for the possible outcome of your cast.
It is important to note that the third rune does not predict any future; it simply predicts the future obstacles in your way while the fourth is the typical "future position" of standard layouts.

Five-Rune Layout

One could also move onto a five-rune layout in which you would pick and place these runes into the shape of a cross with the fifth rune in the center. The far left rune indicates the influence of problems, the top rune shows the influence of solutions and positivity, and the bottom indicates the overall influence of the question. The far right is an immediate answer and the middle is the future of what the question might bring.
Seven-Rune Layout

These spreads can be altered according to preference but we will (for practical purposes) list the two main spreads that are known.

You can opt for the V-shape formation in front of you called the Runic V. Starting from the top left, the meanings follow as such: top left shows the past influence, the next down shows present influences, then future actions, followed by the best actions for positive outcome. Moving upwards towards the right, we see the influence of emotions related to the question, followed by possible problems encountered with the question, and finally, top right is the future outcome of the question. Or, you can opt for the serpent layout where the runes are placed in a flowing formation that guides you from the head to tail of events coming your way. The snaking represents the up and down hills and the path in which you walk along life. It is sometimes referred to as the Serpent of Midgard spread.

Let's picture the seven runes snaking one after the other in front of you, beginning from the tail to the head:
- The first rune can represent the feelings you had in the past relating to the question asked.
- The second rune can be read as the struggles and bumps you will face on the journey to the outcome.
- The third rune points towards our concerns at the present time while we take the journey.

- On the fourth rune we can begin to acknowledge our journey towards an outcome even though there is still some way to go.
- The fifth tells us about our feelings once we can begin to see the outcome at hand.
- The sixth rune is a reminder of the struggles ahead even though the outcome is visible.
- And the final rune is the representation of the goal at hand. This goal can be deceiving though, because just like the Serpent of Midgard that bites its own tail, if you are not careful enough when reading the previous runes, you could end up finding yourself right back at the beginning again.

24-Rune Layout

A much larger 24-rune layout can be read by placing it in a 3 x 8 grid, exemplifying the runic year. This is usually done on New Year's Day to provide answers for the entire year. Read from the top down each of the three columns. They could be interpreted as such:

Row One

- First: how to receive money and prosperity
- Second: how to achieve physical health and strength
- Third: how to achieve defense or destruction
- Fourth: how to achieve wisdom and inspiration
- Fifth: what the direction of your life-path is
- Sixth: what your future wisdom is

- Seventh: skills to be achieved
- Eighth: how to achieve happiness and peace

Row Two

- First: the future changes in your life
- Second: what is needed to achieve these goals
- Third: what obstacles might come your way
- Fourth: your success and achievements
- Fifth: what choices are made and challenges to come
- Sixth: the manifestation of inner skill
- Seventh: situations of life and death
- Eighth: the energy that guides you

Row Three

- First: concerning affairs of a legal nature
- Second: achieve growth and beauty
- Third: your friendships and relationships
- Fourth: your social status
- Fifth: your emotional status
- Sixth: the influences of emotion and sex
- Seventh: your achievement of balance
- Eighth: what wisdom and assets will be gained in the year

The Blank Rune

There is quite a bit of controversy surrounding the use of Odin's Rune. This rune was not as commonly used in traditional rune reading but was later introduced in the 19th century. When drawn from the pouch, it can either be read as a matter of allowing things to just stay secret and unknown or a connection to the fates, destiny, and the knowledge of what is hidden. Some, when presented with Odin's Rune, will simply choose to recast.

"There are many different schools of thought on if to use the blank rune or not in casting. The rune can be a sign that you need to really think about who is the master in your dream" (Auntyflo, 2021).

Chapter 7: Religion

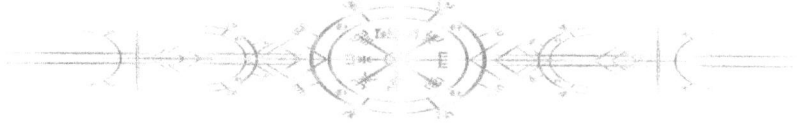

Unlike Christianity, Norse religion is a folk religion. Partaking in a more survivalist and socially focused worship to their many gods, it was often spoken of as the Ásaturu (worship of gods and spirits). The various trans-cultural diffusions between the Sami and Finns, who were their closest neighbors, was most likely what made up their old Norse customs, which were the closest things to religion as a concept at the time. It was animistic, polytheistic, pantheistic (the universe is the manifestation of the deities), and held a cyclical view of time.

The heathen religion was closely related to the different practices performed for different events or gatherings to praise a god according to the theme (war, wealth, health, or fertility). Again, it is vital to understand that because there are not many details regarding their worship, it is suggested that we make an unclear image of interpretations from what survived. What we do know is that the Norse did not put up too much of a fight towards the new religion, because in their polytheistic culture and worshiping a long list of gods, adding Christ to the lot was not the hardest aspect to adjust into.

Public and Private Faith

A clear distinction between private and public faith took play: where your worship was either tied to within the threshold of the house, being private and individualized, or over the social public structure of gatherings and feasts, being open and combined.

Public

There are a few records of sites or dwellings of worship in Norse religion. Halls were likely built and used for dual purposes as places of law and festivities as well as rituals and religious sacrifices from the 6th century to well into the Middle Ages.

Religious festivals normally fell around the time when other practices occurred as well, like *things*. "Things" were the gatherings of free people in the community and presided over by law speakers. The gathering occurred in thingsteads and their main function was to counsel and talk over certain major aspects concerned at the time. Kings and chiefs played a central role in the ritualistic practice of public acts and sacrifices presiding and judging accordingly.

Holy rituals were usually located in very specific places associated with the gods and divine forces connected to them. For instance, sacred groves were found to be places where people left offerings in streams and placed them under rocks or in trees to please the landvættir, who were the spirits of the land. It is basically understood that their public faith was rather nature-oriented and the connection to the world around them was their way of reaching to the divine.

Private

It is still unclear whether there was a complete distinction between the private and personal faith performed within the threshold of a Norse family or if it was somehow integrated with that of their public faith.

Usually, it is thought that the head of the household leads the rituals and also chose whether the thrall (slaves) participated in them as well. These were connected to daily tasks instead of seasons or major calendar events.

Rites of passage were extremely important, symbolizing the change of status in personal life, such as becoming a mother, getting married, or dying. When a child is born, it was believed that the fates or Norns would reveal the örlögs of the child as well as the name.

This was most often accompanied by prayers to the goddesses Freyja and Frigg to protect and bring well-being over the newborn. Names given were connected to the traits that were seen from the parents or sorceress who assisted in the birthing process.

Marriage was also considered to be a solid center of Scandinavian religion and culture. The important transition for the couple and their respective families would either elevate their status or their legacy. It was necessary that a dowry be presented from the groom's family to that of the future bride and it was a staged ritual of some weeks. Even though surely most marriages were decided for wealth and social standing, not thinking too much about the happiness and compatibility of the couple, this was actually quite important too, for the couple had to be able to run a farm and family together and, therefore, get along.

Death & Reincarnation

It was very costly to bury a member of the community. If the practices were to be done right, it could take time and money to prepare and properly finalize. Therefore the physical evidence we see today mainly shows boat graves ornately buried along with the person who was most likely elite or royalty of some sorts. We are not too sure what would have happened to commoners (those who didn't fight battles) when they died, as grave sites are far and few, therefore pointing towards probable cremation.

It is unsure where each person's soul would stay within the grave, haunt the home, or join the gods in their realms.

Parts of the Soul

The concept of souls for the Norse was quite different from what we understand today. According to the Norse the soul was divided into four parts:
- **Hamr** was one's physical appearance. It could change and was associated with shapeshifting.
- **Hugr** was the person's character and personality which followed them after death.
- **Fylgja** was their companion animal that reflected their *hugr*. Stronger individuals had stronger totems.

- **Hamingja** was the person's success in life formed by the *hugr* and would be passed down to close family members, either in good or bad omen.

The soul would split after death and each of the four aspects venture into different directions. This was not controlled by the will of the gods and it seemed to be something more personal; therefore, less information is known about it. The *hugr* is what is thought to be what passed onto a newborn baby in the community, and thus the person's character would show itself in the newborn.

The Afterlife

As with most historical sources from the time, they were heavily influenced by Christian writings, but what we do know from the scripts is a general overview of the destination of the souls:

- **Valhalla**: known as the hall of heroes or Odin's hall. Here the warriors of both men and women would meet like old friends to drink, celebrate, and fight in preparation for Ragnarök.
- **Folkvangr**: this is the field of the people watched over by the fertility goddess Freyja. It was the land of peace and rest.

- **Hel**: situated in the ice world of Niflheim and presided over by the goddess Hel, most people went here after death. Most likely a post-Christian adaptation of the underworld as this was not a concept shown before the conversion.
- **Realm of Rán**: also called the Coral Caves of Rán, this giantess would watch over the treasure and sailors befallen to the seas.
- **The Burial Mound**: some souls never left their graves. If they were prepared correctly with all of their treasures and belongings, they would stay in that vicinity and were known as ghosts.

Ghosts

In Norse literature, we see two types of ghosts: the *haugbui* and the *draugr*. These powerful supernatural beings would guard their former possessions and haunt their community. The haugbui was relatively harmless unless his burial mound was disturbed and deeply attached to places that were comforting to them when they were alive. Some were buried with an open grave-door so that their relatives could bring food offerings, as the dead were known to always be hungry. The draugr, on the other hand, was the more malevolent ghost who haunted their family if they died in bad circumstances or were not buried properly. Some stories say they would wreak havoc in the village by killing animals and destroying property.

Sacrifice

The ritual of sacrifice stood as another central aspect of Norse religion. The Old Norse term *blót* was used to signify the practice, and it was technically an exchange to stay on good terms with their gods. Sacrificing for good weather, luck in battle, and fertility were the most common reasons, but this was also seen at weddings, burials, and birth rights.
Historians believe that there were four fixed sacrifices a year: winter solstice, spring equinox, summer solstice, and the autumn equinox. These were presided over by the magnate or chieftain and accompanied by sorceresses like the völva or the *seiðkona* as a further connection to the deities.
The act of sacrificing an animal to the gods was the central focus of large calendar events. Eating the meat of the sacrificed animal while drinking mead of beer around the fire would bring positive omens to the village and people.
From Snorri's *Hakon* in the *God's Saga* written in the 12th century, we can get a better look at what it entailed and what it meant.
Like his father, Sigurd Hakonsson made sacrifices frequently in their village temple. All sorts of animals were sacrificed, although horses were especially used.

The blood of the sacrificed animal was used to spatter on alters, walls, and the participants. The meat that was cooked and eaten by all in attendance and the beer filled was always blessed by the magnate, their pagan priest. Many toasts were then made, one to honor the god Odin, "to the king and victory," and the other to Njörd and Frey, where the cups would be emptied securing a peaceful future. Each person then emptied their cups while pledging to undertake great exploits, and finally was the toast for the dead who rested in their burial mounds.

Not only animals or humans were sacrificed, but weapons and objects of special meaning to the owner were thrown into lakes or rivers. The same sites were frequently used, believing there to be a strong connection to god in that specific location. Sacrificing to statues in forests and groves or in the cult buildings at the center of villages was a common practice too.

There have been a number of disagreements whether human sacrifices were performed during the Viking Age. With the look at some of the sagas we can see the description of human sacrifices of thralls (slaves) in ritualistic practices at funerals, maybe entailing that the free man who owned the thrall would be buried along with him.

Some remains in temples suggest ritualistic sacrifice of commanders of war bands consecrating enemy warriors to Odin. And other accounts tell us about hanging the sacrifices by trees along with animals like dogs and cats. Christian propaganda influenced the many stories and sagas we see today, therefore it is unsure if that was the actual truth.

Chapter 8: Connection to Nature & the Unseen

The Vikings lived in an enchanted and sacred world. The enchantment was the concept of the way things were. They did not isolate nature from culture but accepted it fully as they found it, understanding the way it was and how it should be.

They worked on sacramental traditions rather than what we know today as moral religiosity. The divine was found in advancing their interests within the world rather than fundamentally changing its character. After all, they believed that events unfolded by fate and thus were completely out of their control.

Paul Tillich, a twentieth century philosopher of religion, explained their romantic-conservatism as such:

The word 'romantic' in this context, points to the experience of the infinite in the finite, as it is given in nature and history. The word 'conservative' in connection with romance emphasized the experience of the presence of the ultimate in the existing forms of nature and history. If a man sees the holy in the flowers as it grows, in the animal as it moves, in man as he represents a unique individuality, in a special nation, a special culture, a special social system, he is romantic-conservative. For him the given is holy and is the content of his ultimate concern. (McCoy, 2019e)

Their Concepts

We can describe the many different realistic concepts that drove the Norse on their daily journey through Scandinavia, so here we would like to bring to your attention some of the most obvious aspects.

Cyclical View of Time

Unlike our idea of time being linear with a past, present, and future, the Norse saw the past as being just as alive and relatable as their present, therefore cyclical. Time was layered and complex, with the past still continuing to shape their futures and their futures being a debt to be paid (known as skuld) for their actions or lack thereof. There was an importance of fulfilling debt and keeping obligations.

In Sweden, for instance, they would hold a festival called the Great Disting every eight years in the halls at Uppsala:

This eight year cycle is known as the octa eteris meaning that the moon cycle would return back to the exact same place relative to the sky years prior. This occurred every nine lunar years, a number sacred to their people. (Burton, 2018) Scandinavians lived so far north that it was impossible to relate to the European times established. Winter days were very short and summer nights even shorter. They divided their days into eight equal parts. They would use daymarks (dagmarks) which were the directions of the sun in the horizon. Their horizon was sectioned into eight parts: north, northeast, east, southeast, south, southwest, west, and northwest. Noon was the most important daymark of the day, when the sun was at its highest. Known as Middag (midday), it marked the midpoint of the sun's path across the horizon.

Geographical location of the sun would change during the year, but the midday point was always in the same place. Mountains were used as identifiers of the midday mark, and many are named after it, like Middagshorn or Hadegisbrekkur (highday). Other landmarks used were fields, bridges, and mountain passes. The closer to the Arctic Circle, the easier it was to establish midday and midnight. Midnight was seen by the slight luminescence of the sun just below the horizon, so one could establish midnight if the sun was due north and midday if the sun was due south.

Herbs and Potions

Archaeobotany has brought up some very interesting findings when it came to the use of plants for healing and magic. The Norse used different plants to remove infection or pain, or a combination of poisonous plants and alcoholic meads that would allow the person to slip into a trance and remove themselves from their physical body to connect to the spirit realm. Each god had an herb that was connected to their theme, which would allow one to interact with this deity when the plant was used for healing, cooking, or potions, called the magical union.

Here are some of the most common plants used at the time:
- Henbane was used in smoking or drinking, which activated its extremely toxic properties, assisting in the arrival of a trance like state.
- Mugwort was used as a diuretic in the household and in rituals for divination.
- Bog Myrtle or Sweet Gale was used as a flavoring additive to many brews and as an antiseptic ointment.
- Meadowsweet was used as a cure for headaches or to reduce indigestion.
- The Elm plant was used as a magical connection to the Alfheim realm and to carry love spells and other charms into the afterworld.

Many other plants were used in conjunction with rituals as well as their household use. Some connected to the dead and ancestors, and some to love and the living.

Sacred Numbers

In paganism, numbers were often recycled to keep their relevance in each story told. In the Norse mythology we see the numbers three and nine. These numbers reflect in the *Poetic Edda* and in the Icelandic Sagas.

The number three is portrayed in many ways:
- Ymir, Búri, and the cow, Audhumla, are the three original beings.
- There are three Norns.
- There are three sacred wells.
- Before Ragnarök has its time, three long winters will ensue.
- Odin sacrificed himself three times at the Yggdrasil tree in search of the runes.
- Many of the sacred possessions of the gods come in three.

The number nine is portrayed in many ways as well:
- There are nine worlds supported by Yggdrasil.
- Odin hangs from the branches of Yggdrasil for nine days and nights.
- The nine mothers of Heimdallr.

- The great feast and sacrifice in Uppsala occurs every nine years.
- Odin's golden ring Draupnir releases nine golden drops every nine nights.
- Freyr is required to wait nine nights before he can consummate his love for giantess Gerðr.

Spirit Worlds

Wights

Landvættir were the spirits and wights of the land and the natural places surrounding Iceland.
People would often worship and ask for advice in rocks, woods, and waterfalls, as the wights controlled the life of the land, its fertility, and health. Some stories implied that they were already there before the Norse settled, like in the Saga of King Olaf Tryggvason in the *Heimskringla*. King Harald Bluetooth wanted to invade Iceland but before he could, he needed a wizard to send out his spirit to scout for locations where it would be easy to infiltrate the land.

The wizard sent his spirit out in the form of a whale, and while swimming around the northern coasts towards Vopnafjörour, he was confronted by a great dragon named Dreki who was followed by many poisonous snakes, lizards, and insects. So he ventured instead west towards Eyjafjörour, and swimming inland he was met by a huge eagle called Gammur, with wings spanning hillsides, followed by many other birds, deterring him to a new course once again. This time he decided to go south from the west coast into Breioafjörour and was confronted by a bull so horrible and large who called himself Grioungur, and many other landvættir followed behind him. He finally attempted the last region south in Reykjanes where he encountered a giant named Bergrisi who was taller than hills and carried an iron staff. This giant was followed by many other jötnars and, therefore, the wizard had to move away at last. It was established that no longships could sail to Iceland as nothing but wasteland and high crashing waves were enveloping the land.

This story shines through till today in Icelandic culture, traditionally dividing the region into four quarters guarded by these landvættir. You can see them on the coat of arms as well.

Útiseta

This was a practice of clarity, where sitting out the night on crossways was not only for invoking spirits and deities to reveal secrets or counsel, but also to meditate and prepare one's energy for other more strenuous practices later.
It required sitting in darkness in nature, covered in a cloak or blanket, and fasting for many days, as Útiseta means "powering down" or "the act of sitting out" to provoke spirits.

The communication received from the outside, such as sounds, smells, and feelings were what grounded the person and clarified their minds so they may hear the spirits around them. The encounter between pupil and spiritual teacher was the goal, looking for answers in the wilderness within and without. Depending on the knowledge you seek, you would invoke the assistance of Odin, Freyja, or Thor.
Here is a passage from the epic Finnish poem *The Kalevala* of a völva's journey through Útiseta:

Many runes the cold has taught me, many lays the rain has brought me, other songs the winds have sung me. Many birds from many forests, oft have sung me lays in concord, waves of sea and ocean billows, music from the whole creation, oft have been my guide and master. (p. 281)

Totemism

The Norse Kingdoms frequently partook in the practice of totemism. This is the spiritual relationship between humans and different types of animals or plants. The totem is considered the guardian or ancestor of the human whom it is connected to and overlaps the human self—meaning that if the owner died, so did the totem.
Before Christianization, their worldview of this state of being and connection to the natural world was separated into two factions, as explained below.

The Fylgjur

These were the personal animal spirits of individuals assigned to them at birth. *Fylgjur* means 'follower' in Old Norse; therefore, we can understand it as a companion that has a direct correlation to the health of the owner.
The sagas talk about animals such as cats, dogs, foxes, wolves, birds of prey, and mice. Each person's character will be affected by the inherent character of the animal they are connected to. The character of a leader would have the untamed nature of the fox, deer, eagle, or lion, whereas the tame nature of a woman for example would be that of a boar, ox, or goat. If you were of noble descent, it was a bear; if you were of a violent person, it was a wolf, and so on.

Gods were often associated with their own totems, like Odin's ravens or Freyr's boars that would guide and assist them through their adventures.

The animal was known to come to them in dreams and offer advice and what future events are to come. Just like the fates, they were not changeable nor could they act on their own. Sometimes a fylgjur, in the form of a woman, would appear in their dreams. This was known as a *dís*, who was not necessarily the totem, but the goddess attached to their fates telling them what is to come.

Militaristic Totemism

During raids and military action, many men would group up in their group totems of victory, usually a wolf or a bear. The initiation period required one to go out into the wilderness alone for some time and hunt or scavenge from neighboring villages, imitating the totem they would accept. This implied the need to cleanse both physically and morally before battle.

When the warrior progressed to the next stage of transition it would be that of identification. So the person would often just burst out in a rage of ferocity and savagery. This was fitting into their fylgjur spirit when the men would wear the pelts of the animals and transform into their totems, in a way of shapeshifting their spirits in a symbolic manner.

Numerous sagas tell of warrior shapeshifting into a bear or wolf before battle. For instance, in the saga of the Völsungs, the hero known as Sigmund trains his apprentice Sinfjötli as they wear wolf pelts and become the wolves themselves, raging through the forest. They are known as *ulfhednar,* or "wolf-hides," taking full animalistic behaviors just like the Berserkers (bear-shirts), who were the warrior groups who wore bear and wolf pelts to give them courage and fearlessness in battle.

Chapter 9: Norse Morality & Ethics

More than what was portrayed, the Norse people abided by certain morals and codes of conduct that ruled their lives and whole existence. Let us take a better look at these various structures.

Law

Kings and chiefs played a central role in the ritualistic practice of public acts and meetings. A *thing* was a gathering of various clans and villages, and the law meetings in halls were presided over by the law speakers. Law speakers had to memorize the *Bjarke* law, which regarded smaller merchant towns. A group of Þing, who were free men and women from the villages, often voted and gave a say in these gatherings, whether criminal or political.

Later in the 11th century, especially in Iceland, law became written text. Depending on the Nordic country, criminal proceedings were addressed slightly differently. Punishment most often included fines and, depending on the severity, outlawing, which meant you were no longer protected by the law and therefore capable of receiving any kind of punishment seen fit, something like village justice. Stealing, murdering, raping free women, and even lying and cheating were concerns brought forward to the earls and leaders of the regions for evaluation.

After the influence of Christianity, the proceedings altered and became more civilized. Slavery was abolished and many painful pagan trials to establish innocence were later abolished too.

Virtues and Values

Family was a central part of Norse culture. The ideals behind marriage, children, and raising a good farm to support you your whole life was the goal, originating from the heathen ideals of the *Ásaturu*.

It is unfortunate that the movies, books, and series these days portray an idea of bloodthirsty savagery with no inner values and peaceful practices. This is wrong as it is known from the *Hávamál* poem in the *Codex Regius* as the ethical code of conduct manual for Viking people:

- Courage: More than just being brave in battle, courage was the ideal of living up to the code and standing your ground when defending your beliefs.
- Truth: Lying was considered cowardice, therefore already breaking the first value: to stay true to who you were and what your heart told you was right.
- Honor: Without honor, one could not be courageous or trustworthy. It all fell in line with their personal integrity and dignity.
- Fidelity: More than just the fidelity to their gods and chiefs, it was especially true towards their family and friends.
- Discipline: their total way of life. No matter the environment or situation, one must practice a great deal of self-discipline to stay true to their virtues and principles.
- Hospitality: also known as the golden rule. Due to the insularity of the visitor being human or a god in disguise, they would offer it because that was the right way.

- Industriousness: Mediocre was not an accepted word for them. You worked your due till it was done with the best interests and full attention.
- Self-reliance: Being extremely independent and frugal for winter months, they strived on having the option to rely on their own thoughts, own families, and own land.
- Perseverance: Finally, to achieve all the above virtues, one needed perseverance. To push and fight through struggles and challenges was what made everything worthwhile.

After Conversion

Some Icelanders and many other Nordic Kingdoms rejected the conversion and began performing *Launblót* (secret offering) to their old gods.
As we have discussed previously, the Viking Age was a time of conversion. Scandinavian people were slowly but surely renouncing their pagan gods. This can be seen archaeologically through the fact that many of the newer graves were lacking grave goods because the converters were buried in standard empty graves.

The conversion was not as hard as it may have seemed. Due to their polytheistic view of gods, accepting a new one into their worldview was not a big challenge. Many of the base values of the Vikings, like plundering, having multiple wives, and engaging in blood feuds, never really changed after their conversion. It seems they really didn't care whether they were going to Heaven or Valhalla, as long as they lived free and favorably.

Christianity tainted the reality of the course of history through their divine eyes, and we struggle to see beyond that due to the lack of original written information. The kings and rulers of greater European regions benefited from the top to bottom conversion, so they were able to use the power of northerner's. The Norse people themselves benefited from the bottom-up conversion, so they could socially evolve and become a stronger nation for it. Baptism was pushed by English Kings onto their Viking leaders who were defeated, not necessarily for the savior of their souls, but for the forced peace that would come of it.

"Ironically, more Norse would be forced into Christian conversion by Vikings than by the kings of Christendom" (Sons of Vikings, 2019).

Conclusion

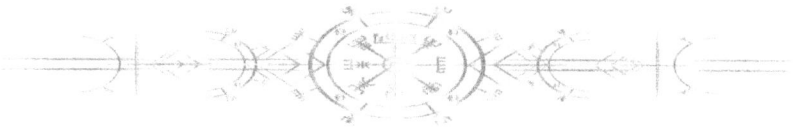

The night is cold and silent. A breeze of snowy wind moves through the mountain pass and encircles Arne and his son as they climb up the same route that has been used for almost a century now.

Arne has grown into a strong and reliable member of his community and now, in turn, takes his young son Frode up the pass to that clearing where he and his own father, Bo, came many moons before. This tradition has stayed firm and true in their family, so that he may be able to tell the same stories and legends that brought him closer to his ancestors and gods. Now that his own son has reached the right age to join him on this trip, it marks a new beginning to manhood and maturity, and it makes Arne very proud.

As they reach the same clearing between the two Ash trees that have been standing vigil there for as long as he can remember, they quietly look up into the night sky and marvel once more at the performance above their heads.

Arne looks at the childlike bewilderment in his son's face and remembers his own excitement when taking the trip and seeing the colors dance in front of him. But he also gets a sense of melancholy for the changes that are happening around them and which he cannot stop.

The stories that are told today are still the same, but Arne knows that another influence is making its way into their lives and culture as a whole. Many priests have come through his village to spread the word of this new god and many of his friends have argued about it around the fires. Arne has had his doubts for years, but still chooses to hold a firm belief in his own gods and their might and allow his family to talk and worship their magic just the same.

Even though he joined many ventures to the lands of the east for trade, he still prefers his freedom here in the place he calls home. His cousins have told him of their raids and riches in the west, but nothing will keep him from his farm and traditions. He will never say this out loud, but he is afraid of the change, and where many seem excited and eager to forget their old ways, he will not. That is why he takes his son up the pass, so that no matter what Frode chooses in his own adult life, he always remembers the stories and songs that make them the men of the north.

The winds of change will not reach them here, in their cold wilderness, under the watchful eyes of their gods, so he quietly begins his tales as his son watches on.

Farewell

Well, there you have it, dear reader and lover of ancient things!

The condensation of historical and cultural content has been broken down for you to be able to return to whenever you need to remember the old ways. We believe that history can always teach a person something new, whether it is for practical and educational purposes or for the knowledge of something deeper within. We are hopeful that you are reading this conclusion with a broader understanding of Norse magic and its surrounding myth. With a smile and an open heart, we thank you for choosing this piece of literature to expand your own ideals, thoughts on their history, and the influences their 600 years of existence have had on the world.

We would have you take a minute to realize just how the Norse were so attuned to another dimensional consciousness and how we can take something from that and mold it into our own busy and noisy world. Whether you were simply hungry for the information and wanted to understand this mysterious culture or you were beginning to master the heathen arts, then you have received some valuable information from this precious book. By bringing to you the modalities of their life, we hope you can take this book and apply it to your inner search for happiness, truth, and the connection to your Wyrd.

We touched on the lives of the common farmers and their practice of paganism with regards to family and surrounding communities. Then we pressed on to their warriors, the Vikings, that made fame and fortune from war and trade which left a lasting mark on the world around them. Touching on their gods and goddesses and the countless worlds which they inhabit, we were then able to take you on the journey through their mythologies and folktales written by pagans and Christians alike.

We loved telling you about their magic and witchcraft and their innate need for answers and guidance from the unseen world. We discussed their use of the markings that you now know to be more than just a language but a means to conjure and manipulate the magical world around them. Then, we broke down how you can start practicing this divination in your own capacity through the runes. Towards the final chapters, we spoke about their spiritual connection to nature and the animals and plants that live within it, to lastly touch on their concepts of honor, valor, hospitality, and the heavy influence of the new god that tamed them and brought an end to their savage ways.

Thank you again for your enthusiasm and interest in a subject that is so intriguing and raw. It resonates with a deeper consciousness that we might have lost many centuries ago, but that can be found again if we decide to listen to the songs and watch for the signs that are all around us.

References

Absolute History. (2021, June 29). *The untold legends of female Vikings who conquered Iceland | Viking women | Absolute History* [Video]. YouTube. https://www.youtube.com/watch?v=9orVsF0pZ1U

Adrien, C. J. (2021). *What was the difference between Danish, Norwegian, Swedish Vikings?* C.J Adrien. https://cjadrien.com/difference-danish-norwegian-swedish-vikings/

Arctic Adventures. (2021). *Icelandic sagas | What makes them so interesting?* Arctic Adventures. https://adventures.is/information/icelandic-sagas/

Auntyflo. (2021). *Rune the unknowable.* Auntyflo.com. https://www.auntyflo.com/rune-stones/rune-unknowable

Britannica. (2019). *Denmark - The Viking era.* Encyclopædia Britannica. https://www.britannica.com/place/Denmark/The-Viking-era

Burton, T. (2018, April 10). *The Anglo-Norse concept of time.* Medium. https://medium.com/@thomburton/the-anglo-norse-concept-of-time-a6aee671ae36

Carter, R. (2020, December 8). *11 Creatures from Scandinavian folklore you should know.* Scandification. https://scandification.com/scandinavian-folklore-creatures/

Crawford, J. [Jackson Crawford]. (2017, June 5). *Writing English in Runes* [Video]. YouTube. https://www.youtube.com/watch?v=A271ohcO7Yc

Crawford, J. [Jackson Crawford]. (2021, May 18). *Poetic of Edda.* YouTube. https://www.youtube.com/watch?v=nbi9mQCRd18&t=454s

Creepyhollows. (2021). *How-to read runes.* Instructables. https://www.instructables.com/How-To-Read-Runes/

Dashu, M. (2016). *Witches and pagans: Women in European folk religion, 700-1100.* Velona Press. (Original work published 2014).

Devereaux, L. (2019, February 7). *Scandinavian time measurement during the Viking era.* The Falcon Banner. http://falconbanner.gladiusinfractus.com/2019/02/07/scandinavian-time-measurement-during-the-viking-era/

Fotevikens Museum. (2016). *Agricultural plants in the Viking*. Fotevikens Museum. https://www.fotevikensmuseum.se/d/en/vikingar/hur/mat/recept/vaxter

Germanic Mythology. (2021). *Grímnismál: Texts and translations*. http://www.germanicmythology.com/PoeticEdda/GRMThorpe.html

Goodrich, R. (2018, August 29). *Viking history: Facts & myths*. Live Science. https://www.livescience.com/32087-viking-history-facts-myths.html

Grimfrost. (2020a, October 3). *Grimfrost Academy: Viking age herbs in food, culture and magic* [Video]. YouTube. https://www.youtube.com/watch?v=mhMHTZ2jfXM

Grimfrost. (2020b). *Grimfrost Academy - Viking religion* [Video]. YouTube. https://www.youtube.com/watch?v=ruQw7ieoGJM

Groeneveld, E. (2017, November 2). *Norse Mythology*. World History Encyclopedia. https://www.worldhistory.org/Norse_Mythology/

Gronitz, D. (2021). *The Rune Site | Casting layouts and spreads.* The Runesite. http://www.therunesite.com/casting-layouts-and-spreads/

Guido. (n.d.). *Chapter 10: The Ætt in rune casting.* Mind Unfolded. https://sites.google.com/site/mindunfolded/chapter-6

Gundarsson, K. (2021). *Space-Craft, seiðr, and shamanism.* Hrafnar.org. https://hrafnar.org/articles/kveldulf/spaecraft/

Hanson, M. (2016, October 27). *Norse mythology.* English History. https://englishhistory.net/vikings/norse-mythology/

Harger, A. (2021, June 30). *Rune divination methods: Introduction* [Video]. YouTube. https://www.youtube.com/watch?v=jJNSfzZuTu0

Harlitz-Kern, E. (2019, October 24). *12 Surprising facts about Viking runestones.* Mental Floss. https://www.mentalfloss.com/article/601594/viking-runestone-facts

History Extra. (2015, April 8). *Top 10 Viking stories.* HistoryExtra. https://www.historyextra.com/period/viking/top-10-viking-stories/

History on the Net. (2018, May 29). *Viking runes and runestones - History*. History. https://www.historyonthenet.com/viking-runes-and-runestones

History.com Editors. (2018, August 21). *Vikings*. History. https://www.history.com/topics/exploration/vikings-history

Iceland Rovers. (2017, January 5). *Mythology of Iceland - The Magical Staves - Icelandic sagas*. Iceland Rovers. https://www.icelandrovers.is/blog/the-magical-staves-of-iceland/

Icelandic Literature Center. (n.d.). *The Edda & the Sagas of the Icelanders*. https://www.islit.is/en/promotion-and-translations/icelandic-literature/the-edda-and-the-sagas-of-the-icelanders/

J. Mark, J. (2018a, December 10). *Norse ghosts & the afterlife*. World History Encyclopedia. https://www.worldhistory.org/article/1290/norse-ghosts--the-afterlife/#:~:text=There%20is%20evidence%20that%20the

J. Mark, J. (2018b, December 20). *Nine Realms of Norse Cosmology*. World History Encyclopedia. https://www.worldhistory.org/article/1305/nine-realms-of-norse-cosmology/

Kneale, A. (2013, July 20). *Celts and Vikings - Scandinavian influences on the Celtic nations.* Transceltic. https://www.transceltic.com/pan-celtic/celts-and-vikings-scandinavian-influences-celtic-nations

Lin, K. (2017, March 21). *Edda.* World History Encyclopedia. https://www.worldhistory.org/Edda/

McCoy, D. (2009). *Loki - Norse Mythology for smart people.* Norse Mythology. https://norse-mythology.org/gods-and-creatures/the-aesir-gods-and-goddesses/loki/

McCoy, D. (2012a). *Baldur - Norse Mythology for smart people.* Norse Mythology. https://norse-mythology.org/gods-and-creatures/the-aesir-gods-and-goddesses/baldur/

McCoy, D. (2012b). *Freyr - Norse Mythology for smart people.* Norse Mythology. https://norse-mythology.org/gods-and-creatures/the-vanir-gods-and-goddesses/freyr/

McCoy, D. (2012c). *Njord - Norse Mythology for smart people.* Norse Mythology. https://norse-mythology.org/gods-and-creatures/the-vanir-gods-and-goddesses/njord/

McCoy, D. (2012d). *Odin - Norse Mythology for Smart People*. Norse Mythology for Smart People. https://norse-mythology.org/gods-and-creatures/the-aesir-gods-and-goddesses/odin/

McCoy, D. (2012e). Ragnarok - *Norse Mythology for smart people*. Norse Mythology. https://norse-mythology.org/tales/ragnarok/

McCoy, D. (2012f). *Valkyries - Norse Mythology for smart people*. Norse Mythology. https://norse-mythology.org/gods-and-creatures/valkyries/

McCoy, D. (2019a). *Elves - Norse Mythology for smart people*. Norse Mythology. https://norse-mythology.org/gods-and-creatures/elves/

McCoy, D. (2019b). *Forseti - Norse Mythology for smart people*. Norse Mythology. https://norse-mythology.org/forseti/

McCoy, D. (2019c). *Odin's discovery of the runes*. Norse Mythology. https://norse-mythology.org/tales/odins-discovery-of-the-runes/

McCoy, D. (2019d). *Seidr*. Norse Mythology. https://norse-mythology.org/concepts/seidr/

McCoy, D. (2019e). *The enchanted world*. Norse Mythology. https://norse-mythology.org/the-enchanted-world/

McCoy, D. (2019f). *The kidnapping of Idun*. Norse Mythology. https://norse-mythology.org/tales/the-kidnapping-of-idun/

McCoy, D. (2019g). *Totemism*. Norse Mythology. https://norse-mythology.org/concepts/totemism/

McCoy, D. (2021). *The Aesir-Vanir War*. Norse Mythology. https://norse-mythology.org/tales/the-aesir-vanir-war/

Newcombe, R. (2019). *Rune guide - An introduction to using the runes*. Holistic Shop. https://www.holisticshop.co.uk/articles/guide-runes

Nikel, D. (2020, April 29). *Norwegian mythology & folk tales*. Life in Norway. https://www.lifeinnorway.net/norwegian-mythology-folk-tales/

Norse Magic and Beliefs. (2021, February 27). *The different types of Norse magic* [Video]. YouTube. https://www.youtube.com/watch?v=VAY6ai4pzvk&t=157s

Raging Seas Blog. (n.d.). *Norse magic: A simplified introduction* [Tumblr post]. Tumblr. https://ragingseas.tumblr.com/post/172717314664/norse-magic-a-simplified-introduction

Personified. (2014, August 16). *Spae-craft & Seidr - Magic forums*. SpellsOfMagic. https://www.spellsofmagic.com/read_post.html?post=666296

Rune, M. (2014, September 13). *Path of the Valkyries*. Novel Ideas. https://www.miriamrune.co.uk/path-of-the-valkyries/

Salvör, B. (n.d.). *A guide to Icelandic runes*. Guide to Iceland. https://guidetoiceland.is/history-culture/a-guide-to-icelandic-runes

Sandra, B. (2016, October 29). *Pesta: The personification of the Black Plague in Norway*. Myths and Microbes. https://mythsandmicrobes.com/2016/09/29/pesta-the-personification-of-the-black-plague-in-norway/

Schellenberg, J. (2015, November 16). *A Viking love story*. Europeana Foundation. https://www.europeana.eu/en/blog/a-viking-love-story-the-saga-of-frithiof

Shweta. (2019, May 29). *The concept of love in Norse mythology*. Scoopify. https://www.scoopify.org/the-concept-of-love-in-norse-mythology/

Sons Of Vikings. (2019, March 26). *Vikings and religion*. Sons of Vikings. https://sonsofvikings.com/blogs/history/the-vikings-and-christianity

Super User. (2014). *Mythology of the northern lights*. The Aurora Zone. https://www.theaurorazone.com/about-the-aurora/aurora-legends

Talisa + Sam. (n.d.). *Rune meanings and how to use rune stones for divination*. Two Wander. https://www.twowander.com/blog/rune-meanings-how-to-use-runestones-for-divination

TED-Ed. (2020). *The secret messages of Viking runestones - Jesse Byock* [Video]. YouTube. https://www.youtube.com/watch?v=wOcVy5dvwjs

The Viking Rune. (2019). *Writing in runes — How to start writing in Norse runes*. Viking Rune. https://www.vikingrune.com/2013/09/guide-to-writing-in-runes/

Timeline. (2018, April 1). *How the Norsemen became the seafaring Vikings | Wings Of A Dragon | Timeline* [Video]. YouTube. https://www.youtube.com/watch?v=hOsTfZ8gTM8&t=431s

Tommy. (2021). *What is the relationship between Vikings and Celts?* Herreira. https://harreira.com/viking/what-is-the-relationship-between-vikings-and-celts/

V.K.N.G. (2020, April 6). *Famous Valkyries [Divine Shield maidens]*. Norse and Viking Mythology [Best Blog] - Vkngjewelry. https://blog.vkngjewelry.com/en/famous-valkyries/

Viking Archaeology. (2021). *Viking Archaeology - Eddaic Poetry*. Viking.archeurope.info. http://viking.archeurope.info/index.php?page=eddaic-poetry

Vikings, S. (2020, May 27). *Learning about the Younger Futhark runes* [Video]. YouTube. https://www.youtube.com/watch?v=a6mxX4kYG10

Wanner, K. J. (2008). Snorri Sturluson and the Edda: The conversion of cultural capital in medieval Scandinavia. University Of Toronto Press, Cop.

Well... Actually. (2016, January 12). *Runology - The study of runes* [Video]. YouTube. https://www.youtube.com/watch?v=YTdPDBBxK8A

Wikipedia. (2020a, December 6). *Younger Futhark*. Wikipedia. https://en.wikipedia.org/wiki/Younger_Futhark

Wikipedia. (2020b, December 14). *Old Norse poetry*. Wikipedia. https://en.wikipedia.org/wiki/Old_Norse_poetry

Wikipedia. (2021a, March 31). *Saga*. Wikipedia.

https://en.wikipedia.org/wiki/Saga

Wikipedia. (2021b, May 27). *Rune poem*. Wikipedia.

https://en.wikipedia.org/wiki/Rune_poem

Wikipedia. (2021c, May 31). *Numbers in Norse mythology*. Wikipedia.

https://en.wikipedia.org/wiki/Numbers_in_Norse_mythology

Wikipedia. (2021d, June 11). *Galdr*. Wikipedia.

https://en.wikipedia.org/wiki/Galdr

Wikipedia. (2021e, June 22). *Settlement of Iceland*. Wikipedia.

https://en.wikipedia.org/wiki/Settlement_of_Iceland

Wikipedia. (2021f, July 16). *Nixie (folklore)*. Wikipedia.

https://en.wikipedia.org/wiki/Nixie_(folklore)

Wikipedia Contributors. (2019a, September 23). *Medieval Scandinavian law*. Wikipedia.

https://en.wikipedia.org/wiki/Medieval_Scandinavian_law

Wikipedia Contributors. (2019b, November 19). *Sagas of Icelanders*. Wikipedia.

https://en.wikipedia.org/wiki/Sagas_of_Icelanders

Wikipedia Contributors. (2021a, March 17). *Frithiof's Saga*. Wikipedia. https://en.wikipedia.org/wiki/Frithiof%27s_Saga

Wikipedia Contributors. (2021b, May 15). *Þorbjörg Lítilvölva*. Wikipedia. https://en.wikipedia.org/wiki/%C3%9Eorbj%C3%B6rg_L%C3%ADtilv%C3%B6lva#cite_note-SEPHTON-1880-12-13-3

Wikipedia Contributors. (2021c, May 17). *Landvættir*. Wikipedia. https://en.wikipedia.org/wiki/Landv%C3%A6ttir

Wikipedia Contributors. (2021d, June 10). *Seiðr*. Wikipedia. https://en.wikipedia.org/wiki/Sei%C3%B0r

Wikipedia Contributors. (2021e, July 11). *Dökkálfar and Ljósálfar*. Wikipedia. https://en.wikipedia.org/wiki/D%C3%B6kk%C3%A1lfar_and_Lj%C3%B3s%C3%A1lfar

Free Bonus from HBA: Ebook Bundle

Greetings!

First of all, thank you for reading our books. As fellow passionate readers of history and mythology we aim to create the very best books for our readers.

Now, we invite you to join our VIP list. As a welcome gift we offer the History & Mythology Ebook Bundle below for free. Plus you can be the first to receive new books and exclusives!

Remember it's 100% free to join.

Simply follow the link below to join.

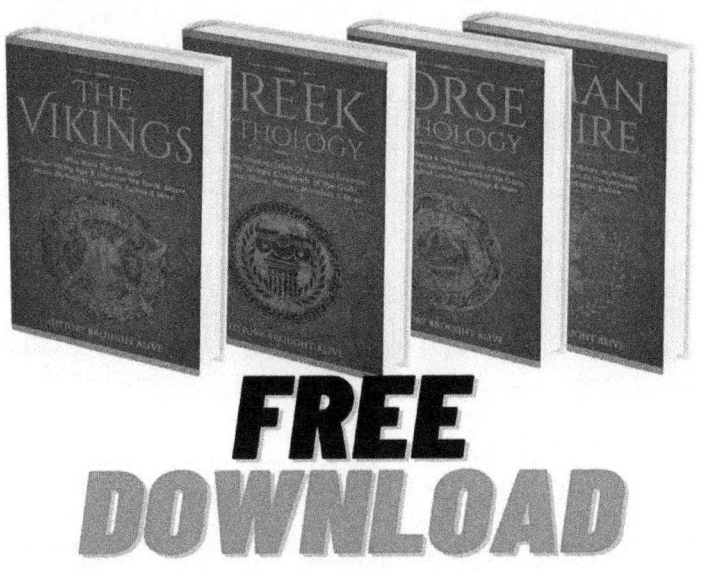

(https://www.subscribepage.com/hba)

Keep up to date with us on:

YouTube: History Brought Alive

Facebook: History Brought Alive

www.historybroughtalive.com

www.ingramcontent.com/pod-product-compliance
Lightning Source LLC
Chambersburg PA
CBHW071704080126
37732CB00082B/70